FAST BIKES

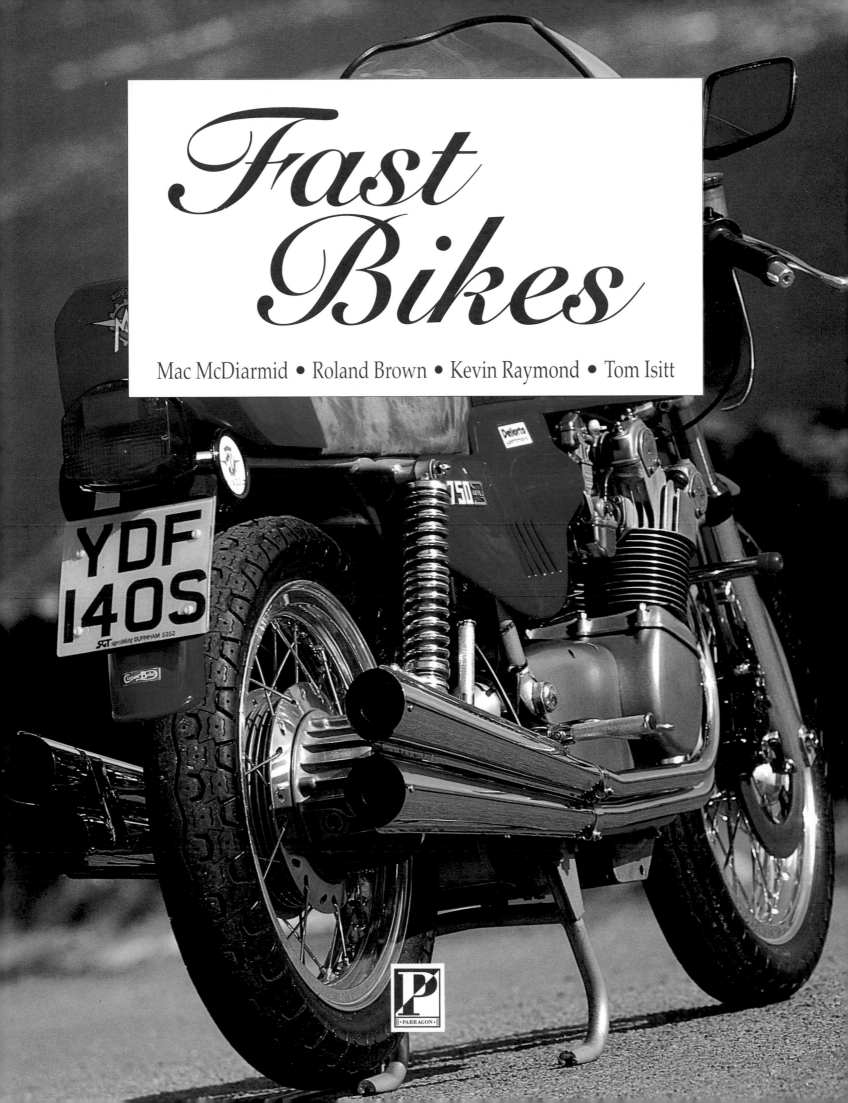

Fast Bikes

Mac McDiarmid • Roland Brown • Kevin Raymond • Tom Isitt

PARRAGON

Page 1 — Ducati's ST2 Sport Turismo combines the Italian firm's traditional high performance and V-twin character with the comfort required of a top-class all-rounder.

Page 2 — The stylish and super-fast ZX-7R, Kawasaki's best 750cc super-sports bike yet, is the end product of many years of development by the Japanese firm.

Page 3 — MV Augusta 757S America, based — if only loosely — on the most successful grand prix 500 ever built.

Opposite — Possibly the most eye-catching British vertical twin, the limited production Rickman Interceptor.

This is a Parragon Book

Parragon
Queen Street House
4 Queen Street
Bath BA1 1HE, UK

Superbikes From Around The World and *Classic Superbikes From Around The World* first published by Parragon in 1995

Copyright © Parragon 1999

Designed and produced by
Stonecastle Graphics Limited
Old Chapel Studio, Plain Road, Marden
Tonbridge, Kent TN12 9LS, UK

ISBN 0-75273-331-2

Printed in Italy

Photographic credits

Roland Brown: pages 1, 17 (top), 18, 20, 36, 37 (top), 51 (below), 76, 170 (top), 171, 174-175
Paul Bryant: page 51 (top)
Jason Critchell: pages 92, 93 (top)
Gold & Goose: pages 4, 5, 40, 41, 50, 56, 58, 59, 74, 75, 77, 78, 79, 87, 88
David Goldman: pages 16, 17 (below), 80, 81 (below), 126-127, 142-143
Patrick Gosling: pages 54, 55, 155
Harley-Davidson: pages 37 (below), 38
Honda UK: pages 48, 49
Mac McDiarmid: pages 9, 24, 27 (right), 28, 29, 34, 35, 44, 45, 46, 47, 53, 60, 81 (top), 90 (top), 91, 94, 95, 96, 97
Phil Masters: pages 14, 15, 19, 30, 31, 42, 43, 64, 65, 84, 85, 176-177, 178-179
Mitsui Yamaha: pages 86, 90 (below)
Kenny P: pages 10, 11, 68, 69, 87
Kevin Raymond: page 52
Dale Stenten: pages 22, 23
Suzuki GB: pages 70, 71, 73 (below right)
Oli Tennant: pages 7, 8, 15, 25, 26, 27, 32, 33, 38, 51, 57, 60, 61, 62, 63, 66, 67, 72, 73 (top), 82, 83, 93 (below), 102-103, 108-109, 154, 164-165
Martyn Barnwell/*Classic Bike*: pages 112-113, 116-117, 118-119, 134-135, 162-163.
Jack Burnicle: pages 180-181, 188-189
Kick Start magazine: pages 166-167
Don Morley: pages 104-105, 128-129
to all of whom, many thanks.

Contents

SuperBikes
FROM AROUND THE WORLD

REVISED AND UPDATED BY ROLAND BROWN
With contributions by
Mac McDiarmid, Tom Isitt and Kevin Raymond

Contents – Superbikes

Opposite – Honda's ultra-light CBR900RR Fireblade stunned the motorcycle world when it was released, and has since been refined to keep it at the front of the sports-bike pack.

Below –Harley-Davidson Heritage Softail – proving there's sometimes more to superbikes than super performance.

Introduction

....

'A Superbike, then, is something which stands out from the common herd of two-wheelers.'

Although the word 'Superbike' didn't exist before 1969, the concept certainly did. Coined to express the sense of wonder at Honda's then new CB750-four, it might equally have been used in an earlier age to describe a Brough Superior, a Vincent Black Shadow, or even the Triumph and BSA triples which preceded the Honda by a mere year.

In some ways it is a trite expression, no more worthy of our esteem than various 'superstars' or 'supermodels'. And there is, after all, nothing very exhilarating about a 'super' market. Yet 'superbike' is also shorthand for the bewildering technical advances of motorcycling over the past 30 years. In previous times, truly outstanding machines might appear perhaps once per decade; by the early 'seventies perhaps once per year; now they're coming at us thick and fast.

So exactly what does put the 'super' into 'Superbike'? Literally, the prefix means 'above'. It can mean, and it certainly does here, 'superior in quality . . . a degree beyond the ordinary meaning'. A Superbike, then, is something set apart from the common herd of two-wheelers. It is so special that the mere words 'bike', or 'motorcycle' cannot fully fully describe it. A Superbike stands out.

It does not simply mean 'faster'. Nor does it refer to price. The very fastest and most expensive motorcycles, certainly, are Superbikes. But so are some of the slowest – at least if you allow Harley-Davidson into the equation. In their case, the 'degree extra' is some indefinable quality. It isn't simply style and it certainly isn't performance, but most motorcyclists recognise it when they see it.

That, perhaps, is the essence of the true

Honda's CBR900RR Fireblade redefined the superbike concept when launched in 1992, and still reigns supreme amongst Japanese supersport fours.

Superbike. Whatever physical properties they may have, they also possess something extra, some indefinable quality which sets them apart. Inevitably, it is subjective and open to argument. And it is by no means always the same. Whatever it is about a Harley that turns people on, Bimotas have something very different but equally desirable.

Whatever that quality might be, all the motorcycles on the following pages have it – from the sensuous good looks of Ducati's 916 to the brutal elegance of Yamaha's XJR1200. From the over-the-top specification of Honda's GL1500 Gold Wing to the sheer bruising speed of Kawasaki's ZZ-

R1100. From the stylised Retro-tech of Harley-Davidson's Heritage Softail, to the brave novelty of Bimota's Tesi 1D. From the breathtaking power-to-weight of the Honda CBR900RR Fireblade, to the understated efficiency of the BMW K1200RS.

Ironically, a common complaint about modern motorcycles is that they are 'all becoming the same'. Yet even a cursory inspection of these Superbikes reveals a mouth-watering diversity of form and function. Turn the pages, relish them, and dream. For these are not merely motorcycles, they are fantasies given physical form. 'Superbike' is really too humble a word to describe them.

Not quite the fastest, but perhaps the sexiest superbike ever built, Ducati's 916 is also almost unbeatable on the track.

Nico Bakker QCS1000

'The svelte bodywork and 'unusual' suspension systems give the QCS a look all its own.'

Only a handful of exotic bikes have single-sided suspension at even one end. Only Nico Bakker's creation boasts such technology at both.

Yamaha were the first company to put an alternative front end into mass production on a motorcycle, but they were by no means the first to experiment with replacing the front forks in favour of a better design.

One of the pioneers of alternative front ends is Dutch 'specials' builder Nico Bakker, a man with several decades of chassis and suspension building to his credit and an impressive consultancy list that includes BMW and Laverda. And his QCS1000 (QCS stands for Quick Change System – both wheels can be changed in a very short space of time) is the latest incarnation of his own very effective design.

Traditional front forks are inherently flexible and can affect a motorcycle's steering geometry as they compress in corners. A method of separating the steering from the front suspension is generally considered to be the way forward for motorcycle design, and as yet only Yamaha and BMW have put alternative front suspension systems into production. But Nico Bakker has a system which he has been using since 1988 which is both clever and effective.

The QCS is a hand-built 'special' that uses a Yamaha FZR1000 engine for its motive power, around which is wrapped an aluminium-alloy square-section chassis onto which are bolted single-sided swingarms front and back. The front suspension system works in a very similar way to that of the Yamaha GTS1000 – the steering is handled via a spar running from the hub of the front wheel to the steering crown, while the suspension is actuated by the single-sided swingarm that bolts onto the front of the chassis. The benefits of this system can best be realised by a high-performance

sportsbike, which makes Yamaha's decision to fit it to a modest-performance sports-tourer surprising.

But the performance of the QCS is anything but modest. The derestricted FZR1000 engine oozes power and torque. The five-valves-per-cylinder in-line four makes 145bhp in the QCS and is capable of whisking it up to 165mph in very short order.

The rear suspension is also a single-sided swingarm affair, but without the necessity for steering the system, is used primarily for fast wheel changes (Honda developed this system for their endurance racing bikes, and it has subsequently been used on road-going machines by Honda and Aprilia).

On the road the QCS delivers exactly what it promises. There is no front end dive when hard on the brakes, and the bike is rock-steady mid-turn. It exhibits none of the drawbacks of traditional front forks and, unlike the GTS1000, the steering response is both fast and positive. A massive front

disc brake gripped by a six-piston caliper helps stop this 160mph beast, and a massive 180/55 section rear tyre helps the QCS grip tenaciously in the corners.

The svelte bodywork and 'unusual' suspension systems give the QCS a look all of its own – the swoopy styling and bright red paint tells the world that this is one serious, and very purposeful, motorcycle.

Very much more than a mere styling exercise, the QCS combines stability and agility in unprecedented proportions.

SPECIFICATION: NICO BAKKER QCS1000	
ENGINE	Water-cooled DOHC 20-valve in-line four
DISPLACEMENT	1002cc
HORSEPOWER	145bhp @ 10,000rpm
CARBURETTORS	4 x 38mm Mikuni
GEAR BOX	Six speed
FRAME	Aluminium-alloy twin beam
WHEELBASE	57ins
WEIGHT	418lbs dry
TOP SPEED	165mph

Bimota YB11 Superleggera

The format of Bimota's YB11 Superleggera is familiar: a blend of four-cylinder Yamaha engine, twin-spar aluminium frame and top-class cycle parts. For almost a decade the Italian firm has been building Yamaha-engined fours. But none of them matches the style or the sheer performance of the YB11, which is powered by the awesome 1002cc motor from the Japanese firm's YZF1000R Thunderace.

Superleggera means 'superlight' in Italian, and the name suits Bimota's exotic flagship just fine. With its lean, aggressively sculpted styling, the YB11 looks like a more muscular, slimmed-down version of the Thunderace. At 403lbs the Bimota is 30lbs lighter than the Yamaha, and matches Honda's less powerful CBR900RR Fireblade exactly.

The YB11 certainly has heaps of pedigree. It is the latest of a long line of aluminum-framed, Yamaha-powered sportsters developed from the 750cc YB4 on which Virginio Ferrari won the Formula One world championship back in 1987. The YB6 roadster of 1988 was the first to use Yamaha's FZR1000 powerplant, and since then the big-bore motor has powered a string of Bimotas with names such as Tuatara and Furano.

Those bikes all used similar versions of the familiar twin-spar alloy frame, which was advanced in the late '80s but looks unexceptional almost ten years later. Bimota's main change for the YB11 is to relocate the main cross-member closer to the steering head, adding rigidity while slightly reducing weight.

The YB11's slim, muscular styling perfectly complements the bike's blend of light weight and potent four-cylinder engine. Compared to the Yamaha Thunderace whose powerplant it shares, the Bimota is an aggressive machine that makes very few concessions to road-riding comfort.

Even crouching as far forward as possible can't prevent the aptly-named Superleggera's front wheel from coming up when the throttle is wound open to unleash the stunning midrange power of the 20-valve Yamaha engine.

The Bimota's slim, aerodynamic bodywork and compact chassis contribute to its mind-warping acceleration and 170mph top speed. The whole bike is light, firm and superbly precise — built for speed both in corners and a straight line.

Even the standard Thunderace's thick 48mm front forks are dwarfed by the Superleggera's huge 51mm diameter stanchions. The Paioli units are adjustable for compression and rebound damping; the same Italian firm also provides the YB11's multi-adjustable rear shock.

There are no internal changes to the 20-valve, liquid-cooled Thunderace engine, which in standard form produces a claimed 145bhp at 10,000rpm. But the airbox is new and larger, fed via ducts running back from the nose of the Superleggera's sleek glass-fibre fairing. Bimota claim the airbox adds two or three horsepower in conjunction with a new four-into-one pipe and rejetting of the Yamaha's 38mm Mikuni carbs.

Although the YB11 shares its engine, chassis type and even its wheelbase with the YZF1000R, the two bikes feel distinctly different. The Bimota's

suspension is firmer, its seat thinner and its riding position more racy, with hands forward, head down and feet high. By comparison Yamaha's YZF is roomy and softly sprung.

The Superleggera's reduced weight gives a slight edge to straight-line performance. A crack of the throttle sends the Bimota hammering off into the distance with its front wheel reaching for the sky. Given enough room it's good for 170mph. There's usable torque from as low as 2000rpm, and the fearsome acceleration from 5000rpm makes the YB11 an easy bike to ride very, very fast.

Although the Superleggera's race-ready suspension feels harsh on bumpy roads, on smoother surfaces the bike handles superbly, combining light steering with impeccable stability. Brembo's blend of big front brake discs and four-piston calipers gives heaps of stopping power, and Michelin's fat, grippy Hi-Sport tyres allow maximum use to be made of the YB11's almost limitless cornering clearance.

Inevitably this Bimota can't match the performance advantage that its YB6 predecessor once held over the opposition, and equally inevitably the hand-built Superleggera is horribly expensive. But with its looks, handling and outrageous performance, the YB11 is a fitting addition to Bimota's dynasty of mighty Yamaha-powered roadburners.

SPECIFICATION: BIMOTA YB11 SUPERLEGGERA	
ENGINE	Water-cooled DOHC 20-valve in-line four
DISPLACEMENT	1002cc
HORSEPOWER	148bhp @ 10,000rpm
CARBURETTORS	4 x 38mm Mikuni
GEAR BOX	Five speed
FRAME	Aluminium alloy twin beam
WHEELBASE	55.9ins
WEIGHT	403lbs dry
TOP SPEED	170mph

'The bike handles superbly, combining light steering with impeccable stability.'

13

Bimota SB6R

....

Bimota's SB6R had a hard act to follow. This bike's predecessor, the SB6, was a huge success for the tiny Rimini company, selling over 1200 units in the three years following its release in 1994. Such a total is insignificant by the standards of most manufacturers – but it's enough to make the SB6 Bimota's all-time best-selling bike, so its replacement had to be good.

The SB6R is more than good, it's one of the world's great sports bikes. Rather than make dramatic changes to the SB6's format, Bimota produced the SB6R by tuning, tweaking and restyling the existing model. The extra digit supposedly stands for 'Racing', although the list of modifications adds up to a bike that is fractionally faster but, more importantly, has a slight edge over its predecessor in looks, sophistication and handling.

The basic SB6 format remains, which means that the SB6R combines the watercooled, 16-valve four-cylinder engine from Suzuki's GSX-R1100 with a short, immensely strong aluminium frame of Bimota's own design. The main frame spars run all the way from the steering head past the swing-arm pivot – hence the 'Straight Connection Technology' logo on the 6R's streamlined fibreglass fairing.

Styling is subtly different to the SB6's, from the fairing's sharper nose all the way to the carbon-fibre tailpiece, which in grand prix style is self-supporting so requires no subframe. As before, the rear shock, a multi-adjustable unit from Swedish specialist Öhlins, sits horizontally on the right of the bike. Its spring is softer than the SB6's, and has a revised rising-rate linkage.

In Bimota tradition the GSX-R engine remains internally standard, and its output is modified by

The SB6R's styling is subtly different to that of its SB6 predecessor. But the two bikes share a basic format of Suzuki GSX-R1100 motor in a 'Straight Connection Technology' frame, whose aluminium spars run all the way from steering head to swing-arm pivot.

With a claimed 156bhp on tap the SB6R is awesomely fast in a straight line. It's also impressive for the way that Bimota's system of rubber-mounting the cylinder head tames the big four-cylinder Suzuki motor's vibration.

induction and exhaust modifications. New, shorter exhaust downpipes are claimed to increase power at high revs. The airbox is bigger and the 40mm Mikunis carburettors are fed by a ram-air system. Bimota chief engineer Pierluigi Marconi says the ram air helps add a total of 10bhp, although the gain shows up only at high speed and the official maximum remains 156bhp at 10,000rpm.

Whatever the increase, the Bimota's straight-line performance is utterly fearsome. When you crack open the smooth-action throttle the SB6R flies, its torquey GSX-R motor providing shoulder-splitting midrange acceleration and a thrilling charge towards the redline. Top speed is somewhere around 170mph, and the lightweight Bimota gets there phenomenally quickly.

The SB6's rather buzzy feel at some engine speeds is notably reduced by the 6R's system of rubber mounts where the cylinder head bolts to the frame. Other changes from the SB6 include a new vacuum fuel pump, designed to prevent the SB6's occasional starvation problems, a larger, 22-litre fuel tank, and a single battery above the airbox, instead of two hidden in the fairing nose.

Handling is subtly different to the SB6's, because the 6R's suspension has been tuned to give a slightly more compliant ride. Compression damping both in the 46mm Paioli forks and the Öhlins shock is reduced which, along with the rear unit's other changes, gives a smoother feel on bumpy roads. And although steering is quick and the 6R is short and light, its stability remains excellent.

All this, allied to racy steering geometry, the grip of fat Michelin Hi-Sport rubber and the predictably powerful bite of twin Brembo front discs with four-piston calipers, makes for a stunningly quick and deliciously agile bike. The hand-assembled Bimota's price is inevitably high, but the SB6R looks set to continue its predecessor's sales success for several years to come.

Simply sitting astride the super-light SB6R is enough to make the adrenalin start flowing – and this is no ordinary motorbike saddle. The Bimota's beautifully shaped seat unit is cut away to reveal the exhaust's twin tailpipes. In grand prix racebike fashion, the unit is a self-supporting structure made from carbon-fibre.

SPECIFICATION: BIMOTA SB6R

ENGINE	Water-cooled DOHC 16-valve in-line four
DISPLACEMENT	1074cc
HORSEPOWER	156bhp @ 10,000rpm
CARBURETTORS	4 x 40mm Mikuni
GEAR BOX	Five speed
FRAME	Aluminium alloy twin beam
WHEELBASE	55.1ins
WEIGHT	418lbs dry
TOP SPEED	175mph

Bimota Tesi 1D

·····························

The Bimota Tesi is one of the most radical, extraordinary and most interesting superbikes ever built. With the Tesi, the small Italian factory took a giant leap forward in motorcycle design, one that only Yamaha (and to a lesser extent BMW) have dared to follow, although 'specials' builders such as Nico Bakker have produced similar machines in very small numbers. What Bimota did was put into production a superbike that featured hub-centre steering rather than traditional telescopic front forks.

The problem with conventional telescopic forks is that they flex under braking and cornering, and because they compress under braking, the steering geometry of the bike is altered. In an ideal world the suspension and steering of a motorcycle should be separate and independent to each other. With telescopic forks this isn't possible, no matter how good the forks are, but with hub-centre steering the suspension can be separated from the steering.

So instead of wrapping the motorcycle's engine in a conventional frame and then bolting a pair of forks to the headstock and a rear swingarm to the back, Bimota have wrapped their chassis around the sides of the engine and then bolted a swingarm on at the front and at the back. The rear swingarm pivots in the traditional way and actuates the rear shock, while the front shock is bolted to the left-hand spar of the front swingarm and to the chassis. A complicated system of linkages joins the steering column to the front wheel to allow almost 30 degrees of steering movement.

One of the advantages of using a twin-sided front swingarm (as opposed to a single-sided one like the Yamaha GTS1000) is that it allows two brake discs to be used. And with twin 320mm front discs gripped by four-piston Brembo calipers, the Tesi has one of the best brake set-ups of any superbike.

All Bimotas are beautiful. The Tesi adds technical novelty to the usual aesthetic flair of Rimini products.

'Tesi' is Italian for degree thesis — of Bimota designer Pierluigi Marconi. If only all university courses looked like this.

The engine itself is a modified version of the Ducati 904cc water-cooled eight-valve desmo-dromic V-twin engine which uses a development of the Weber-Marelli fuel-injection system to produce a hefty 117bhp.

If all this doesn't sound exotic enough, the whole bike is clad in carbon-fibre bodywork and equipped with a pair of Kevlar silencers. The finished result is a bike that scales a featherweight 407lbs dry and which has a wheelbase more akin to a 400cc machine than a litre bike.

On the road the Tesi is quite unlike anything else. The lack of dive when slowing, and the fact that the suspension continues to work during hard braking, means that the Tesi can be braked later and cornered harder than anything else on the road. The fire-breathing Ducati engine means that top speeds of 160mph are a breeze and that in terms of performance the Tesi will stay with the very best that Japan has to offer.

The down side is that the Tesi is a solo machine, with no accommodation for pillion passengers, and it costs twice as much as a Yamaha GTS1000. In fact, except for the Honda NR750, the Tesi is the most expensive production bike in the world. But then it is also arguably the best production bike in the world.

Unique Tesi front suspension comes into its own, howling into bumpy corners hard on the brakes.

SPECIFICATION: BIMOTA TESI 1D	
ENGINE	Water-cooled SOHC 8-valve Desmo V-twin
DISPLACEMENT	904cc
HORSEPOWER	117bhp
CARBURETTORS	Electronic fuel injection
GEAR BOX	6 speed
FRAME	Twin aluminium-alloy plates
WHEELBASE	55.5ins
WEIGHT	407lbs dry
TOP SPEED	160mph

BMW K1200RS

With its striking styling, aluminium frame, innovative front suspension system and powerful four-cylinder engine, BMW's K1200RS is every millimetre a modern superbike. It's also a very long way indeed from being a traditional BMW – mainly because its engine's 130bhp output blasts a huge hole in the German firm's long-held limit of 100bhp.

Even BMW's sportier models have been restrained in the past, but there is nothing dull about the K1200RS's stylishly streamlined bodywork. And nor is there anything remotely boring about the way the 16-valve RS rockets smoothly to a top speed of over 150mph.

The K1200RS is still very much a BMW, for all that. When its makers describe the RS as a sports-tourer, unlike most manufacturers they place as much emphasis on the touring side of the equation as the sports. This BMW might have plenty of speed, but it also has adjustable ergonomics, anti-lock brakes and shaft final drive.

Its engine is a revamped version of the German firm's familiar longitudinally mounted inline four, its capacity increased to 1171cc by use of a longer-stroke crankshaft. More performance is added by use of lightweight pistons and valvegear, and a higher compression ratio – all of which contribute to its peak output of 130bhp at 8750rpm.

The RS's chassis is completely new and very different to that of its K1100RS predecessor, not just because its frame is made from aluminium instead of steel, but because the engine is rubber-mounted to reduce vibration. Front suspension is by a revised version of BMW's Telelever system, which links hollow fork legs via rods to a vertically mounted shock absorber. The single-sided rear swing-arm also works a single shock, placed diagonally on the right of the bike.

The K1200RS is a radical bike by BMW standards, combining its 130bhp four-cylinder engine with eye-catching styling and an aluminium frame. The RS is fast, and it's also built for long-distance comfort – a sports-tourer that fully lives up to the description.

Being a BMW, the RS is naturally available with numerous rider-friendly accessories including a tank-bag and panniers. The big difference between this bike and its predecessors is that even when loaded with luggage, the K1200RS is capable of cruising smoothly at 140mph.

'This is not a bike for knee-scraping cornering antics.'

What sets the RS apart from its predecessors is the exhilarating performance from its fuel-injected engine, which manages to combine its new-found high-rev power with the K-series motors' traditionally generous midrange torque. Twisting the throttle sends the big BMW storming forward almost regardless of where its tachometer needle is pointed, which makes for effortless overtaking.

Not that changing gear is a problem on the K1200RS, whose new six-speed gearbox is not just the best ever fitted to a BMW, but the first to meet Japanese standards. A slight buzz intrudes at about 4500rpm, ironically the useful 85mph-in-top-gear cruising zone. But at all other speeds the BMW feels supremely smooth and refined.

Handling is very good, too. Although, at 260kg dry, the RS is no heavier than several rival sports-tourers, it is a big machine that can be intimidating. This is not a bike for knee-scraping cornering antics; as well as the weight, it's too long, its steering geometry is too conservative and its suspension too soft.

But the RS has a pleasantly neutral and stable steering feel, excellent grip from broad radial tyres, and enough ground clearance to allow plenty of fun on a twisty road. Its Telelever front suspension eradicates fork dive under braking almost completely, soaking up bumps even when the powerful brakes – fitted with an uprated and very impressive ABS anti-lock system – are used hard.

One surprising limitation is lack of fuel capacity. The engine's thirst when used hard means that the 21-litre fuel tank gives a range of under 150 miles. But that's only a problem because the BMW is so comfortable that it allows all-day riding with no aches. If long-distance speed, comfort and style are what you require, very few bikes even come close to matching the K1200RS.

Features such as the adjustable windscreen and Telelever front suspension system are typical of BMW's innovative approach to bike design. Both work well, contributing to the way the RS swallows long distances at speed and in comfort.

SPECIFICATION: BMW K1200RS	
ENGINE	Water-cooled DOHC 16-valve longitudinal four
DISPLACEMENT	1171cc
HORSEPOWER	130bhp
CARBURETTORS	Motronic fuel-injection
GEAR BOX	Six speed
FRAME	Aluminium alloy spine
WHEELBASE	61.2ins
WEIGHT	572lbs dry
TOP SPEED	152mph

BMW R1100RS

BMW have a reputation for building top-quality touring motorcycles rather than high-performance superbikes, but in recent years they have managed to bridge the gap between the two concepts. Arguably the most eye-catching of this new breed is the R1100RS.

The R1100RS is a unique departure for BMW. Since the 1930s they have been building horizontally-opposed twin-cylinder machines with two valves per cylinder actuated by push-rods. But with the R1100RS the 'Boxer' engine (as it is commonly known) has joined the latter half of the 20th Century. It is still air cooled, but the number of valves per cylinder has been doubled to four, and their camshafts are now actuated by a series of belts driven from the crankshaft.

The old Bing carburettors, always a distinctive feature of the two-valve Boxer, have also been replaced – the R1100RS is the first Boxer to feature electronic fuel-injection.

But if all that is a major departure, the innovative 'Telelever' front suspension system of the R1100RS is a quantum leap into the next century for the German marque. Just as Yamaha has looked at alternative front suspension and steering systems for motorcycles, BMW has also taken the brave step of introducing their own solution to the problem. And that problem is that ideally the steering and suspension systems for a motorcycle's front end should be separate and independent from each other. Traditional telescopic forks flex, the steering geometry of the machine is altered when the front brake is being used, and often much of the fork's movement is taken up with braking, leaving little to deal with bumps in the road.

Yamaha's solution to the problem is the hub-centre-steered GTS1000, but BMW have taken a lower-key approach. They still use a pair of telescopic forks on the R1100RS, but they deal with the steering only. The suspension is handled by a single shock absorber bolted to the headstock and actuated by a wishbone-shaped bracket that joins the forks to the chassis. In effect the forks are merely sliders that join the front wheel to the headstock, while the wishbone actuates the shock absorber. Thus the suspension and steering are separated, creating an anti-dive effect when the front brake is applied.

This system is much simpler than that used by the Yamaha GTS1000, but is no less effective. Indeed the consensus of opinion is that the BMW

'BMW designed this bike to be a superlative sport-tourer.'

This odd-looking thing is Bavaria's answer to riders who want '90s technology in a bike they can understand.

As well as scratching well (above), the *Bee-eM* offers more user-friendly 'goodies' than practically any other motorcycle.

Boxer engine is inevitably wide (left) but the RS still has plenty of ground clearance to exploit.

Telelever system is actually more effective than that of the Yamaha. Certainly the R1100RS gives more feedback to the rider, and retains the traditional look of telescopic forks – an important consideration for the normally conservative BMW buyer.

But there's more to the R1100RS than an all-new Boxer engine and a 'funny' front end. BMW designed this bike to be a superlative sport-tourer, so comfort and the ability to cover ground effortlessly are also essential. To this end BMW have equipped the R1100RS with a host of user-friendly features that include adjustable seat height, handlebars and windscreen to enable the owner to tailor the bike to his own requirements. Hard luggage as an optional extra which, allied to a five-gallon fuel tank and a frugal 45mpg fuel consumption, means the R1100RS can cover well over 200 miles to a tankful of fuel and pack a decent amount of luggage for the two-wheeled tourist.

Weighing in at 526lb, the BMW needs good brakes, so the R1100RS has a pair of 305mm discs at the front gripped by four-piston calipers. BMW's excellent anti-lock braking system is also fitted, making this a very safe and well-braked machine. With the engine putting out 95bhp the R1100RS is capable of topping 135mph, but it is its ability to cruise all day at three-figure speeds that is its forte.

What BMW have done is build a thoroughly modern motorcycle that should appeal to the traditionalist buyer in search of something a little different. It's not the fastest machine on the roads, but it is supremely capable, and – the Bavarian hallmark – resolutely unorthodox.

SPECIFICATION: BMW R1100RS SE	
ENGINE	Air-cooled horizontally-opposed eight-valve flat twin.
DISPLACEMENT	1185cc
HORSEPOWER	95bhp @ 7250rpm
CARBURETTORS	Electronic fuel injection
GEAR BOX	Five speed
FRAME	Tubular steel
WHEELBASE	58ins
WEIGHT	526lbs wet
TOP SPEED	135mph

Buell S1 Lightning

Nothing on two wheels packs the visual punch of the Buell S1 Lightning. The barrel-chested Buell combines its big Harley-Davidson V-twin engine with a tiny seat and tail section. The result is uniquely aggressive – motorcycling's answer to the American Pit Bull terrier.

The Lightning's launch capped an exciting few years for Buell, the firm founded by Erik Buell, a former road-racer and Harley engineer. Buell made his name with a series of quick and fine-handling Harley-engined bikes such as the RR1000 and RS1200. But he was limited by lack of capital, which kept output low and prices high.

Then, in 1993, Harley-Davidson took a 49-per-cent stake in the renamed Buell Motorcycle Company, adding finance plus development and marketing expertise. The firm moved to a new and

larger factory near Harley's base at Milwaukee, increased production to ten bikes a day, and developed several new models – the most striking of which is the Lightning.

Like previous models its engine is Harley's 1203cc Sportster unit, for the first time tuned for extra horsepower. Compression ratio is increased from 9:1 to 10:1, and breathing is improved by combining the 1200 motor's big valves with the 883cc Sportster's cylinder heads. Other changes include Screamin' Eagle camshafts, lighter flywheels and a new ignition system.

Harley's engineers were commissioned to produce a super-efficient airbox and silencer. The results, a massive black plastic airbox on the right of the bike, and an even bigger silencer running beneath the motor, are ugly but effective. Peak

Is this the most distinctive profile in all motorcycling? The S1 Lightning's combination of big Harley V-twin engine, tubular steel frame, underslung exhaust pipe and tiny seat gives a lean and muscular look that leaves no doubts about the Buell's aggressive personality.

Erik Buell and his engineers work magic on Harley-Davidson's 1203cc V-twin engine. The Lightning produces a peak of 91bhp and delivers arm-wrenching acceleration to a top speed of 130mph. Buell's clever Uniplanar mounting system means the ride is smooth, too.

'The result is uniquely aggressive – motorcycling's answer to the American Pit Bull terrier.'

power output is 91bhp at 5800rpm, a massive 50 per cent more than a stock Sportster's figure.

The tubular steel frame is based on Buell's traditional design, with its 'Uniplanar' system of rubber mounts and rods that restrict vibration to the vertical plane. As before, suspension is by Dutch specialist WP, with 40mm upside-down forks and a single shock, situated horizontally beneath the engine and operated in tension rather than the conventional compression.

The S1 exhaust's soft, tractor-like chugging sound is disappointing, but the tacho needle races round the dial with unfamiliar enthusiasm at the blip of the throttle. At very low revs the S1 vibrates noticeably, but by 4000rpm it has cleared to give a ride as smooth as a magic carpet.

And the way the Lightning makes power is little short of amazing. The V-twin motor pulls strongly from as low as 50mph in top gear, giving a pleasantly relaxed ride. And by the short time that it takes to reach 80mph the S1 is really into its stride, living up to Buell's slogan – 'America's Faaast Motorcycle' – as it accelerates smoothly towards its 130mph top speed.

Suspension at both ends is sports-bike firm, with the 40mm WP forks doing a good job of soaking up bumps while giving a taut, racer-like feel. The rear

SPECIFICATION: BUELL S1 LIGHTNING	
ENGINE	Air-cooled pushrod OHV 4-valve 45-degree V-twin
DISPLACEMENT	1203cc
HORSEPOWER	91bhp @ 5800rpm
CARBURETTORS	40mm Keihin
GEAR BOX	Five speed
FRAME	Tubular steel ladder
WHEELBASE	55ins
WEIGHT	425lbs dry
TOP SPEED	130mph

Such is the Lightning's blend of acceleration and cornering power that many riders of other bikes have seen the Buell's diminutive seat and fat back tyre disappearing into the distance.

shock is well-controlled, but harsh on rough tarmac. In combination with the tiny seat and upright riding position, that makes for an uncomfortable ride.

Other chassis parts work well. The bike can be slowed abruptly with its huge, 340mm single front disc and six-piston Performance Machine caliper, then flicked into turns quickly and fired out hard using the torque of the V-twin motor. Its Dunlop radial tyres are very grippy, and there's plenty of ground clearance.

The S1 quickly became a big hit in America, and spearheaded Buell's expansion into export markets including Japan and Europe. With its unique style, smooth performance, sharp handling and V-twin charm, the Lightning is proof that America has a serious high-performance motorcycle manufacturer at last.

Cagiva 900 Elefant

*'As a road
bike the
Elefant is
surprisingly
capable.'*

Although based on Cagiva's successful desert racers, the Elefant is surprisingly adept at back-road scratching.

The popularity of the Paris-Dakar Rally in Europe has spawned a whole generation of enormous on/off-road superbikes, and none of them is more impressive than the Cagiva 900 Elefant.

The Paris-Dakar covered thousands of miles of desert in northern Africa, and the major motorcycle manufacturers spent many years, and enormous quantities of money, building bikes that would win it. Success in the Paris-Dakar translated directly to sales in Europe.

But the demands of the Saharan marathon meant that these trailbikes had to be very big and very fast, not something normally associated with off-road bikes. They also had to be immensely rugged and capable of carrying a lot of fuel and water with them – the two-wheeled equivalent of a Landcruiser.

The Cagiva 900 Elefant is a production version of the bike which triumphed in the Paris-Dakar a few years back, and is one of the biggest and best

Paris-Dakar replicas available. It's also one of the most interesting in that it uses a 900cc air and oil-cooled overhead cam 90-degree V-twin motor with desmodromic valve gear (as used on countless Ducati road and race bikes). Electronic fuel-injection helps the Elefant to produce a healthy 70bhp at 8500rpm, although brute power is less important with this kind of off-road machine than a usable spread of torque.

A high level of suspension equipment is *de rigeur* for desert-racers, and here the Cagiva gets full marks for Marzocchi forks at the front and an Öhlins multi-adjustable monoshock at the back. Rugged long-travel suspension is a must for this type of machine, and the Elefant has it in abundance.

Hefty twin front disc brakes give the Elefant plenty of stopping power, with twin-pot Nissin calipers providing bite. A large-capacity fuel tank (although not as large as the pukka desert race

bike's) and twin-headlamp fairing are also part of the essential P-D package, as is a vertiginous seat height of over 35ins.

As a road bike the Elefant is surprisingly capable. Although lacking the kind of power to compete directly with road-going sports 900s, the Elefant has a wide spread of power and torque which makes it very usable on twisting back roads. And with a top speed of 120mph the Elefant offers plenty of thrills along the way.

But it is off-road where the Cagiva really excels. That lazy, low-revving motor and low gearing make the Elefant a superb dirt bike that is equally at home idling along narrow gravel tracks or blasting at speed across open desert. The flexibility of the V-twin engine means that gear-changes are kept to a minimum, allowing the rider to concentrate on picking the right line across whatever terrain he happens to be traversing.

The long-travel suspension soaks up all but the biggest bumps, giving a soft manageable ride under almost all road and off-road conditions. That suspension travel also makes the Elefant a comfortable long-distance road mount, too.

Although bikes like the Elefant can't offer the kind of searing performance a high-performance road-bike can, their go-anywhere, do-anything capabilities give them an appeal all their own. The Cagiva 900 is undoubtedly the pinnacle of on/off-road engineering.

Gutsy V-twin power makes stunts such as this almost second nature. But if you want wild revs, look elsewhere.

Despite bash-plate and off-road styling, 900 Elefant is more a go-anywhere tourer than a true dirt machine.

SPECIFICATION:	CAGIVA 900 ELEFANT
ENGINE	Air/oil-cooled SOHC 90-degree Desmo V-twin
DISPLACEMENT	904cc
HORSEPOWER	70bhp @ 8500rpm
CARBURETTORS	Electronic fuel-injection
GEAR BOX	Five speed
FRAME	Aluminium-alloy cradle frame
WHEELBASE	61.8ins
WEIGHT	414lbs dry
TOP SPEED	120mph

Ducati 900 Monster

'All the elements come together to make a bike that is a real pleasure to ride, and even more of a pleasure to look at.'

Ducati made their reputation by building uncompromising sports bikes for those with the discernment and money to appreciate them, but in recent years they have branched out in another direction. In late '92 Ducati unveiled the M900 Monster to a stunned public, proving that they could build exciting bikes for all tastes, not just for the race replica sports rider.

The M900 was the first Ducati for many years to appeal to a wide range of riders, from the traditional Ducati fan to the rider in search of something 'a little different'. And the Monster is certainly different. Although it uses the same engine as the Ducati 900SS, the Monster is designed to be a muscle-bike. A bike that accelerates with startling rapidity, and which is more at home cruising the urban jungle looking for traffic-light Grands Prix to take part in than jockeying for position into turn one at Monza.

The Ducati 900SS has an engine blessed with masses of low-down power and usable torque, so to make it into a serious muscle-bike Ducati lowered the gearing and slotted the engine into the steel trellis frame that is their trademark. The engine puts out 84bhp at 7000rpm, power enough to hustle the Monster to a top speed of almost 130mph. That's not all that fast for a 900cc machine, but this is a bike built for cruising and back-road riding, so there is no fairing and the riding position is very upright. That makes it great in town or on country lanes, but painful at speed on motorways.

Where the Monster is really at home is cruising the *Promenade des Anglais* in Nice or parked outside *Tre Scalini* in the *Piazza Navonna* in Rome. This is a bike for being seen on, for posing on, for getting you around town in style and comfort, and with a large grin on your face.

And that grin is there not only because the Monster is very fast from a standing-start, not only because it is equipped with the best suspension and brakes around, but because it is a stupendous-looking machine. The feel-good factor gained from riding *Il Mostro* is enormous. Of course it does help that the Monster will out-drag all but the most powerful sports bike or supercar, that it comes with state-of-the-art 41mm upside-down forks and a multi-adjustable rear monoshock, and that it wears a massive pair of Brembo disc brakes equipped with four-piston calipers. All the elements come together to make a bike that is a real pleasure to ride, and even more of a pleasure to look at.

For the hard-core Ducati fan (a devotee of rock-solid suspension, agonising riding position, and 'idiosyncratic' electrics) the Monster will be a disappointment. But to everyone else the combination of good looks, lightning-quick steering, excellent suspension, eyeball-popping brakes and a lusty motor will ensure a huge grin and a much-depleted bank balance.

SPECIFICATION: DUCATI M900 MONSTER	
ENGINE	Air/oil-cooled SOHC 90-degree Desmo V-twin
DISPLACEMENT	904cc
HORSEPOWER	84bhp @ 7000rpm
CARBURETTORS	2 x 38mm Mikuni
GEAR BOX	Six speed
FRAME	Steel trellis
WHEELBASE	56.3ins
WEIGHT	408lbs
TOP SPEED	130mph

A rare picture of a M900 with both wheels on the ground. 'Wheelies' and 'stoppies' are more its natural territory.

Monster frame (above) comes from the 888 superbike, air-cooled engine from the familiar 900SS.

'Il Mostro' — the Monster — someone dubbed the prototype. Not surprisingly, the name stuck.

Ducati 916

....

'The spread of power is so immense that almost any gear will do.'

To many, Ducati's 916 is not merely a superbike, but *the* Superbike. Part motorcycle, part fantasy, part erotic art, few motorcycles of the past 20 years have aroused such passion amongst the motorcycling public.

Just look at it. Is there such a thing as Repetitive Strain Injury of the desire muscles? There is now. Within nanoseconds of its UK launch in late 1993, a whole generation of bikers had instantly put the 916 top of their lust list. Practically overnight, every one of the 200 destined for Britain in 1994 were sold. And the first 100 due in '95. Even at £11,800 apiece, it seemed cheap.

Not only does the 916 have looks in abundance, it has pedigree. Essentially, it is a racer, with the almost desultory addition of lights and a number plate. It is little more than a spin-off from World Superbike regulations which insist that if you can't find the same frame, engine castings and induction system in the shops, you can't put them on the track, either. For this reason, Honda would probably never have built their RC45 were it not for their Superbike racing ambitions. Ducati, on the other hand, almost certainly would have built the 916 – because they're Italian and Italians are into that sort of thing.

The 916's predecessor, the 888, had already won the World Superbike crown in 1990, '91, '92. Hot off the drawing board, the 916 followed suit, taking Carl Fogarty to memorable victory in the 1994 title chase. By the time you read this, he'll probably have won it again. And if Fogarty doesn't, another 916 almost certainly will.

Despite the leanness of its lines, the 916 is an extraordinarily complex box of tricks. That slim

SPECIFICATION: DUCATI 916	
ENGINE	Liquid-cooled DOHC 8-valve Desmo V-twin
DISPLACEMENT	916cc
HORSEPOWER	114bhp @ 9000rpm
CARBURETTORS	Programmed fuel injection, 50mm chokes
GEAR BOX	Six speed
FRAME	Tubular steel trellis
WHEELBASE	55.5ins
WEIGHT	430lbs dry
TOP SPEED	160mph

Not surprisingly, it was lust at first sight for a generation of bikers when the 916 was first unveiled. No previous machine had embodied quite the same combination of race-bred performance and sensuous good looks as the road-going counterpart of the machine which would take Carl Fogarty to his first World Superbike title.

fairing hides an engine which may 'only' be a twin, the latest in a line of Ducati V-twins dating back to 1972. But the latest Dukes have four valves per cylinder, four camshafts, six gears, liquid-cooling, computer-controlled electronic fuel injection and desmodromic valvegear.

All this advanced technology makes the 916 quite unlike most racing engines. Instead of a diet of pure, giddy revs, the twin pours out irrepressible, visceral urge almost from tickover. Solid, hard power begins as low as 3000rpm, and from 6000-upwards the universe is thrown into reverse. Top speed is a blistering 160mph.

In 955cc Superbike racing trim, the '916' develops the thick end of 150bhp. As a roadster it claims 114bhp at 9000rpm, but feels even stronger, more usable. The spread of power is so immense that almost any gear will do. And the booming roar when downshifting into corners is one of the joys of motorcycling.

The Ducati's chassis, too, is of the highest class. Compared to the 888, the 916 is shorter, more agile, more racer-like. The Japanese Showa suspension offers a huge array of settings, but there is very little wrong with the Duke straight out of the crate. With its short wheelbase and its lively geometry, it is in its element through turns – blindingly fast sweepers and hairpins alike.

Anyone buying the 916 takes custody of a dream as much as reality. As a practical street bike it has its faults, not the least of which is comfort. In a racing crouch – what it was designed for, after all – it fits like a glove. As a tourer, it makes a good plank. This is not a practical motorcycle, and every red-blooded rider in the world should want one.

Ducati 900 Superlight

·························

'Given a crack of the throttle the Superlight thundered off.'

Essentially a lightened version of the Ducati 900SS, the Superlight is a worthy descendant of the first Ducati superbikes of the mid-'seventies – lean, light and uncompromisingly purposeful.

Red, raw and unashamedly singleminded, Ducati's 900 Superlight proved conclusively that a sports bike could provide high performance – not with excessive horsepower but through simplicity, light weight and agile handling. By modern standards the Superlight was only moderately powerful – but it was rapid, exciting and every last millimetre a pure-bred Ducati sportster.

The Superlight was launched in 1992 as a racer, more aggressive relative of the 900SS, which had been introduced in 1989 and revamped to good effect two years later. Essentially the new model was a hard-charging, single-seat version of the SS, complete with reduced weight and numerous other changes intended to cash in on Ducati's early-'90s domination of the World Superbike race series.

Most of the Superlight's 90-degree V-twin engine was derived from the 900SS, which meant it was a 904cc, single overhead camshaft unit with two valves per cylinder and desmodromic valve operation (valves closed positively, instead of by springs). The gearbox remained a six-speed unit; the only transmission difference was a ventilated cover for the Superlight's dry clutch.

The 900SS's pair of 38mm downdraft Mikunis was retained, which helped give an identical claimed peak output of 73bhp at 7000rpm. The Superlight's lack of a pillion seat allowed the free-breathing exhaust pipes to sit higher. At the other end, the new bike gained a front mudguard of lightweight carbon-fibre, instead of the conventional plastic.

In Ducati tradition the Superlight's chassis was based around a tubular steel ladder frame, and featured low-set clip-on handlebars and rearset footrests. Most of the chassis was shared with the 900SS, including the sturdy 41mm upside-down front forks from Showa, and the same Japanese firm's multi-adjustable rear shock, working directly on a cantilever swing-arm.

To that successful format the Superlight added composite wheels with aluminium rims and lightweight magnesium spokes, wearing Michelin's Hi-Sport radial tyres in suitably broad sizes. Brakes

Gutsy V-twin powerplant allows the Superlight to power hard out of bends, almost regardless of gear and revs. Handling is similarly forgiving.

were Brembo's finest: twin 320mm discs up front, gripped by four-piston Gold Line calipers.

As much as its pure performance, it was the Superlight's purposeful attitude and uncompromisingly sporty feel that made the bike so addictive. Its racy red styling, aggressive riding position and rich exhaust note gave a sporty, unmistakably V-twin feel, and the Ducati's blend of gutsy midrange torque, light weight and crisp throttle response made for a wonderfully eager and easy-to-ride machine.

That 73bhp peak output resulted in a top speed of almost 140mph, which could be bettered by several Japanese 750s. But the Ducati's combination of superlightness and broad power delivery meant the V-twin could stay with almost any competition on all but an arrow-straight road. Given a crack of the throttle the Superlight thundered off, remaining reasonably smooth all the way to its 9000rpm redline.

Handling was excellent too, thanks to the Superlight's rigid frame and its collection of top-quality cycle parts. Steering was light and neutral, giving the 388lbs Ducati the feel of a genuine middleweight. The adjustable forks gave a ride that was firm without being harsh, and the firmly sprung rear end was superbly well-controlled, even when being worked hard by the aggressive cornering encouraged by the grip of the fat and sticky rear Hi Sport tyre.

Whether the Superlight's 15lbs weight advantage, compared to the 900SS, was strictly noticeable was debatable, and the two models were certainly very

closely related in performance, as well as specification. The new bike's price was considerably higher, too. But for riders addicted to the speed, style and simplicity of Ducati's two-valves-per-cylinder V-twins, the 900 Superlight was second to none.

SPECIFICATION: DUCATI 900 SUPERLIGHT	
ENGINE	Air/oil-cooled SOHC 4-valve Desmo V-twin
DISPLACEMENT	904cc
HORSEPOWER	73bhp @ 7000rpm
CARBURETTORS	2 x 38mm Mikuni
GEAR BOX	Six speed
FRAME	Tubular steel ladder
WHEELBASE	56ins
WEIGHT	388lbs dry
TOP SPEED	137mph

Despite the fashion for aluminium beam frames, Ducati remain devoted to a steel trellis design, for the simple reason that it works.

Egli Harley-Davidson

'Vibration from the solidly-mounted motor added to the sensation of speed, too.'

Former Swiss racing champion Fritz Egli has been building beautifully engineered bikes around his own chassis for over 25 years. When Egli adapted his traditional steel spine frame to hold a tuned, 1607cc Harley-Davidson V-twin engine, the result was an exciting machine that was outrageous by any standards – and especially those of environment-conscious Switzerland, notorious for its strict limits on motorcycles' power and noise.

Big, basic and muscular, the first Egli Harley, built in 1992, had an aggressive and vaguely classic look, thanks to bodywork fashioned from 1960s-style unpainted aluminium. A huge petrol tank curved over the top of the grey-finished Evolution engine. Large triangular sidepanels ran below a one-and-a-half-person seat. Front and rear mudguards were also made from bare alloy sheet.

The frame consisted of a main steel spine, which doubled as the oil reservoir, plus narrower tubes that held the motor in a conventional twin cradle. Egli himself built numerous parts, including the 38mm diameter front forks and their yokes. At the rear, the triangulated steel swing-arm worked a single, multi-adjustable White Power shock absorber.

The motor was far from standard, having been built by Egli to incorporate a long list of tuning parts including Cosworth pistons, Carrillo rods and Manley valves. Plumbed with a 36mm Mikuni carburettor and an Egli-made exhaust system, the result was an increase in the V-twin's capacity from 1340cc to a massive 1607cc, raising peak output to 120bhp at 5500rpm.

When the big Harley burst into life, it did so with enough noise to start an avalanche. The view from the pilot's seat was intimidating. There was a long stretch across the alloy tank to adjustable clip-on bars that were set low and wide. Standard Harley clocks perched above the protruding fork-tops, the tacho needle flicking across the dial with every blip of the throttle.

Riding the Egli Harley confirmed that it was no docile modern sportster but a big, old-fashioned bruiser of a bike that needed a firm hand to give of its best. Its wheelbase was compact by Harley standards, at 60ins. But conservative steering geometry, an 18-inch front wheel and a high centre of gravity meant a good deal of effort was needed to change direction.

Raucous, raw and very, very rare, Fritz Egli's radical reworking of the Harley theme has more than double the power of the original.

Suspension was firm and worked well on smooth roads, the forks feeling reassuringly rigid and the well-damped rear unit keeping the back end under control. Despite its much-increased output, the engine was as tractable as any Harley motor. Crack open the throttle, and the bike hurtled forward to the accompaniment of an increasingly frenzied barrage of sound from the exhaust.

Vibration from the solidly-mounted motor added to the sensation of speed, too. Below 3000rpm the big V-twin was smooth, giving a relaxed feel up to 60mph in top gear. But the vibes arrived at that figure and increased steadily. Although the Egli stormed past 100mph on the way to a top speed of about 130mph, fast cruising was best limited to short bursts.

Rubber-mounting the engine would have been one solution – but, as Fritz Egli pointed out, much of the bike's appeal came from its raw feel, to which the untamed V-twin lump was a major contributor. At least there was no pretence with an Egli Harley. What you saw was a big, old-fashioned V-twin brute of a machine, and that was precisely what you got. Plenty of sports bikes were faster and more agile than the Egli. Few were more thrilling to ride.

SPECIFICATION: EGLI HARLEY-DAVIDSON	
ENGINE	Air-cooled pushrod OHV 45-degree V-twin
DISPLACEMENT	1607cc
HORSEPOWER	120bhp @ 5500rpm
CARBURETTORS	36mm Mikuni
GEAR BOX	Five speed
FRAME	Steel main spine and duplex cradle
WHEELBASE	60ins
WEIGHT	520lbs dry
TOP SPEED	130mph

130mph and no fairing gives the rider two choices: tuck in, or get blown away.

Steel spine frame, bespoke forks and White Power suspension still struggle to cope with a machine weighing well over 500lbs.

Harley-Davidson Dyna Glide

'The essence of any Harley is that pounding V-twin beat.'

The Dyna Glide features Harley-Davidson's latest chassis, which Harley themselves proudly claim is the result of computer-aided design (CAD). But it's a far cry from the exotic aluminium beam frames favoured by the latest Japanese race replicas. This one's steel, good ol' US steel, a direct spiritual descendant of an earlier generation of American iron horses.

Seemingly sculpted from solid billets of Milwaukee metal, Harleys spurn 'crotch rocket' styling in favour of timeless V-twin appeal. Well-spaced fork legs mark this as the 'Wide Glide' version.

But the frame is, in its modest way, a new departure for Harley-D as they progress ever-so-cautiously into the future. First seen on the 1991 Sturgis model, it features a refinement of the system of rubber engine mounting previously fitted to Glide and Low Rider models. And for the first time, it is possible for a normal person to ride a Harley at sustained speed without going numb from the wrists down.

Purists might frown. The essence of any Harley is that pounding V-twin beat. Unlike the anodyne whirr of Japanese multis, you're *supposed* to feel it. Dyna Glide's endeavour to offer the best of both worlds: you can tell there's 80 cubic inches of Milwaukee muscle down there, all right, but it doesn't put your circulation in a sling.

To ride, these are the smoothest Hogs yet, by a margin. Even sensitive souls will use power outside the Evolution engine's hitherto rev-range without worrying that the entire bike's about to fall to bits. Now you can happily ride at low revs where other Hogs quake and shudder. Or at high revs where your fillings used to be in danger of shaking out. Without laying a hand on the engine, rubber mounting has effectively widened the big Vee's powerband.

Harley themselves bill the Dynas as 'combining '70s Low Rider looks with the handling and rubber-isolated ride of today's Low Riders'. Both standard, 'Low Rider' and 'Wide Glide' models have been produced, the latter with the fork legs widely spaced. These are lean, low machines by Harley standards, styled according to whatever passes for grace in Milwaukee.

The rest, as is Harley's way, is largely in the hands of the cosmetic engineers. Using just two engines (Sporters of 883 & 1200cc, plus the 1340cc twin), and a handful of frame designs, the Milwaukee company typically produces around 20 models per year. It follows that many of the differences are cosmetic, and there are truly only four types of Harley: Sportsters, Low Riders, Softails and Glides. Dyna Glides are essentially a variation of the Low Rider theme.

This is precisely the point. Whilst owners of European and Japanese sports machines might discuss the number of valves per cylinder, or the thousands of suspension options available, Harley owners are interested in style. If it's paint, badging, chrome or tassels, Harley can supply it from a bewildering accessory list. And if they can't, an entire industry of custom goodies manufacturers will be happy to oblige.

Equally, whilst outright performance is rarely at the top of any Harley owner's shopping list, mild performance options are popular. Again, there's a Harley catalogue of bolt-on 'Screaming Eagle' parts.

Such are the number of variables that it's impossible to describe in detail how any particular model performs: on the whim of the stylists different Dyna Glides, for instance, feature one or two front disc brakes. So some stop, and some don't. Dyna Wide Glide's have poor ground clearance, even by Harley standards. Others are adequate, just about.

Inescapably, functionality is not the point. It's how a Harley looks that makes it Super. Beauty might be in the eye of the beholder, but nothing turns heads quite like a Hog.

SPECIFICATION: HARLEY-DAVIDSON DYNA GLIDE	
ENGINE	Air-cooled OHV 45-degree V-twin
DISPLACEMENT	1340cc
HORSEPOWER	55bhp @ 5000rpm
CARBURETTORS	40mm Keihin
GEAR BOX	Five speed
FRAME	Tubular steel twin cradle
WHEELBASE	65.5in
WEIGHT	599lb
TOP SPEED	105mph

Upper digits of speedo are redundant, but on a Hog it's style, not speed, that counts.

Unmistakably 'born in the USA', but modern rubber-mounting of the engine insulates the rider from the shuddering twin's customary vibes.

Harley-Davidson Electra Glide

·······················

The Electra Glide has to be one of the most famous names in motorcycling. Ask anyone to name a make and model of motorcycle and the chances are they'll say Harley-Davidson Electra Glide. Immortalised by the film *Electra Glide in Blue*, and by the California Highway Patrol, the Electra Glide is the archetypal American superbike.

The Electra Glide has been around for 30 years, and has remained pretty much unchanged during that time. Harley-Davidsons aren't renowned for their speed or sporting prowess, and the Electra Glide is no exception. Using a large-capacity but low-revving V-twin engine, the Electra Glide is built for comfort rather than speed.

The engine is something of a curiosity in the motorcycle world these days – people just don't build 1340cc air-cooled push-rod V-twins anymore. With increasingly stringent noise and emissions regulations being put in place by governments around the world, the future of the traditional Harley engine looks rather bleak. But until the day arrives when they can't get through the homologation procedures, the big twins will continue to delight their fans.

Harley-Davidsons have been described as being as high-tech as a mangle, and although that is somewhat overstating the case, the appeal of Harleys is their simplicity. That, and their classic

'Undoubtedly gorgeous- looking machines, Harleys have become a cult icon.'

Possibly the biggest item of designer jewellery ever created, the Electra Glide legend rumbles on and on.

The wheels of choice for film stars and rock legends, but the 'Glide is also the Stateside tourer *par excellence*.

good looks. Undoubtedly gorgeous-looking machines, Harleys have become a cult icon. Not all that long ago the Harley was the mount of the outlaw biker, but these days the Harley rider is more likely to be a stockbroker, film star or rock legend. Harleys have become the chic and expensive playthings of the rich and famous.

So what is the Electra Glide like? The engine is a vast unit, heavily over-engineered and built to last a life-time. Although it displaces 1340cc it produces a meagre 55bhp, allowing the Electra Glide to rumble to a top speed of around 110mph. That's not what you'd call fast, but the engine is blessed with an abundance of torque that means you put it in top gear and allow the motor to chug away in its own leisurely way.

The thing to remember about Harleys is they were designed for use in the USA, where 65mph is as fast as you can go and where the distances are huge. For this reason the Electra Glide is designed to cover ground slowly but effortlessly. Unlike machines such as the Honda Gold Wing, which bristle with state-of-the-art electrical gizmos, the Electra Glide relies on soft suspension, a plush seat, and a low-revving engine to make it a fine long-distance tourer. And a very accomplished tourer it is – it will cover 200 miles without having to stop for fuel, and when you do stop you aren't suffering the aches and pains experienced with some other touring machines.

Harleys have never had good brakes, high-tech suspension, or any of the other things the

Japanese, British, German or Italian motorcycle manufacturers use to make their machine better than anyone else's. Instead, Harleys are built to a competent level and the Harley image and name does the rest. The fact that they look fantastic and are very desirable means that Harley-Davidson sell every one they make without any effort at all. The Electra Glide might not be fast, it might not be powerful, but it is certainly one of the most stylish and prestigious superbikes around today.

Only something this big could make 1340cc of air-cooled twin appear dainty.

SPECIFICATION: HARLEY-DAVIDSON ELECTRA GLIDE	
ENGINE	Air-cooled OHV 45-degree V-twin
DISPLACEMENT	1340cc
HORSEPOWER	55bhp @ 5000rpm
CARBURETTORS	40mm Keihin
GEAR BOX	Five speed
FRAME	Steel double-cradle
WHEELBASE	62.9ins
WEIGHT	741lbs dry
TOP SPEED	110mph

Harley-Davidson Heritage Softail

....

'Not for Harley the headlong race for performance.'

Nostalgia, as they say, isn't what it used to be. It's better. For this, ladies and gentlemen, is Retro-tech. It is Harley-Davidson's shatteringly successful attempt to sell back to the motorcycling public those dreamy days of the 'fifties when the sun always shone and the Platters presided over a million teenage romances.

Not for Harley the headlong race for performance. Of overhead camshafts, they have none. Two valves per cylinder is all you get, and liquid-cooling is strictly for cars. What you get instead is style, American-style, in huge imposing motorcycles deliberately engineered to ape a bygone age: Retro-tech.

Although the Glide range has now evolved into something distinct (see page 36), the Heritage Softail is not unlike the original Glide, the Hydra-Glide of 1949. This was the first Milwaukee machine to feature telescopic forks, and the Softail's are shrouded to emulate the earlier design.

Glides didn't boast swing-arm rear suspension until the Duo-Glide of 1958. A cursory inspection of any Softail suggests that it, too, is a pre-'58 design. But what the designers have done is style a rear suspension which looks 'hardtail', but is in fact fully sprung. A pair of damper units reside discreetly under the gearbox as though ashamed to own up to the 1990s. This is 'Softail' and, like most things Harley, even the name is copyright.

Between '49-style forks and the *appearance* of no rear suspension is slung the classic Harley V-twin. Like the chassis, on first examination it could have been built pretty well any time between 1920 and the present. But yet again, appearances are deceptive. This is a 1340cc 'Evolution' unit, dating from 1985. Modernisation has improved reliability, without sacrificing the V-twin's classic charm.

All these things the Heritage has in common with the rest of the Softail range – the 'standard' Softail Custom and the Fat Boy. The Springer Softail goes even further down the retro route in wearing forks which mimic '30s girders. All are massive machines – the lightest is 617lbs – with distinctly modest power outputs, and the power-to-weight of a not very sporting car. Cruising, not scratching, is where Softails are at.

So riding any Harley is more a spiritual experience than an adrenaline-soaked thrill. The Heritage Softail, arguably the biggest fashion accessory in the world, takes this to extremes. It rolls around amiably on its ponderously fat tyres, vibrates like mad at any sort of revs and changes gear only in its own good time.

Since, unlike Glides, Softail engines are not rubber-mounted, vibration is acute at high revs. You're never left in any doubt that the shuddering lump under the petrol tank is a real engine producing prodigious torque at low revs, the two-wheeled equivalent of generations of Detroit V-eights. This, more than anything else, is a Harley's soul.

The rear suspension, meanwhile, is better than it looks without actually being much good. Despite the constraints inherent in the styling, Softails in fact boast more rear suspension travel – 4.06in – than any other models in the Harley range. But hit something hard, and you'd better hope your vertebrae are in good shape. Braking is similarly feeble by current standards. It is actually possible to lock a Softail

Despite rumours to the contrary, with the Softail, nostalgia definitely *is* what it used to be – or as near as Harley can make it. And very lucratively so.

front wheel, but you need a helluva fright to work up the necessary energy. Like all Harleys, you use plenty of rear brake to slow down.

But slow and stately is the point. Legends, after all, are not to be hurried.

SPECIFICATION:	HARLEY-DAVIDSON
	HERITAGE SOFTAIL
ENGINE	Air-cooled OHV
	45-degree V-twin
DISPLACEMENT	1340cc
HORSEPOWER	55bhp @ 5000rpm
CARBURETTORS	40mm Keihin
GEAR BOX	Five speed
FRAME	Tubular steel twin cradle
WHEELBASE	62.5in
WEIGHT	710lb
TOP SPEED	105mph

Cruisin' is what Harleys do best, whether loping across the American Prairies or ambling along English country lanes.

Lazy, low-revving 'Evolution' engine has deservedly banished the reputation Harleys once had for unreliability.

Harley-Davidson
XL1200S Sportster Sport

·····························

The profile is classical Sportster: raised bars, peanut gas tank and V-twin motor with 'staggered shorty dual' pipes. But this is the sportiest Sportster yet – thanks to uprated, multi-adjustable suspension, twin floating front disc brakes and sticky radial tyres. Handling, roadholding and braking are still a long way from grand prix standard – but this Harley is a whole lot of fun on a twisty road.

Harley-Davidson's Sportster is a rolling, rumbling two-wheeled legend – but it's one that hasn't lived up to its name for many years. Shortly after its launch back in 1957, the lean, tuned-up 883cc V-twin really was a sports machine, boasting 110mph top speed, fierce acceleration and respectable handling. But then the Sportster was outpaced first by British twins and then by Japanese multis, changing little in style or performance as its name became less apt with every passing year.

That hasn't prevented Harley's most basic bike from remaining hugely popular right up to the present day. Thanks largely to its good looks, character and competitive price, the Sportster has often been the best-selling motorcycle on the American market. And in 1996, Harley's

management gave the bike back a little of its ancestors' aggression by producing the XL1200S Sportster Sport – the closest thing to a truly sporty Sportster for years.

The key to the Sportster Sport is its considerably uprated chassis. Its Showa 39mm front forks and twin rear shocks are fully adjustable for preload, compression and rebound damping – a major first for Harley. The front brake features not one but two drilled 292mm floating discs, and is bolted to a cast wheel which, like its rear counterpart, wears a wide radial tyre. Compared to the cycle parts worn by previous Sportsters, this is serious stuff.

Much of the rest of the bike is familiar, including the faithful 1203cc, aircooled 45-degree motor whose only change is a revamp to the five-

The Sportster Sport's peak output is little more than 50bhp, but there's a fair amount of midrange torque and the Harley has more than enough power to lift its front wheel when the occasion demands.

'The Harley trundles up to about 120mph given enough time.'

speed gearbox, aimed largely at reducing noise. That means the aircooled, pushrod-operated motor's peak output remains somewhere in the modest mid-50bhp range, delivered at about 5000rpm.

Straight-line performance is unchanged from other recent 1200 Sportsters. The XL pulls cleanly at low revs and rumbles easily along with a pleasantly laid-back feel at legal speeds, accelerating crisply until it's cruising quite smoothly at 70mph with just 3000rpm showing on the tacho. At fairly slow speeds the upright riding position is comfortable, and the gearbox allows easy short-shifting to make the most of the strong low-rev performance.

Inevitably the Harley is less impressive when revved harder, beginning to vibrate noticeably by 4000rpm. By 5000rpm there's a fair amount of

buzzing coming through the handlebars. The Harley trundles up to about 120mph given enough time, but it's a tough rider who can hold high cruising speeds for long.

If this Sportster's engine performance remains much the same as ever, then happily that's not true of its chassis. This is still a basic and old-fashioned motorbike, with a simple twin-cradle steel frame, a 19-inch front wheel and a substantial 497lbs of weight. But its chassis parts are an improvement on anything that Harley has previously fitted.

Most noticeable is the front brake, which despite its feeble-looking single-action calipers gives very respectable stopping power. The grippy Dunlop tyres fitted as standard are well up to coping with this, and combine with the Sport's reasonably generous ground clearance to allow lots of fun on a twisty road. Most important, though, is the Harley's uprated suspension, which is comfortable on its standard settings in town – and can be fine-tuned to give more control for hard riding.

Even these modifications and the Sportster Sport name do not make this Harley a genuine high-performance motorcycle. But the charismatic V-twin remains as stylish and as endearingly simple as ever, and the 1200S handles and stops well enough to make for an entertaining twisty-road ride. It's the best Sportster yet, and is sure to help the legendary name rumble on for many more years to come.

Harley's 1203cc, 45-degree V-twin powerplant is cooled by air and operates its valves via pushrods, just like its predecessors. This motor has a revised five-speed gearbox, but the Sportster Sport's extra performance comes from its chassis.

SPECIFICATION: HARLEY-DAVIDSON XL1200S SPORTSTER SPORT	
ENGINE	Air-cooled OHV 4-valve 45-degree V-twin
DISPLACEMENT	1203cc
HORSEPOWER	55bhp @ 5000rpm
CARBURETTORS	40mm Keihin
GEAR BOX	Five speed
FRAME	Tubular steel duplex cradle
WHEELBASE	60.2ins
WEIGHT	497lbs dry
TOP SPEED	120mph

Honda F6C Valkyrie

Honda's F6C is quite simply the most surprising superbike of recent years. At first sight the gigantic, chrome-covered, six-cylinder F6C looks more like a two-wheeled burger bar than a serious motorcycle. But looks can be deceiving. One ride on the improbably fast and agile Honda is guaranteed to put a helmet-splitting grin on the face of even the most sceptical rider.

The F6C is built in America (where it is known, rather more imaginatively, as the Valkyrie) and is Honda's attempt to create a new two-wheeled category: the 'performance cruiser'. That meant combining the all-American style of high handlebars, big fenders and fat tyres with the sort of performance more commonly associated with low bars and streamlined fairings.

Honda's engineers were determined that the bike should be stamped with the Japanese marque's own identity, so they utilised the 1520cc flat-six engine of the legendary Gold Wing tourer. The motor is tuned slightly with hotter camshafts, a new exhaust system and six carbs in place of the Wing's two. The result is a maximum power output of 100bhp – heady stuff by cruiser standards – and generous torque production from very low revs.

The shaft-drive motor sits in a tubular steel frame developed from that of the Wing. Suspension is seriously heavy-duty, with massive 45mm upside-down forks up front. A pair of chrome-covered rear shocks holds up the back end of a bike which, at almost 700lbs dry, is heavy even for a giant cruiser.

Happily the F6C is far more manageable than

With its outrageous combination of cruiser styling, huge flat-six engine and remarkably capable chassis, the Valkyrie is a motorcycle like nothing else on two wheels. Predictably it has been a big success in the American market, where cruisers dominate and Honda's six-cylinder Gold Wing is a legend.

For such a big bike the F6C handles amazingly well. It stays stable right up to its top speed of almost 130mph. And despite its weight, it corners well thanks to fairly firm and well-damped suspension, adequate ground clearance and grippy tyres.

its size and spec sheet suggest. The bike's low centre of gravity, conservative steering geometry and long wheelbase combine to provide a solid feel. The wide bars help give reasonably light steering, allowing easy slow-speed manoeuvring.

The big bike's user-friendly feel is also due to its engine, which is just about the most flexible powerplant ever suspended between two wheels. The Valkyrie has so much low-down grunt that it barely needs a gearbox at all. On this bike you often find yourself short-shifting into top at just 2000rpm, and when requested the big six will pull from much lower than that.

Yet the Valkyrie very much lives up to its billing as a 'performance cruiser' too. Keep the tacho needle flicking towards the 6500rpm redline, and

the six is a seriously rapid motorcycle. Top speed is over 125mph, and the F6C will happily cruise at over 100mph until your neck muscles have had enough.

If the engine's performance is impressive, the fact that the chassis encourages you to use it is even more so. The Honda remains stable at speed despite all its weight, and its suspension is good enough to make quick cornering not only possible but enjoyable. The Valkyrie gives a slightly less plush ride than many cruisers but it can be banked into a bend with real confidence.

The Honda's Dunlop radials grip well and are certainly wide – the 180-section rear is as fat as most superbike tyres. Ground clearance is generous by cruiser standards, too. And the F6C has plenty of braking power, thanks to twin discs up front plus a slightly larger disc at the rear.

Of course the big, heavy six still has limitations as a performance machine, but it's impossible not to be impressed by the way it goes about its business. The F6C blends distinctive looks with a smooth, powerful, supremely flexible engine and a remarkably good chassis. Honda set out to build a giant cruiser with the performance to match its size – and they succeeded handsomely.

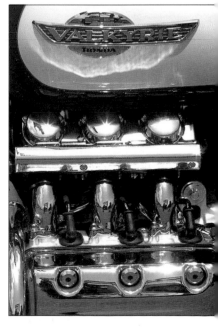

The Valkyrie's 1520cc flat-six powerplant produces an impressive maximum of 100bhp, but it's the Honda's low-rev torque that takes its rider's breath away. Simply winding open the throttle at almost any engine speed sends the big Six surging smoothly forward.

SPECIFICATION: HONDA F6C VALKYRIE	
ENGINE	Water-cooled SOHC 12-valve flat six
DISPLACEMENT	1520cc
HORSEPOWER	100bhp @ 6000rpm
CARBURETTORS	6 x 28mm Keihin
GEAR BOX	Five speed
FRAME	Tubular steel cradle
WHEELBASE	66.5ins
WEIGHT	682lbs dry
TOP SPEED	128mph

Honda CBR900RR Fireblade

·····························

The Fireblade is simply the superbike by which all others are currently judged. At the cutting-edge of superbike technology, the Fireblade combines superlative performance with light weight and peerless handling to create a bike that many have tried to imitate but none has equalled.

Motorcycle manufacturers love to announce 'revolutionary new concepts' in motorcycle design, but realistically few of them ever come up with any such thing. Yet the Fireblade is one such machine. Launched in 1992, it re-wrote the rule book for performance motorcycles, combining litre bike power in a package the size and weight of a 600. Overnight, the rest of the supersport litre bike class became dinosaurs. What previously was thought to be the pinnacle of motorcycle performance was suddenly rendered obsolete.

Britain's best-selling superbike packs a heavyweight punch into a middleweight parcel. When launched in 1992, it re-wrote the rules.

So what makes the Fireblade so special? Very simply, it is the combination of a powerful engine in a small, lightweight machine, fitted with state-of-the-art suspension and brakes. The engine itself is nothing exceptional, being a very familiar water-cooled DOHC 16-valve in-line four putting out 125bhp – pretty much the industry standard for a 1000cc machine.

The chassis is an aluminium-alloy beam, again an industry standard in the supersports category, with a pair of hefty 45mm telescopic forks at the front and a multi-adjustable rising-rate monoshock at the back. Interestingly, Honda ignored the current trend for fitting inverted telescopic forks and a 17-inch front wheel to the Fireblade, instead opting for ordinary telescopic forks and a 16-inch wheel. Brakes are a pair of 296mm discs at the front

'The nature of the Fireblade means that this is not a bike for the faint-hearted or for the touring motorcyclist.'

with four-piston calipers, and a single 240mm disc at the back.

Looking at the specification sheet of the Fireblade, it's hard to work out quite why this is such an exceptional motorcycle. The sum of the parts doesn't seem to add up to anything more than what is on offer from the other manufacturers of superbikes, yet in use the Fireblade stands head and shoulders above everything except the priciest hand-built exotica from Italy.

On the road the Fireblade is so light and so nimble it feels like a race-bred middleweight, yet it packs the punch of a bike from the heavyweight division. The steering response is razor-sharp and allows the Fireblade to be flicked through corners at tremendous speed and with absolute precision. Although the Fireblade may not be the fastest bike on the roads (a top-speed of 165mph is a good 10mph down on machines like the Kawasaki ZZ-R1100), it is almost certainly the fastest bike point-to-point. The ease with which it corners, brakes and accelerates means that off the motorway there's nothing to touch it (except another Fireblade).

The nature of the Fireblade means that this is not a bike for the faint-hearted or for the touring motorcyclist. It is cramped and not at all comfortable, nor is it very practical. But for pure, hedonistic motorcycling at the very edge of the performance envelope there isn't much that comes close.

The Fireblade has raised superbike performance to a level now where the only limits are those of the rider rather than those of the machine. Motorcycle manufacturers will continue to produce better and better machines, but the Fireblade will be remembered as the bike that brought perfection to the masses, and at an affordable price.

SPECIFICATION: HONDA FIREBLADE	
ENGINE	Liquid-cooled DOHC 16-valve in-line four
DISPLACEMENT	893cc
HORSEPOWER	124bhp @ 11000rpm
CARBURETTORS	4 x 38mm Keihin CV
GEAR BOX	Six speed
FRAME	Aluminium-alloy twin beam
WHEELBASE	55.3ins
WEIGHT	407lbs dry
TOP SPEED	165mph

Searing acceleration makes keeping the front wheel down the hardest trick in the Fireblade book.

Honda GL1500 Gold Wing

'On the open road the Gold Wing performs faultlessly, as long as you never forget it weighs 800lbs and isn't designed as a sportsbike.'

When it comes to sheer size, superbikes don't come any bigger than Honda's GL1500 Gold Wing. This leviathan of the two-wheeled world is the ultimate in motorcycling comfort, designed solely to transport two people in as much style and luxury as is possible.

The Gold Wing has been around for two decades, during which time it has evolved from a fairly basic naked tourer into an everything-but-the-kitchen-sink machine for the discerning traveller. It began life as a 1000cc flat-four, grew to an 1100cc flat-four, a 1200cc flat-four, and finally into a 1500cc flat-six.

Yes, six cylinders power this mighty beast, producing 98bhp at 5200rpm and a massive 110ft/lb of torque at 4000rpm. Despite weighing in at a hefty 800lbs dry, the 'Wing is capable of a top speed of 130mph, although it takes its time getting there.

But top speed isn't what the Gold Wing is about. Smooth, effortless power delivery, luggage-carrying capacity, and supreme comfort, are what the Gold Wing is all about. And it is justly famous for achieving its purpose. The barn-door-like fairing is large enough to keep the wind and rain off the rider (although internal vents in the fairing allow you to direct cooling air at yourself when the weather gets hot). The saddle is a masterpiece of the furniture-makers art, coddling the behinds of rider and pillion, and adding to the almost total absence of vibrations from the engine to give the smoothest ride known to motorcycling.

Further to enhance the comfort and quality of ride, an on-board air-compressor allows the rider to pump up the rear suspension, and the adjustable

windscreen allows riders of any height the optimum view of the road ahead. Cruise-control is a prerequisite on this kind of bike (designed, as it is, primarily for the US market where speeds are low but sustainable for hours on end), and the Gold Wing has an effective and easy-to-use one.

But the *pièce de résistance* is the Gold Wing's sound system. The radio-cassette player is an amazing piece of technology that allows you to listen to your favourite music as you cruise the highways. Even at three-figure speeds the stereo system is clearly audible thanks to the sensor that automatically adjusts the volume to compensate for ambient wind noise.

When it comes to transporting your belongings, the Gold Wing is similarly impressive. The panniers and top-box will swallow huge amounts of luggage, and the top-box even boasts an interior light and vanity mirror!

On the open road the Gold Wing performs faultlessly, as long as you never forget it weighs 800lbs and isn't designed as a sportsbike. Fully-loaded the 'Wing will cruise all day at 90mph while you and your passenger sit comfortably behind the huge fairing listening to your favourite radio programme. With a range of over 200 miles from a tankful of fuel the 'Wing can cover 1000 miles in a day with ease, and still leave the rider fresh enough to do the same again the next day. And the day after that.

And that is the sole purpose of the Gold Wing, to make travelling by motorcycle as comfortable and pleasant as possible. It doesn't offer adrenaline-pumping speed or svelte good looks, it just makes touring a uniquely majestic experience.

More dials and gizmos than IBM's latest, the 'Wing offers creature comforts few living rooms can equal.

The only 'six' still in production, the low-tuned Boxer engine offers effortless torque at almost any revs.

SPECIFICATION: HONDA GOLD WING	
ENGINE	Water-cooled SOHC horizontally-opposed flat-six
DISPLACEMENT	1520cc
HORSEPOWER	98bhp @ 5200rpm
CARBURETTORS	2 x 33mm Keihn
GEAR BOX	Five speed
FRAME	Steel double-cradle
WHEELBASE	67ins
WEIGHT	798lbs dry
TOP SPEED	130mph

Honda VTR 1000F Fire Storm

....

> *'Its riding position is sporty without putting too much weight on the wrists.'*

With its combination of torquey 996cc motor and agile yet stable handling, the FireStorm rapidly made its mark as the most practical large-capacity V-twin sportster. Some riders thought its styling bland, but the twin side-mounted radiators provided evidence of clever and original design.

Like Honda's ever-popular VFR750F, the FireStorm is designed to be sporty yet also comfortable. With an efficient half-fairing, not-too-radical riding position and compliant suspension, the VTR can cover long distances effortlessly — yet it also has the sheer performance of a much more singleminded superbike.

Honda's VTR1000F FireStorm is so rapid, so capable and above all so much fun to ride that it begs one simple question: why did the world's largest motorcycle manufacturer take such a long time to build its first big V-twin sports bike? The distinctive character and user-friendly power delivery of the VTR, coupled with its compact size and light weight, made the twin seem a natural part of Honda's range from the moment it was launched.

Unlike Suzuki's TL1000S, which appeared simultaneously, the FireStorm is not a singleminded super-sports machine built to trade blows with Ducati's 916. Instead the VTR is a sporty yet versatile superbike that is more in the style of Honda's own VFR750F. Yet it's a machine which, despite a degree of compromise in its design, is capable of running with the fast crowd too.

The VTR engine shares its watercooled, 90-degree layout and even its bore and stroke dimensions and 996cc capacity with the TL1000S, but in other respects the two motors are very different. Instead of fuel-injection the Honda uses twin 48mm Keihin carburettors. And that big eight-valve motor is tuned for midrange torque as much as for top-end power, developing a respectable peak output of 110bhp at 9000rpm, but impressing even more with its healthy output at lower engine speeds.

Its chassis is conventional, being based on an aluminium beam frame that is most notable for holding novel side-mounted radiators, which are used to free up space in front of the engine. Suspension is a typical Honda blend of 41mm conventional front forks and Prolink monoshock rear. Styling is pleasant without being particularly exciting – but any complaints about that disappear the moment you pull away.

The FireStorm's most memorable characteristic is that midrange power delivery, which makes the big Honda a hugely easy and enjoyable bike to ride very fast indeed. Winding open the throttle with the tacho needle anywhere between 2000 and 7000rpm sends the V-twin surging smoothly forward, providing relaxed yet swift top-gear travel. At higher revs the 'Storm starts to run out of breath, but it keeps pulling to the 9500rpm redline in the lower gears, and to a top speed of about 160mph.

The Honda's user-friendly power characteristics are perfectly complimented by its chassis, which gives light steering and stable handling without approaching the razor-sharp feel of an out-and-out super-sports bike. Relatively conservative chassis geometry and a fairly long wheelbase mean that the VTR isn't quite as agile as some rivals on a twisty road, but it gains by remaining stable in situations that would upset more racy machines.

Part of the reason for that is the Honda's suspension, which is slightly soft for ultra-hard riding, but has enough damping to keep control on a bumpy road. For less than flat-out riding the FireStorm gains by being quite comfortable, too. Its riding position is sporty without putting too much weight on the wrists, even when the powerful Nissin front brakes are used to the full. The half-fairing is reasonably protective, and the footpegs allow a fair amount of legroom without compromising ground clearance.

Mention of comfort should not detract from the VTR's outright performance, particularly as back-to-back tests have shown that in some situations the Honda's stability and broad power-band actually

SPECIFICATION:	HONDA VTR1000F FIRESTORM
ENGINE	Water-cooled DOHC 8-valve 90-degree V-twin
DISPLACEMENT	996cc
HORSEPOWER	110bhp @ 9000rpm
CARBURETTORS	2 x 48mm Keihin
GEAR BOX	Six speed
FRAME	Aluminium alloy twin beam
WHEELBASE	56.3ins
WEIGHT	422lbs dry
TOP SPEED	160mph

make the bike faster than its more singleminded rivals. The FireStorm's competitive price makes a great bike seem even more attractive. This might be Honda's first big V-twin sportster, but it certainly won't be the last.

Honda CBR1100XX Super Blackbird

onda's aim with the CBR1100XX Super Blackbird was crystal clear: to build the world's fastest production motorcycle. For five years the world's largest bike manufacturer looked on while Kawasaki's 175mph ZZ-R1100 held that unofficial title. In designing a new four-cylinder flagship, Honda's engineers were determined to capture the crown.

And with the Super Blackbird, they did just that. When the CBR1100XX was released in late 1996, it did not quite succeed in matching the pre-launch publicity that had estimated its top speed at close to 190mph. But the Blackbird – named after an ultra-rapid American spy-plane – was Super enough, flying to 180mph thanks to slippery aerodynamics and a supremely powerful engine.

Honda's mission was accomplished; Kawasaki were pushed back to second place. That fact alone was enough to ensure the Honda's impact, although in other respects the CBR1100XX – which, like the ZZ-R1100, was more of a sports-tourer than a pure-bred sports machine – is far less outrageous than its specification suggests.

That is certainly true of its styling, which was designed for aerodynamic efficiency rather than looks. The slim fairing, whose shark-like pointed nose was achieved by placing the headlight's twin lenses one above the other (rather than side-by-side as normal), helps give a remarkably low drag coefficient. But the bike's appearance is restrained, thanks partly to paint schemes of grey, black or dark red.

The Super Blackbird's straight-line performance is truly memorable, but the same can't be said of the Honda's thoroughly anonymous looks. The polite way of describing the CBR1100XX's appearance is to say that aerodynamic efficiency took precedence over eye-catching styling when the bike was being designed.

'The furnace-like power unit is the Blackbird's undoubted star attraction.'

Although the Blackbird's peak output of 162bhp at 10,000rpm is exceptional, the 1137cc motor itself is a thoroughly conventional liquid-cooled, 16-valve twin-cam four. Its most novel feature is the inclusion of not one but two balancer shafts, which make the engine so smooth that it is able to aid chassis rigidity by being solidly mounted in the aluminium twin-beam frame.

The furnace-like power unit is the Blackbird's undoubted star attraction, producing a violent surge of acceleration when the throttle is opened anywhere between 5000rpm and the 10,800rpm redline. The Honda is typically sweet and refined at low revs, too, although it has a slight flat-spot at 4000rpm that can hinder top-gear overtaking.

Handling is excellent, although this CBR is no lightweight rival for Honda's CBR900RR Fireblade. The Blackbird's longish wheelbase and 491lbs of weight mean that it's more suited to high-speed motorway travel than to scratching round a racetrack. Straight-line stability is flawless; steering reasonably light; suspension compliant and well-damped.

The Blackbird's braking system incorporates the latest update of Honda's Dual-CBS system, as used by the CBR1000F, which applies balanced force to front and rear discs when either the hand lever or foot pedal is activated. Many riders rate the system highly, although others prefer the more direct feel of a good conventional set-up.

In contrast to the ultra-sporty Fireblade, the Blackbird incorporates a number of rider-friendly details such as a clock and fuel gauge in the dashboard, a broad dual-seat with pillion grab-rail, and clear mirrors that hold the indicators. The low screen, designed to boost top speed, is less impressive. It directs wind straight at a normally seated pilot's head, generating noise at speed.

That detracts from the Super Blackbird's efficiency as an all-round superbike, and there is no doubt that Honda were forced to make some compromises in the search for big numbers. Despite that, though, the CBR1100XX outperforms the ZZ-R1100 in most key areas. And in the one that matters most — top speed — the Super Blackbird succeeds in putting Honda on top of the world.

The Blackbird's fairing and front mudguard are shaped to keep air-flow as smooth as possible. The headlight's lenses are set one above the other, instead of side-by-side as normal, to reduce width.

SPECIFICATION: HONDA CBR1100XX SUPER BLACKBIRD	
ENGINE	Water-cooled DOHC 16-valve in-line four
DISPLACEMENT	1137cc
HORSEPOWER	162bhp @ 10,000rpm
CARBURETTORS	4 x 42mm Keihin
GEAR BOX	Six speed
FRAME	Aluminium alloy beam
WHEELBASE	58.7ins
WEIGHT	491lbs dry
TOP SPEED	180mph

Honda RC45

·····················

'Racers and road riders alike queued up to place their orders for the new bike.'

This is very much more than a motorcycle. This is Honda's attempt to wrest world superbike dominance back from Ducati and Kawasaki. The result simply bristles with high technology.

onda's RC30 was a tough act to follow. It had firmly established itself as one of the all-time great race bikes, and was also a favourite amongst discerning (and well-off) road riders. But by 1993 it had reached the end of its development as far as the increasingly competitive World Superbike Championship was concerned.

Honda still had the exotic works RVF750 race bikes – similar in basic design to the RC30, but representing development work worth millions of dollars. But now the World Endurance series and the Isle of Man TT were to be held under Superbike rules, and the RVF would no longer be eligible.

Honda's answer was to base a new road bike on the RVF, specifically built to win at World Superbike level. Like the RC30, it would be a no-expense-spared, limited production model, and race kits would be available from day one.

It was called the RVF750R, but it's known everywhere by its factory code name – the RC45.

Superficially, it was clearly closely related to the RC30, with its twin spar alloy frame, V-four engine,

single-sided swing arm – even a similar paint scheme. But not a single part is interchangeable between the two.

Superbike rules allow scope for changing engine internals, suspension parts, exhausts and wheels, but they don't allow a complete change of fuel system. This was one of the main reasons the RC30 lost its competitive edge – its carburettors were simply no longer up to the job. With the RC45, Honda took the plunge and fitted an electronic fuel injection system. In terms of pure peak power there's probably little advantage in an injection system, but it simplifies the job of altering the fuelling characteristics to suit different atmospheric conditions or engine set-ups. Instead of dismantling a bank of carburettors to change the jets (notoriously difficult with a complex engine layout like the RC's), all a mechanic has to do is alter the settings on an easily-accessible control box.

Racers and road riders alike queued up to place their orders for the new bike – after all, the RC30 had been superb, so what would its replacement be like? Some road riders, in particular, were disappointed. On the road, the RC45 has no real advantage over the RC30. This is partly because the RC30 had already set such high standards: although the RC45 is faster, has better brakes and suspension and more low-down power, there simply isn't anywhere that an average rider can exploit its advantages. The RC45 operates on a plane of efficiency that doesn't mesh very well with speed limits, blind corners and traffic travelling 100mph slower then the RC45 wants to go.

On the race track, too, the RC45 took a while to come good. It was quickly on the pace and running near the front in Superbikes, and was often fastest through the speed traps, but never seemed to translate that into a winning performance. The Ducati 916 had a weight advantage over the Honda

which gave it better acceleration out of corners. The ZXR750 Kawasaki had the benefit of several years' continuous development. The Honda had a handling problem – lack of traction out of corners. It was eventually traced to the rear suspension linkage, which was quickly revised. Soon the RC45 started to notch up race success, with victory in the prestigious Suzuka Eight Hour race and its first World Superbike success in the hands of Aaron Slight at Albacete in Spain. The RC had already proved its reliability with two victories at the Le Mans 24-hour race, and had taken over from the factory RVF as king of the Mountain Course at the Isle of Man. But, two seasons into its Superbike career, it still can't match those damn Ducatis.

Despite persistent problems on the race track, RC45 handling is utterly beyond reproach on the road.

SPECIFICATION: HONDA RC45	
ENGINE	Water-cooled DOHC 16-valve, 90° V-four
DISPLACEMENT	749cc
HORSEPOWER	118bhp @ 12,000rpm
CARBURETTORS	PGM FI fuel injection
GEAR BOX	Six speed
FRAME	Aluminium twin spar
WHEELBASE	55.5ins
WEIGHT	417lbs dry
TOP SPEED	165mph

Kawasaki 1100 Zephyr

Kawasaki were the first Japanese company to look back on their own history for inspiration when designing new bikes. The result was the Zephyr range, introduced in 1991. The 550 and 750 Zephyrs, both styled like Kawasaki's muscle bikes of the 'seventies, sold well to people who were attracted to the simplicity and spirit of a 'seventies bike, but who wanted 'nineties reliability and a warranty. The 'retro' movement was born. But what real muscle bike fans wanted was the true successor to the hairy-chested Z1 and the later Z1000.

They got it in 1992, with the Zephyr 1100.

In stark contrast to the firm's other flagship 1100, the ZZ-R, the Zephyr is a model of simplicity, consisting of little more than an engine, two wheels and just enough other equipment to hold them together. Visually, the Zephyr takes its styling cues from the Z1. But not a standard Z1. What Kawasaki did was to build a bike that incorporated all the modifications people made to their old Zeds as technology moved on and parts from later bikes became available.

So, the Zephyr has an alloy box-section swinging arm at the rear, operating remote reservoir twin shocks with adjustable damping. At the front, huge twin brake discs and four-piston calipers from the ZZ-R1100 are a far cry from the Z1's single front disc and single-piston caliper. Alloy wheels fitted with wide, sticky tyres complete the picture.

The result of all this attention to the running gear is a bike that's superbly balanced, with plenty of ground clearance for fast back-road riding, and impeccable low-speed manners. The Zephyr is a

Kawasaki were the first to exploit the Retro concept, and after-market suppliers have been happy to leap into the same niche. The Cyclone reflects a growing trend towards customised variants.

Tracing its mechanical ancestry all the way back over 20 years to the Z1, the biggest Zephyr's handling is not for the faint-hearted.

heavy bike, but it carries its weight low, making for good manoeuvrability The low seat and upright riding position help here, too – a relief for many after the race crouch of most modern sports bikes.

But it's the engine that gives the Zephyr its real character. The air-cooled unit is based on the old GPz1100 – strong, almost over-engineered, and still a favourite with drag racers and tuners. Freed from the need to produce awesome peak power figures for maximum speed, the engine designers were able to concentrate on getting smooth, strong, useable power from as little as 2,000rpm all the way up to the relatively lowly 9,500rpm red line.

The only concession to the technological advances made since the 'seventies is the air-cooled motor's twin plug set-up. The use of two spark plugs per cylinder helps improve combustion efficiency and beefs up an already fearsome midrange power curve – there are few bikes that give the same impression of arm-tugging acceleration as an 1100 Zephyr. In the real world, the Zephyr's power characteristics make it easy to drive off the line fast, or power hard out of turns without worrying what gear you're in.

If the midrange is impressive, the Zephyr's high speed manners are less so. Flat out at around 140mph, the combination of old-tech chassis and

suspension components, and a riding position that turns you into a sail, means the Zephyr weaves and wobbles along seemingly on the very edge of control. Unless you want to lie flat on the tank, 130mph is a more realistic top speed, and the lack of a fairing means anything over 90mph is uncomfortable for long distances.

But paradoxically, it's this very aspect that makes the Zephyr so popular. Not everyone wants a bike that can do 170mph and handles so well you have to be a budding racer to take it to its limits. There's definitely a place for the Zephyr's low tech, low cost, high fun factor approach, as Honda, Suzuki and Yamaha have since proved by following Kawasaki's lead and producing their own contributions to the retro revolution.

'There are few bikes that give the same impression of arm-tugging acceleration as an 1100 Zephyr.'

SPECIFICATION: KAWASAKI 1100 ZEPHYR	
ENGINE	Air-cooled DOHC 8-valve in-line four
DISPLACEMENT	1062cc
HORSEPOWER	91bhp @ 7900rpm
CARBURETTORS	4 x 34mm Keihin
GEAR BOX	Five speed
FRAME	Tubular steel double cradle
WHEELBASE	59.1in
WEIGHT	534lbs dry
TOP SPEED	140mph

Kawasaki ZX-9R

....

'Accelerating effortlessly from a standstill up to an indicated 170mph without pausing for breath.'

Almost as fast as the awesome ZZ-R1100, the ZX-9R packs a ferocious punch into a far more compact package.

Kawasaki have long been known as manufacturers of superlative superbikes. From the days of the Z1, through the 900 Ninja, to the ZZ-R1100, they have built an enviable reputation for building ultimate in-line fours. Rather than expending time and money on innovation for its own sake and technological dead-ends, the Big 'K' has stuck to what it knows, and perfected it. They have taken the water-cooled DOHC 16-valve in-line four and made it their own.

In recent years Kawasaki have concentrated their efforts in the superbike market on large capacity sports-tourers such as the ZZ-R1100, with the ZXR750 presenting the pinnacle of supersports development in their range. But with the advent of Honda's all-conquering Fireblade, Kawasaki had to produce a fire-breathing 900cc race-replica of their own. The ZX-9R is it, although this is a street racer with a difference.

Rather than produce a bike that featured state-of-the-art handling and race-track performance, Kawasaki attempted to bridge the gap between race-replica and sports-tourer, to produce a bike that had the looks and speed of a race-replica, but which was comfortable for two-up road-riding. They reasoned that some motorcyclists want the style and image of a race-replica, but the comfort and practicality of a more traditional road bike.

To achieve this Kawasaki made it just a little bit bigger and heavier than a mere Kawasaki 'Fireblade'. Without the need to save weight wherever possible they could concentrate on building a superbike that looked suitably aggressive but which was big enough and comfortable enough to satisfy the demands of the man in the street.

But that doesn't mean the ZX-9R isn't a fine sportsbike in its own right. With a water-cooled DOHC 16-valve in-line four cylinder engine pumping out 125bhp, and a lightweight but strong aluminium-alloy beam frame, the ZX-9R is a performance superbike capable of exceeding 165mph. Multi-adjustable inverted telescopic front forks and a rising-rate rear monoshock give the ZX-9R up-to-the-minute suspension technology and ensure that the handling is as impressive as the engine performance.

Weighing in at 475lbs dry the ZX-9R is no lightweight (it's 70lbs heavier than a Honda CBR900 Fireblade), but that doesn't count against it anywhere except on a race track. On the road the ZX-9R is lightning-quick, blessed with masses of mid-range power and a top-end delivery that takes your breath away. Accelerating effortlessly from a standstill up to an indicated 170mph without pausing for breath, the ZX-9R is the kind of bike that will cover distances quickly, comfortably and with the minimum of fuss. Not quite as quickly and effortlessly as a ZZ-R1100, but not far off, and with the styling and looks of a bike that belongs on a race track.

SPECIFICATION: KAWASAKI ZX-9R	
ENGINE	Water-cooled DOHC 16-valve in-line four
DISPLACEMENT	899cc
HORSEPOWER	125bhp @ 10,500rpm
CARBURETTORS	4 x 40mm Keihin
GEAR BOX	6 speed
FRAME	Aluminium-alloy twin beam
WHEELBASE	56.7ins
WEIGHT	475lbs dry
TOP SPEED	167mph

Kawasaki ZX-7R

....

'It accelerates with a restrained but still spine-tingling growl from the large exhaust can.'

The ZX-7R is the impressive result of several years of relentless development work by Kawasaki. The ZX-7R's predecessor was the ZXR750: a raw, four-cylinder race-replica that was gradually turned into a rapid and refined roadburner in the years following its launch in 1989. When the ZX-7R appeared in 1996, it carried the process of improvement several steps further – without losing the sense of sheer excitement that characterised the ZXR.

The ZX-7R's basic format is identical to that of the ZXR, not to mention several rivals in the competitive 750cc sports bike class. Its water-cooled, 16-valve four-cylinder engine sits in a twin-beam aluminium frame. Its bodywork is sleek and all-enveloping; its riding position stretched-out; its attitude uncompromisingly aggressive.

That was certainly true of the ZXR750, which retained its distinctive character while being updated many times throughout the '90s. Its engine first received more midrange power, then more top-end thanks to the adoption of a ram-air intake system. Its chassis gained frame and brake modifications, and most importantly improved suspension.

The ZX-7R has a new name and a new look, thanks to bold one-colour bodywork in place of the ZXR's contrasting shades, but essentially the new bike is a further development of the same theme. Kawasaki claim its frame is 30 per cent stiffer, thanks to thicker main rails and a larger steering head area. The 43mm front forks are thicker, have polished stanchions to reduce friction and, like the new rear shock, are fully adjustable for the first time.

Numerous engine changes include the adoption of 'short-stroke' dimensions, allowing higher revs. The ram-air system is revised to allow more air in

Kawasaki's 750cc race-replicas have been notable for their aggressive good looks ever since the original ZXR750 of 1989, and the ZX-7R upholds the tradition. Ram-air intakes are clearly visible to each side of the twin headlamp lenses.

via the large ducts alongside the ZX-7R's twin headlamps. New valvegear and a modified four-into-one exhaust system help increase midrange power, although the official maximum output is unchanged at 120bhp. Features such as a bigger radiator and revised cooling system help keep the engine in one piece.

More power or not, the Kawasaki certainly feels mighty fast as the revs climb and it accelerates with a restrained but still spine-tingling growl from the large exhaust can. Although it's a refined machine, the ZX-7R retains the ZXR engine's slightly harsh feel as it heads for the 12,500rpm redline. With a top speed of over 160mph, the ZX is a match for any 750cc four in a straight line.

For rapid riding the ZX-7R's only real drawback is its weight. At 440lbs dry the Kawasaki is fully

35lbs heavier than Honda's more powerful CBR900RR or Suzuki's GSX-R750. Compared to the GSX-R, in particular, the ZX-7R is rather heavy and slow-steering, meaning its rider has to work harder when the pace hots up on a twisty road.

The chassis works well, though, its modifications combining to make this the fastest and best-handling 750cc Kawasaki yet. The ZX is supremely stable, yet turns into corners easily with a light, neutral feel. Its sophisticated suspension soaks up bumps that would have punished a ZXR rider's kidneys, and the six-piston Tokico brake calipers combine with big 320mm discs to give fearsome stopping power.

The ZX-7R might struggle against lighter rivals on a racetrack, but as a roadbike it is up there with the best. Its clean looks, extra midrange power and added chassis sophistication make this the best 750cc Kawasaki yet. And the way in which the ZX-7R blends its raw feel with its new-found refinement ensures a hugely entertaining ride.

Although it's heavier than many rivals, the ZX-7R goes round corners as well as the best of them. Its neutral steering, excellent suspension and fat, grippy tyres make this the best-handling 750cc Kawasaki yet.

In typical Kawasaki style the ZX-7R emits a slightly harsh feel and an evocative exhaust note as the powerful 16-valve engine spins towards its redline – which is set at a heady 12,500rpm.

SPECIFICATION: KAWASAKI ZX-7R

ENGINE	Water-cooled DOHC 16-valve in-line four
DISPLACEMENT	748cc
HORSEPOWER	120bhp @ 11,800rpm
CARBURETTORS	4 x 38mm Keihin
GEAR BOX	Six speed
FRAME	Aluminium alloy beam
WHEELBASE	55.9ins
WEIGHT	440lbs dry
TOP SPEED	163mph

Kawasaki ZZ-R1100

·····················

The Kawasaki ZZ-R1100 is one of the ultimates in the superbikes world. Hugely powerful, stunningly fast and very sleek, the ZZ-R1100 brings eye-watering performance to the mass-market.

Capable of out-performing just about any car on the roads (even the like of Ferarris and Porsches), the ZZ-R1100 costs less than the price of a family saloon. With a top-speed nudging 180mph and a 0-60mph time of less than three seconds, the ZZ-R1100 is a true king of the roads.

So what is surprising about the ZZ-R1100 is how ordinary it really is. It doesn't rely on complicated suspension systems, fancy fuel-injection or curiously-shaped pistons. No, the ZZ-R1100 uses solid, well-proven engine technology and state-of-the-art aerodynamics to produce one of the most impressive superbikes ever seen.

The heart of the ZZ-R1100 is its water-cooled, double overhead cam, 16-valve, in-line four-cylinder engine. Power output varies from country to country according to local laws, but in unrestricted form the ZZ-R1100 makes a whopping 147bhp at 11,000rpm. With a dry weight of 514lbs, that gives the ZZ-R1100 a power-to-weight ratio five times higher than a *very* fast car. One hundred and eighty miles per hour and a standing quarter of a mile in under 11 seconds is territory normally reserved for Italian supercars, but the ZZ-R1100 makes it available to the man in the street!

And what of the rest of the ZZ-R1100? The svelte bodywork is a major contributor to the awesome top speed and it also helps to keep the wind and rain away from the rider. Suspension is handled by a hefty pair of 43mm multi-adjustable telescopic forks at the front and a rising-rate, multi-adjustable monoshock at the back. Twin 320mm front discs seized by four-piston calipers give the ZZ-R much-needed stopping power, with a single 250mm rear disc gripped by a twin-piston caliper to complete the set-up.

The ZZ-R1100 isn't a pure sportsbike, nor was it ever intended to be. Kawasaki have eschewed the race-replica route for their litre bikes, preferring instead to make them potent all-rounders. As a

More 'super' than most, the ZZ-R1100 is the fastest production motorcycle ever built, capable of humbling cars costing ten times the price.

Although not so nimble as Honda's Fireblade, the big 'Kwacker' scratches better than anything *this* big has a right to do.

'The ZZ-R1100 brings eye-watering performance to the mass-market.'

result the ZZ-R1100 is an excellent two-up sports-tourer capable of covering long distances quickly and easily. A large fuel tank and reasonably frugal consumption make the ZZ-R a good long-distance machine, and the rider and pillion accommodation are appropriately comfortable.

There aren't many superbikes with the all-round capabilities of the ZZ-R1100. On the one hand it is a fast, sure-footed sportsbike capable of delivering exceptional performance at the twist of the wrist, while on the other hand it will carry two people a long way in reasonable comfort and with the minimum of fuss. Small wonder, then, that Kawasaki sell so many of them.

Whether it's tricks you want (left), or 1000 touring miles in a day, the ZZ-R1100 effortlessly delivers.

SPECIFICATION: KAWASAKI ZZ-R1100	
ENGINE	Liquid-cooled DOHC 16-valve in-line four
DISPLACEMENT	1052cc
HORSEPOWER	147bhp @ 11000rpm
CARBURETTORS	4 x 40mm Keihin CV
GEAR BOX	Six speed
FRAME	Aluminium-alloy twin beam
WHEELBASE	58.8ins
WEIGHT	514lbs dry
TOP SPEED	175mph

Magni Australia

....

'It was on a twisty road, though, that the Australia came into its own.'

A red-and-silver tribute to countless MV *Grand Prix* winners, but the transverse V-twin is every inch a Moto Guzzi – with added Magni class.

Its sleek styling, big V-twin engine and enormous rear tyre showed that this was a serious sports bike, but it was the red-and-silver paintwork that revealed most about the Magni Australia. Those were the colours of the legendary MV Agusta race team once run by Arturo Magni, the Australia's creator.

Magni had prepared the 'Gallarate Fire Engines' raced to glory by John Surtees, Mike Hailwood and Giacomo Agostini. Then, when MV stopped racing after winning 17 consecutive 500cc world titles between 1958 and 1974, Magni set up business with his son Giovanni to build high-quality roadsters from a workshop near Agusta's old base at Gallarate, north of Milan. Several used engines from Moto Guzzi, notably the 1990-model Sfida, a

retro-styled sportster powered by the two-valves-per-cylinder engine from the Le Mans.

Two years later came the fastest and best Magni yet: the Australia, so-called because it was a direct descendent of a Guzzi-engined Magni racebike that had notched up a string of impressive results Down Under. The Australia was powered by the V-twin engine from the Daytona 1000, Guzzi's fuel-injected, eight-valve flagship. To ease homologation the 992cc 'high cam' unit was retained in its entirety from airbox to silencers.

Almost everything else was new, though, most notably the frame. In place of the Daytona's large-diameter spine was a more conventional arrangement, based on three 34mm diameter chrome-molybdenum steel tubes running back

Unlike more commonplace Guzzis, the Australia's steering is light and precise, a tribute to the exceptional quality of its chassis and suspension.

from the steering head. A pair of front downtubes helped secure the engine.

The swing-arm was a single-shock version of Magni's proven Parallelogramo design, created to combat torque-reaction. Rear suspension was provided by a single shock from Dutch firm White Power. The Australia's swing-arm was wide enough to allow fitment of a wide, 180-section rear tyre.

At the front were upside-down Forcelle Italia forks – adjustable, like the shock, for both compression and rebound damping. The 17-inch wheels held 320mm Brembo brake discs with four-piston calipers. Both mudguards were lightweight carbon fibre, helping to keep weight to a respectable 450lb dry.

The cylinder heads visible at each side of the Australia made the Guzzi connection clear, and there was no doubting the engine's origins when it fired up to send the bike rocking in characteristic fashion with every blip of the throttle. At most engine speeds the Australia had a wonderfully loose, rev-happy feel, aided by the Weber-Marelli fuel-injection's crisp response.

With a peak output of 95bhp, the slippery Australia had a top speed of about 140mph, plus generous acceleration from low revs. The Magni pulled strongly almost from tickover, with a slight surge at around 4000rpm that sent it charging along

with a rustling from the aircooled engine's sticking-out cylinders, and a typically long-legged Guzzi feel at high speed.

It was on a twisty road, though, that the Australia came into its own. Its Brembo brakes were superbly powerful, steering was light and the Magni could be cornered easily and with great precision. Suspension was compliant but very well-controlled at both ends, and the drive shaft barely noticeable.

That blend of good looks, effortless engine performance and nimble handling made the Australia a very impressive special, with a captivating blend of pace and grace. Its price was high – but not excessively so for a machine hand-built in tiny numbers. Especially when those hands had once built bikes for legends such as Surtees, Hailwood and Agostini.

Fuel injection helps give the big Guzzi motor impressive responsiveness and punch throughout the rev range, with an un-Guzzi-like eagerness to rev.

SPECIFICATION: MAGNI AUSTRALIA	
ENGINE	Air-cooled high-cam 8-valve 90-degree transverse V-twin
DISPLACEMENT	992cc
HORSEPOWER	95bhp
CARBURETTORS	Weber-Marelli fuel-injection
GEAR BOX	Five speed
FRAME	Tubular steel
WHEELBASE	58ins
WEIGHT	450lbs dry
TOP SPEED	140mph

Moto Guzzi Centauro

'Suddenly, the big V-twin hits its sweet spot and the Centauro comes alive.'

With its blend of bold, streetwise styling and traditional transverse V-twin engine, the V10 Centauro is rolling proof of Moto Guzzi's re-emergence as a motorcycling force. For years the famous old Italian firm suffered from lack of ideas and investment. But in 1996, under fresh management and making a profit once again, Guzzi confirmed its revitalisation with a striking new model.

The Centauro, whose name comes from the centaur, a half-man, half-horse of Greek mythology, is a naked V-twin with a distinctly aggressive personality. This radically styled bike may have no fairing, but its heart is the 992cc, eight-valve V-twin motor from Guzzi's Daytona flagship – detuned slightly with a softer camshaft but still producing an impressive 90bhp at 8200rpm.

The Centauro's chassis, too, is borrowed from its sportier siblings. The roadster's familiar rectangular-section steel spine frame is identical to that of the 1100 Sport, and the same is almost true of the suspension. Dutch specialist WP's 40mm upside-down forks and rear shock are simply retuned slightly to suit the unfaired V10.

Thanks to the Centauro's flat, large-diameter handlebars and forward-set footrests, there's a distinct feel of Harley-Davidson as you settle into the low, broad seat. But this rumbling, aircooled V-twin motor's torque-reaction roll from side to side when it fires up confirms its origins at Guzzi's base in Mandello del Lario, rather than Milwaukee.

The upright riding position, low seat and generous steering lock combine to make the V10 comfortable and manoeuvrable at slow speed.

With its bulbous bodywork and Moto Guzzi's familiar transverse V-twin engine, the Centauro is a striking bike that rarely fails to make an impact. Even those who dislike its looks can't deny that it's different.

Transmission modifications mean it shifts more cleanly and reliably than many previous Guzzis, too, although the five-speed gearbox still requires a deliberate action.

Weber-Marelli's fuel-injection system, a remapped version of the Daytona set-up, gives a crisp low-rev response. There are no flat-spots, and the big V-twin pulls cleanly even when its throttle is cracked open at only 2000rpm in top gear. But although the V10 chugs forward obediently, its low-rev power pulses quickly smoothing out in typical Guzzi style, the bike doesn't stretch its rider's arms through the lower midrange in quite the way that might be expected of an unfaired big-bore twin.

The reason for that becomes clear when the white-faced tachometer's needle reaches 4500rpm: this motor is still very much a rev-happy sportster powerplant. Suddenly, the big V-twin hits its sweet spot and the Centauro comes alive. The surge of acceleration, made even more vivid by the wind tearing at the rider's chest, transforms the docile Centauro into a stampeding stallion.

An indicated 120mph arrives rapidly and with considerably more to come, though you would need a strong neck and arms to hold high speeds for long. Top speed is 135mph, but more importantly the Centauro cruises at 80mph with a typically relaxed Guzzi feel.

Stability at speed is excellent, with no sign of the wobbles that afflict many unfaired bikes. Steering is neutral although at 451lbs the V10 is no lightweight, and quick direction changes require a firm tug on the bars. The well-damped suspension, grippy Pirelli tyres and powerful Brembo brakes give this Guzzi enough cornering performance to show up more than a few race-replicas.

Ultimately much of the Centauro's appeal – or otherwise – comes down to your opinion of its unmistakable looks. For those who appreciate its style, the V10 works well as a distinctive unfaired roadster with the performance of a sports bike. Either way, it's proof that rejuvenated Moto Guzzi is heading for an exciting future.

The Centauro's eight-valve V-twin engine produces more power at high revs than in the midrange. Handling is typically Moto Guzzi: slow-steering but very stable at speed.

Despite its unusual styling the Centauro looks very much like a Guzzi, thanks to the way the big aircooled cylinders of its transverse V-twin engine stick out to each side.

SPECIFICATION: MOTO GUZZI V10 CENTAURO	
ENGINE	Air-cooled SOHC 8-valve V-twin
DISPLACEMENT	992cc
HORSEPOWER	90bhp @ 8200rpm
CARBURETTORS	Weber fuel-injection
GEAR BOX	Five speed
FRAME	Steel spine
WHEELBASE	58.1ins
WEIGHT	451lbs dry
TOP SPEED	135mph

Moto Guzzi 1100 Sport Injection

Few superbikes combine old-fashioned charm and modern technology to such good effect as Moto Guzzi's 1100 Sport Injection. The Italian firm's original 1100 Sport model, launched in 1994, was a handsome and charismatic roadburner, powered by an enlarged version of the traditional aircooled, transverse V-twin engine that Guzzi have been building for decades.

That first Sport model was respectably rapid and very stable, but in comparison with Guzzi's own fuel-injected Daytona (let alone almost every rival firm's sportsters) it was a little rough round the edges. Two years later, Guzzi revamped the big V-twin with fuel-injection and a host of chassis changes – and the result was a resounding success.

Unlike the eight-valve motor of Guzzi's Daytona flagship, the Sport Injection motor has only two valves per cylinder, operated by old-fashioned

pushrods. But in place of the old Sport model's carburettors, the 1064cc unit has a Weber fuel-injection system similar to that of the Daytona. Other changes include reshaped gearbox teeth and a new cush-drive in the rear wheel.

The Injection uses a slightly revised version of the old Sport's steel spine frame, a new swing-arm constructed from elliptical-section steel tubes, and a multi-adjustable WP shock. The same Dutch firm also supplies the front forks, 40mm upside-down units with adjustable damping. Brakes are by Brembo, as before, uprated to semi-floating 320mm discs with four piston calipers up front.

The Injection's list of modifications does nothing to alter the basic Guzzi feel, which makes itself known the moment the 90-degree transverse V-twin fires-up to send the bike rocking from side to side. Nor do the engine-related changes increase

The 1100 Sport Injection is visually very similar to its predecessor, the 1100 Sport – but the adoption of fuel-injection and numerous other changes improve the big V-twin's throttle response and give it a more refined feel, without losing the Guzzi's traditional long-legged character.

'Once into its midrange stride the Guzzi really begins to pull hard.'

The Sport Injection's Weber-Marelli fuel system doesn't alter the 1064cc V-twin's 90bhp peak output, but the injected bike has a smoother throttle action and a crisper low-rev response than its predecessor.

the Sport's peak power output of 90bhp at 7800rpm. But they certainly make the bike nicer to ride.

The Guzzi pulls away with noticeably less of a transmission clunk than its predecessor. And the fuel-injected bike's throttle action is both light and quick-action – something that was never possible with the original Sport's 40mm Dell'Orto carburettors.

Best of all, though, is the injected bike's behaviour when the throttle is wrenched open at low revs. Even from well below 3000rpm in top gear, the Sport Injection responds crisply, its motor juddering slightly but sending the bike rumbling instantly forward when its carburetted predecessor would just have coughed and spluttered in protest.

Once into its midrange stride the Guzzi really begins to pull hard, accelerating with an effortless feel typical of the marque when it reaches its sweet zone between 5000 and 7000rpm. The old pushrod unit gets a bit breathless and rough after that, and there is little point in taking it to the 8000rpm redline. But given enough room the Injection will rumble up to a top speed of about 140mph.

Handling is good, too, despite the Injection's substantial 486lbs of weight. Guzzis are traditionally very stable, and this one is no exception. The bike steers slowly by modern sports bike standards, but it is still flickable enough to be fun on a twisty road. And although the Injection's Pirelli Dragons are not

the widest of superbike tyres, they certainly give plenty of grip.

The Sport Injection's excellent throttle response and reliable handling make this a very easy machine to ride fast. Along with the old Sport model's retained good looks and V-twin character, the result is a bike that excels at the things Moto Guzzis traditionally do well, and has far fewer of the old faults. No wonder many enthusiasts consider it quite simply the best big Guzzi yet.

SPECIFICATION:	MOTO GUZZI 1100 SPORT INJECTION
ENGINE	Air-cooled OHV 4-valve 90-degree transverse V-twin
DISPLACEMENT	1064cc
HORSEPOWER	90bhp @ 7800rpm
CARBURETTORS	Weber fuel-injection
GEAR BOX	Five speed
FRAME	Tubular steel spine
WHEELBASE	58ins
WEIGHT	486lbs dry
TOP SPEED	140mph

Like any big Guzzi, the Sport Injection steers slowly by modern superbike standards. But its suspension is good and it's stable in corners.

Suzuki GSX-R750

....

When Suzuki unveiled the long-awaited successor to its GSX-R750 sportster in 1996, few people believed that the new bike could make the same sort of impact as its predecessor. After all, the original GSX-R750, introduced 11 years earlier, had become a legend. Powerful, outrageously light and stunningly fast, it had annihilated all opposition and sparked the cult of the aluminium-framed Japanese race-replica.

Those doubters reckoned without Suzuki's peerless ability to build singleminded high-performance motorcycles. Sure enough, with the new-generation GSX-R, Suzuki has managed to create a machine with precisely the original model's no-compromise approach. It's arguably the leanest, fiercest, most gloriously irresponsible vehicle on two wheels.

Statistics don't come close to telling the whole story, but they are revealing all the same. The GSX-R750's peak power output of 126bhp matches that of Honda's mighty CBR900RR Fireblade and exceeds all other 750s. The Suzuki weighs just 394lbs, making it lighter than most *600cc* fours. It has the same steering geometry and wheelbase as the Suzuki RGV500 grand prix bike ridden to the 1993 world championship by Kevin Schwantz.

Although the GSX-R's approach is unchanged, it shares very few components with its predecessor. The engine's dramatically increased power output and reduced size and weight required some major modifications, notably the adoption of a ram-air intake system. Internal changes to the 16-valve, watercooled engine include more oversquare cylinder dimensions, the camchain moved to the end of the crankshaft, cylinders set closer together, and many other parts made smaller and lighter.

The frame is a conventional twin-beam aluminium construction, in contrast to the old GSX-R's taller and less rigid aluminium cradle. Despite its neat styling and distinctive, swoopy tail-piece, this makes the Suzuki look slightly ordinary – but any notion that this is just another Japanese in-line four changes the second you ride it. Even at a standstill the GSX-R feels outrageously light and manoeuvrable. Once under way, the ultra-responsive Suzuki flicks into corners almost before its rider realises they've arrived.

Such a short, light, quick-steering bike can't help being a bit frisky when accelerating hard, and on a bumpy road the GSX-R can be a real handful. The original GSX-R750 pushed frame, suspension and tyre technology to the limit, resulting in occasional tank-slappers, and the current model inherits the family trait.

But in most situations the handling is superb, thanks to the frame's rigidity and the control provided by sophisticated, multi-adjustable upside-down forks and monoshock. Fat, sticky radial tyres make good use of the generous ground clearance. And the front brake combination of twin 320mm

The modern GSX-R750 is a much more compact and streamlined machine than its famous forebear from 1985, but the two bikes have much in common – notably mind-blowing acceleration at high revs, ultra-light weight and a tendency to feel twitchy at speed.

discs gripped by six-piston calipers, although rather wooden in town, is phenomenally powerful at speed.

Inevitably the GSX-R thrives on revs, requiring frequent tune-playing with the slick six-speed gearbox to give of its best. Keep the tacho needle flicking towards the redline at a heady 13,500rpm, and the Suzuki provides searing acceleration towards a top speed of 165mph. Although there is nothing like as much power available lower down, for such a highly-strung machine the GSX-R is reasonably tractable.

Naturally, a bike as singleminded as this has its drawbacks. The GSX-R is cramped and firmly suspended, it requires too much rider input ever to

be remotely relaxing, and its low screen gives little wind protection. But when you ride the Suzuki on the right road, none of those things matters at all. It's super-fast, supremely agile and absolutely crazy – every bit a true GSX-R750.

This GSX-R's most distinctive feature is its exaggerated seat hump, which combines with the low, swept-back screen to give smooth air-flow for maximum straight-line performance.

Few other superbikes come even close to matching the GSX-R's superbly light and precise steering feel, but inevitably the drawback is marginal stability.

SPECIFICATION: SUZUKI GSX-R750	
ENGINE	Water-cooled DOHC 16-valve in-line four
DISPLACEMENT	749cc
HORSEPOWER	126bhp @ 12,000rpm
CARBURETTORS	Four 39mm Mikuni
GEAR BOX	Six speed
FRAME	Aluminium alloy beam
WHEELBASE	55.1ins
WEIGHT	394lbs dry
TOP SPEED	165mph

'The Suzuki provides searing acceleration.'

Suzuki GSF 1200 Bandit

Due to its slightly raised handlebars and lack of a fairing, Suzuki's GSF1200 Bandit is commonly referred to as a retro-bike – and in one sense that's just what it is. The Bandit brings to mind Suzuki's GSX1100, a bike which, back in the early '80s before the Japanese manufacturers discovered fairings, was perhaps the best of the powerful, heavy but increasingly well-mannered fours.

Like the old GSX, the Bandit is a naked machine with a 16-valve four-cylinder engine. The modern bike's clean-cut styling is similar to that of its predecessor, too. But that's where relevance of the 'retro' tag ends. Because far from being a softly-tuned piece of nostalgia, the Bandit is a powerful, fine-handling, wheelie-loving and thoroughly modern superbike.

Its engine is based on the oil-cooled unit from the fearsome GSX-R1100 sportster, bored-out by 1mm to 1157cc and detuned slightly to give more midrange torque at the expense of top-end power. Lowered compression ratio plus revised ignition and cam timing reduce peak power output to 98bhp, and allow maximum torque to be produced at just 4500rpm.

If the Bandit's engine is an ideal powerplant for a big naked bike, its chassis is every bit as good. The 1200's tubular steel frame is similar to that of the GSF600 Bandit, strengthened and fitted with a bigger aluminium swing-arm. The 1200's wheelbase is short by the standards of big retro-bikes, its steering geometry is steep, and most importantly the Bandit is light – at 464lbs it weighs less than all its closest rivals.

Suzuki didn't skimp on the Bandit's cycle parts, either. Its forks are sturdy 43mm units with adjustable spring preload and, instead of the old-style pair of rear shocks fitted to most so-called retros, the GSF has a modern monoshock complete with rising-rate linkage. Fat, low-profile tyres and fully-floating brake discs with four-piston calipers complete an impressive picture.

The big GSF1200's styling and basic layout are traditional, owing much to the aircooled, 16-valve GSX1100s of the early 1980s. But the Bandit's compact chassis and riding-rate monoshock rear suspension hint that it's much more fun to ride than the average retro-bike.

SUZUKI GSF1200 BANDIT

Happily the Bandit is every bit as much fun as its spec sheet suggests. The engine is smooth and strong, responding instantly to a crack of the throttle to send the bike hurtling forwards at a thrilling rate. Overall gearing is lower than the GSX-R1100's. Combined with the generous low-rev torque and short wheelbase, this means a Bandit rider requires great self-control to avoid leaving every set of traffic lights with the front wheel in the air . . .

The gutsy motor is equally impressive on the open road, where its crisp midrange power delivery makes for effortless overtaking. Top speed is

140mph, although the naked bike's windblown riding position keeps cruising speed well below three figures. (If that's a problem, the Bandit is also available with a half-fairing.)

Just as the old GSX1100 was generally the best-handling big four back in the early '80s, so the GSF1200 is the pick of the modern naked bikes on a twisty road. Its frame is strong, suspension at both ends is well-controlled, steering is light without being twitchy, and the big twin discs give plenty of stopping power.

The Bandit is even commendably practical for an unfaired bike, although its small fuel tank requires frequent top-ups. The riding position is roomy; the seat is well-padded and big enough for a passenger. And despite the GSF's general air of high quality production, it retails at a remarkably competitive price.

Given all those attributes, it's no surprise that the GSF1200 has become a best seller for Suzuki. Its success is thoroughly deserved. The Bandit is one of those bikes that puts a huge smile on the face of everyone who rides it.

There's nothing special about the Bandit's peak power figure of 98bhp, but cracking open the throttle reveals the 1157cc four's wonderfully strong midrange output. This picture shows the version with half-fairing, which makes for more comfortable high speed cruising.

'The engine is smooth and strong, responding instantly to a crack of the throttle.'

SPECIFICATION: SUZUKI GSF1200 BANDIT
ENGINE	Oil-cooled DOHC 16-valve in-line four
DISPLACEMENT	1157cc
HORSEPOWER	98bhp @ 5500rpm
CARBURETTORS	Four 36mm Mikuni
GEAR BOX	Five speed
FRAME	Tubular steel duplex cradle
WHEELBASE	56.5ins
WEIGHT	464lbs dry
TOP SPEED	140mph

Suzuki RF900

··························

'Suzuki saw the gap for a slightly softer-edged machine.'

When Honda's Fireblade rekindled interest in the 900 class in 1992, the other manufacturers were caught on the hop. For Suzuki the matter was urgent – overnight the Fireblade had usurped both the GSX-R1100's position as the definitive nutter's bike, and the GSX-R750's top spot in the handling stakes. But it had also gained a reputation as a bike which was hard to get the best out of – a real racer on the road. Suzuki saw the gap for a slightly softer-edged machine, easier to use and more practical, but still possessing awesome straight-line performance. The RF900 – styled and badged as a big brother to the existing RF600 – was launched for 1994.

Like the RF600, the 900 was built to a tight budget, developing existing technology rather than starting from scratch with a whole new design.

The water-cooled engine is based on the well-proven GSX-R range, and combines the free-revving nature of the 750 with the low-down pulling power of the 1100. But it's far more than just a sleeved-down 1100 or a big-bore 750. The RF's engine is so well-developed it has a character all of its own. The carburation, in particular, is perfect, allowing the rider to crack the throttle open at any revs and be rewarded with instant performance. Whilst the 900's outright performance doesn't set any records – slightly faster in still conditions than a Fireblade but a long way off the class-leading 170mph+ of the ZX-9, its real strength is in its all-round performance.

The surprise package of '94, Suzuki's RF900 exploded onto the scene with blistering performance at a truly amazing bargain price.

The RF's styling, inherited from its RF600 stablemate, isn't to everyone's taste. But as in so many other areas, the RF's policy of getting the job done first and worrying about appearances later pays off. The fairing does an excellent job of directing air around the rider, and the bulbous tail unit carries a seriously wide and comfortable seat with a proper pillion grab rail. The RF is one of the few serious performance bikes that are genuinely comfortable two-up.

Despite pushing it very close in the performance stakes, the steel-framed RF was never meant to compete head-on with the Fireblade, and weighs in around 40lbs heavier than Honda's rocketship. In theory that puts the Suzuki at a serious disadvantage, but in the real world the extra weight gives the RF a comfortable ride, with a feeling of solidity that the pared-down 'Blade can't achieve. It does this with old-tech, but well-matched, suspension components – no fashionable upside-down forks or single-sided swingarms here. But that doesn't mean the RF can't corner hard – it can. The weight distribution's more sporty than touring, and the emphasis is on stability. 120mph sweeping bends are the RF900's favourite stamping grounds, but it tackles everything from backroads to the occasional racetrack with the same easy, do-anything, go-anywhere competence.

For anyone trying an RF900 for the first time, there are two surprises. First, that something apparently styled for long-distance comfort offers such shattering performance and competent, hard-charging handling. Second, that it's cheap – nearly ten per cent cheaper than Suzuki's own GSX-R750. If the Fireblade broke the mould by proving that big bikes didn't need to be bruising heavyweights, the RF did the same by proving that high performance need not cost the Earth.

The RF's prodigious horsepower gleefully shrugs off the limitations of a heavy steel frame and slightly down-market suspension.

SPECIFICATION: SUZUKI RF900	
ENGINE	Water-cooled DOHC 16-valve in-line four
DISPLACEMENT	937cc
HORSEPOWER	124bhp @ 10,000rpm
CARBURETTORS	4 x 36mm Mikuni
GEAR BOX	Six speed
FRAME	Pressed steel twin spar
WHEELBASE	56.7ins
WEIGHT	447lbs dry
TOP SPEED	165mph

Comparatively restrained styling reflects the 900's role as a high-speed all-rounder rather than a race track escapee.

Suzuki TL1000S

....

'The Suzuki's handling adds to the bike's ultra-sporty, take-no-prisoners attitude.'

With a powerful V-twin engine, a light and innovative chassis and an uncompromisingly aggressive attitude, Suzuki's TL1000S is a stunning machine that heralds a new era for Japanese sports bikes. Suzuki's GSX-R fours have long defined the limits of cutting-edge race-replica design – and the TL follows their example to end Ducati's domination of the V-twin super-sports bike market in emphatic style.

Such was the secrecy with which Suzuki developed the TL that the bike's launch at the Cologne Show in late 1996 shocked not only Ducati but also Honda, whose own VTR1000 V-twin was revealed at the same time. Compared to the rounded VTR, the TL1000S is a no-compromise machine in typical Suzuki mould, complete with fuel-injection, radical steering geometry and even race-compound Metzeler tyres as standard fitment.

Tucked below the strikingly styled Suzuki's half-fairing is a watercooled, 8-valve, 90-degree V-twin engine whose pair of huge 98mm pistons combines with a short 66mm stroke to give a capacity of 996cc. The motor is fed by a ram-air system and uses a specially-developed Mikuni-Denso fuel-injection set-up to help develop impressive horsepower. Peak output is a claimed 123bhp, giving the Suzuki a distinct edge over the 916 and VTR.

The all-new engine is superb, but it's the TL's chassis that reveals Suzuki's engineering at its best. The frame is an aluminium lattice design, developed for visual impact as well as performance, which incorporates a unique rear suspension system consisting of a single spring (placed near-horizontally on the right) and separate rotary damper. This compact arrangement allows the engine to be placed further back, with its rear cylinder where a conventional shock would be, giving a short wheelbase for extra manoeuvrability.

Other cycle parts are conventional and of high quality, notably the multi-adjustable, upside-down Kayaba forks, and the front brake combination of 320mm discs and four-piston Nissin calipers. The TL's dry weight is just 411lbs, and its steering angle is a racy 23.7 degrees – so it's no surprise that the

The TL1000S's half-fairing leaves the big V-twin engine on display, and also reveals the distinctive aluminium frame. Rear suspension is a unique combination of single spring and separate rotary damper.

Suzuki is a thrilling, quick-steering machine that requires its rider to keep totally alert at all times.

That big V-twin motor pulls crisply at low and medium revs, giving enough instant acceleration to lift the front wheel with just a twist of the throttle. And the free-revving engine really takes off at 6500rpm, sending the tacho needle shooting round to the 10,500rpm redline, and hurling the TL forward towards a top speed of 160mph.

The Suzuki's handling adds to the bike's ultra-sporty, take-no-prisoners attitude, as the bike's light weight and radical geometry combine with its awesome acceleration to make the steering very light – sometimes to the point of instability. But if the inevitable drawback of providing effortless steering response and rapid direction changes is twitchiness on a bumpy road, that's a price many riders are willing to pay.

In other respects the TL's chassis is exemplary. Suspension control at both ends is excellent (that unique rotary damper really works), the brakes are powerful and have lots of feel, ground clearance is almost limitless, and the sticky standard-fitment Metzelers complete a package that puts the Suzuki right up there with the world's best and fastest sports bikes of any engine configuration.

Better still, the TL1000S combines its cutting-edge performance and technical sophistication with a very competitive price tag. For riders who always lusted after a rapid V-twin but lack the commitment (financial and otherwise) to own Ducati's demanding 916, the TL1000S provides a challenging and exhilarating alternative.

Motorbikes don't come much more outrageous than the TL1000S, which combines razor-sharp handling with a gloriously free-revving engine. Cracking open the throttle in first or second gear makes the front wheel reach for the sky.

Much of the credit for the TL1000S's crisp throttle response goes to the Mikuni-Denso fuel-injection system.

SPECIFICATION: SUZUKI TL1000S	
ENGINE	Water-cooled DOHC 8-valve 90-degree V-twin
DISPLACEMENT	996cc
HORSEPOWER	123bhp @ 8500rpm
CARBURETTORS	Mikuni-Denso fuel-injection
GEAR BOX	Six speed
FRAME	Aluminium alloy trellis
WHEELBASE	55.7ins
WEIGHT	411lbs dry
TOP SPEED	160mph

Triumph T595 Daytona

There's no mistaking that the T595 Daytona is a pure-bred sports bike, from the tip of its twin-headlamp fairing to the end of its equally streamlined seat unit. Smooth aerodynamics contribute to the Triumph's impressive top speed of over 160mph.

The stylish and super-fast T595 Daytona is the machine that British sports bike enthusiasts dreamt of following Triumph's comeback in 1991. The Hinckley firm's rapid growth since then has been based on its modular format, by which many components are shared between different models. The compromises this involves do not allow a competitive super-sports bike – but in planning the new-generation Daytona, Triumph's engineers had no such constraints and made an all-out attack.

The engine of the T595 (the production bike uses the factory code-name, in the tradition of the old Meriden-based Triumph company) is based on the original watercooled, 12-valve triple. But so much has been changed that it is effectively a completely new motor. Increasing the bore by 3mm to 79mm pushes capacity out to 955cc. New semi-forged pistons ensure that there's no increase in weight.

Lotus Engineering helped tune the motor by allowing it to breathe better. The valves are larger, lighter and reshaped to improve gas flow. Camshaft profile is revised, and the crankshaft and balancer are lightened. Engine weight is further reduced by magnesium covers, modified crankcases and a redesigned gearbox and clutch.

The Daytona's three-into-one exhaust uses stainless steel castings designed for efficient flow, and ends at an oval-section single silencer. A redesigned airbox feeds a sophisticated Sagem fuel-injection and ignition system, whose black box delivers a claimed three million instructions every second.

In place of Triumph's traditional and rather tall steel spine frame is a distinctive perimeter design based around twin oval-section aluminium extrusions. Styling was a key factor in the chassis design, hence the Daytona frame's polished-and-lacquered tubes and the thick single-sided swing-

Handling is superb, the T595's combination of fairly light, neutral steering and confidence-inspiring stability proving just about perfect for rapid road riding. At 436lbs dry the Triumph is slightly heavier than its sportiest rivals, and requires a little more steering effort, but the British bike is correspondingly more stable.

The rather top-heavy feel of previous Triumphs is completely gone, replaced by a pleasantly manageable feel, and backed-up by excellent control from the compliant yet well-controlled suspension from Japanese firm Showa. Brakes, too, are Japanese – and Nissin's front-brake combination of 320mm fully-floating discs and four-piston calipers gives supremely powerful stopping.

However long you examine the T595, and however hard you ride it, there's no doubting that Triumph has really got it right. The new Daytona is every bit as good as it looks. Britain once again has a sporting superbike that stands comparison with the very best in the world.

Although the T595 is designed for fast road riding, with a blend of light steering and high-speed stability, the triple is more than capable of holding its own at high speed on a racetrack.

Triumph's management is happy to admit that styling was regarded as a key element of the T595's design, and the triple combines good looks with high-quality engineering. With its curvaceous bodywork, distinctive oval-section tubular aluminium frame and single-sided rear swing-arm, the Daytona is a stunning bike that heralds an exciting new era for the reborn British manufacturer.

arm. The bike is much more compact than previous Triumphs; its riding position a typical race-replica crouch to fairly wide clip-ons.

The new powerplant is much punchier than its predecessors, kicking super-hard anywhere above 6000rpm to send the bike howling forward urgently and the tacho needle flicking towards the 10,500rpm redline. Peak output is a claimed 128bhp at 10,200rpm, 15bhp up on the old Super Three figure and competitive with the world's best sports bikes. It's enough to send the sleek, fully-faired T595 screaming to a top speed of about 165mph.

Low-rev response is crisp, too, although there is a distinct torque dip at about 5500rpm, which can be frustrating because it's the engine speed at which you quite often find yourself dialling in some extra throttle for overtaking. The Daytona's only other slight disappointment is its rather inconsistent six-speed gearbox – surprising considering previous Triumphs' excellent boxes.

SPECIFICATION: TRIUMPH T595 DAYTONA	
ENGINE	Water-cooled DOHC 12-valve in-line triple
DISPLACEMENT	955cc
HORSEPOWER	128bhp @ 10,200rpm
CARBURETTORS	Sagem fuel-injection
GEAR BOX	Six speed
FRAME	Aluminium alloy tubes
WHEELBASE	56.7ins
WEIGHT	436lbs dry
TOP SPEED	165mph

Triumph T509 Speed Triple

'The Speed Triple will go very fast if you want it to.'

Triumph's new-generation Speed Triple roadster, the T509, is one of the most entertaining bikes on the road – as well as one of the most visually striking. With its twin frog-eye headlights up front, and its three-cylinder engine on show to the world, the T509 has a raw, aggressive 'streetfighter' look that many riders love, some dislike but none can fail to notice.

The original Speed Triple was one of Triumph's most popular models worldwide, and its 1997 replacement combines a similar naked musclebike image with many of the components developed for the T595 Daytona. The T509's motor uses a combination of old and new parts, while its chassis is almost identical to that of the T595. The updated Speed Triple might not have a fairing, but in every other respect it's a seriously sporty machine.

Its engine is closer to that of the T595 than the old Speed Triple unit. The original 855cc capacity is retained, as are the cylinder head, pistons and con-rods. But everything else is new, including the aluminium cylinder liners and the lightened crankshaft and clutch. The new Triple's Sagem fuel-injection system is a revised version of that used by the T595, and the airbox and three-into-one exhaust system are also similar. The result is a claimed peak output of 106bhp at 9100rpm, 9bhp up on the old Speed Triple.

The T509's chassis is even closer to that of the T595. This bike's oval-section aluminium frame differs only in that it is painted, instead of polished and lacquered as on the Daytona. The naked Triumph also features identical multi-adjustable 45mm Showa front forks, fully-floating Nissin front brake discs with four-piston calipers, and single-sided swing-arm. All are top-class components of a kind that many unfaired machines make do without.

Differences in engine tune, as well as the lack of a fairing, mean that the T509 is a very different bike to ride to its T595 relation. Rather than delivering its best power at high engine speeds, the Speed Triple is designed to punch out torque in the midrange zone where it's most useful on a naked roadster. Its engine's flexible nature means there's no need for frequent use of the six-speed gearbox – just flick into top and enjoy the ride.

The T509 is most impressive between 3000rpm and about 7000rpm, after which the motor starts to run out of breath as it heads towards the redline at 9500rpm. The Speed Triple will go very fast if you want it to – accelerating hard to a top speed of about 135mph – but on the road it's happiest cruising at up to 120mph. At those speeds the rider gets some wind-protection from the instruments, and the Triumph feels pleasantly smooth and refined.

The naked T509 gives a clear view not only of its oval-section aluminium frame – which is identical to that of the T595 apart from its paint finish – but also its 885cc three-cylinder engine, which uses parts from both the old Speed Triple and new T595 powerplants.

SPECIFICATION:	TRIUMPH T509 SPEED TRIPLE
ENGINE	Water-cooled DOHC 12-valve in-line triple
DISPLACEMENT	885cc
HORSEPOWER	106bhp @ 9100rpm
CARBURETTORS	Sagem fuel-injection
GEAR BOX	Six speed
FRAME	Aluminium alloy tubes
WHEELBASE	56.7ins
WEIGHT	431lbs dry
TOP SPEED	135mph

Handling, braking and roadholding are every bit as good as might be expected of a bike with such a high-tech chassis. At 431lbs the T509 is light for a big naked machine, and its aluminium frame is supremely rigid. Showa's suspension is firm without being harsh, and very well-damped. Both ends keep control even when the Triumph is putting down lots of torque through its massive and very grippy 190-section rear tyre.

Inevitably the T509's striking styling is the feature that attracts the attention initially, but after riding the Triumph it's the way the bike performs that stays in the mind.

If a lean, muscular roadster with twin headlamps, plenty of torque, a fat back tyre and a thoroughly nasty image appeals to you, then rest assured. The T509 Speed Triple delivers everything it threatens.

For a naked roadster the T509 handles superbly, thanks to its rigid frame, top-quality Showa suspension and broad radial tyres. The Speed Triple makes an impact even when it's parked, with its frog-eye twin headlamps. The optional-extra flyscreen adds the finishing touch to a very distinctive bike.

Triumph Sprint 900

....

'The quality of paint and plating is as high as anything in motorcycling.'

The 900 Sprint, like the rest of the Triumph range, is part Superbike, part miracle. After the once-mighty British motorcycle industry self-destructed during the '60s and '70s, the prospects of regeneration on anything like its former scale were as likely as an (old-style) Triumph twin that didn't vibrate or leak oil. True, there had been occasional flourishes from the likes of Norton and Matchless, but these were very small scale and, it turned out, ill-fated.

Triumph is different. To date John Bloor, the Midlands builder who owns the new company, has sunk around £80 million into the venture. The Hinckley, Leicestershire factory is as modern and efficient as any in the world. Its state-of-the-art computer-controlled machinery will produce well over 10,000 motorcycles during 1995. And, most important of all, the product is good.

The Sprint is a case in point. It eschews race replica performance, in favour of a formula which simply works. Yet originally it wasn't even Triumph's idea. When the naked Trident range first appeared in 1991, a number of customisers, notably in Britain and Germany, produced a half-faired variant. One year later Triumph themselves responded with the Sprint.

But there was a difference. Where the 'unofficial' Sprints had simply been modified Tridents, the official version was actually more of a defrocked version of the fully-faired Trophy. So from the outset the Sprint had the Trophy's dual-rate front springs and both pre-load and rebound damping adjustment at the rear. Although still too softly sprung for out-and-out sport riding, the latter is a useful bonus, allowing the suspension to be fine-tuned to suit conditions. On maximum damping, there is less of the mild wallow to which the unfaired bike is prone.

The result not only *looks* like a motorcycle ought, but makes for a versatile and practical all-rounder. Highish 'bars and lower seat offer a riding position as relaxed as anything this side of a full-blown tourer (and better then several of those). Once you've become used to wielding the wide 'bars from low behind the bulbous tank, the bike is beguilingly easy to control. The half fairing largely eliminates wind fatigue. For long trips by motorway or fast A-roads, it is almost indispensable.

SPECIFICATION: TRIUMPH SPRINT 900	
ENGINE	Liquid-cooled DOHC 16-valve transverse four
DISPLACEMENT	885cc
HORSEPOWER	100bhp @ 9500rpm
CARBURETTORS	3 x 36mm Mikuni CV
GEAR BOX	Six speed
FRAME	Tubular steel spine
WHEELBASE	58.7ins
WEIGHT	474lbs dry
TOP SPEED	136mph

'Invented' by aftermarket specialists, the 900 Sprint quickly became one of the most successful models in the Triumph range, offering a rare brand of performance and practicality.

As well as the rider, the fairing gives the engine an easier time. 100 horsepower shoving a naked Trident through the air has a much tougher time than the same power pushing a comparatively slippery fairing. As with the 900 Daytona, the simple appliance of a dash of aerodynamics makes an already potent engine seem even stronger.

In just a few short years we have come to expect a high standard of finish from Triumph, and the Sprint does not disappoint. The quality of paint and plating is as high as anything in motorcycling, BMW included. Carburation and clutch action are equally refined, and the gear change is superbly precise.

And the three-cylinder engine, of course, is special: flexible, inexhaustible and strong. It thrives on revs, yet punches hard through the mid-range. Like all its siblings, it employs a balance shaft to reduce vibration, but not at the expense of 'character'. Somehow, something distinctive gets through to the rider. You can't quite put your finger on it, but there's a rumble, a cadence, *something*, which says 'I am not a four, and especially not a Japanese four: I am *different*'.

No concealing race-replica styling here, and the Sprint's superb powerplant certainly has no reason to be bashful.

Triumph Thunderbird

'The Thunderbird's chassis was well up to containing its engine performance.'

Although the T-bird's striking styling slightly compromised its performance, the first Retro Triumph instantly vaulted to the head of Hinckley's sales figures. It now accounts for 30 per cent of total production.

One glance at the Thunderbird said everything about the bike that Triumph created to spearhead its return to the American market in 1995. The three-cylinder cruiser was built for nostalgia, echoing the British firm's 1950s and '60s look from its high bars and chrome headlamp all the way to its wire wheels and old-style 'peashooter' silencers. The name added to the period feel, too, for the original 650cc Thunderbird parallel twin had been a big US hit for Triumph in the '50s, and was the bike famously ridden by Marlon Brando's character, Johnny, in *The Wild One*.

The Thunderbird represented a big step for the fast-expanding Hinckley firm, as it was the first model to move significantly away from the modular concept on which Triumph's range had been based. Although the basic layout of this bike's watercooled, twin-cam, 12-valve powerplant was shared with the eight other triples in the range, numerous engine and chassis components were unique, making the Thunderbird more complicated and expensive to produce.

Triumph retained the big triple's familiar 885cc capacity, but the T-bird's cylinder head, crankcases and covers were restyled to mimic those of old aircooled models. Internal changes, including different cams and a lower compression ratio, reduced peak power to 69bhp from the normal 97bhp. Like the Speed Triple, the new triple also had five, rather than Triumph's more common six ratios in its gearbox.

The frame's main spine was similar to the other models', but joined a modified rear section that allowed a slightly lower dual-seat. Bodywork was all new, and did a great job of recapturing the look of the old twins. The classical 'mouth-organ' tank-badge was almost identical to the '50s original. The fuel tank's shape, the chrome carb-covers and wire-spoked wheels (in 18-inch front, 16-inch rear sizes) all added to the period effect.

Triumph's previous triples had been superbly tractable, yet the detuned engine was even stronger at low revs (peak torque arrives at just 4800rpm). Given a handful of throttle, the Triumph surged forwards almost regardless of how far the tacho needle was from its 8500rpm redline. The motor was wonderfully smooth, too, and the gearbox typically slick. Top-end performance was less impressive, as the T-bird began running out of breath well before its modest top speed of 122mph.

The Thunderbird's chassis was well up to containing its engine performance. The frame was stiff, and suspension at both ends firm by cruiser standards. Hard riding, particularly over a series of bumps, sometimes revealed the handling's limitations with a slight twitch. Unlike other Triumphs, this bike made do with a single front disc brake, but it was effective providing the lever was given a solid squeeze.

For short trips and gentle cruising the Thunderbird was comfortable, manoeuvrable and very pleasant indeed. Inevitably, some practicality had been sacrificed to style. This bike's fuel tank held only 3.3 gallons, compared to the 5.5 gallons of most other Triumphs, limiting range to about 100 miles. By then, the wind-blown riding position had normally made the rider glad of a stop, despite the broad and comfortable dual seat.

Triumph offered extra practicality – and style – with a range of accessories including a screen and panniers. But many riders preferred the added retro image of cosmetic options such as traditional two-tone paintwork and rubber knee-pads for the fuel-tank. That carefully cultivated air of nostalgia, combined with good performance and excellent build quality, rapidly made the new Thunderbird a big hit – not just in America but all over the world.

SPECIFICATION:	TRIUMPH THUNDERBIRD
ENGINE	Water-cooled DOHC 12-valve in-line triple
DISPLACEMENT	885cc
HORSEPOWER	69bhp @ 8000rpm
CARBURETTORS	3 x 36mm Mikuni
GEAR BOX	Five speed
FRAME	Tubular steel spine
WHEELBASE	61ins
WEIGHT	484lbs dry
TOP SPEED	122mph

The Thunderbird's name, 'mouth organ' tank badge and acres of chrome plate hark back – and forward? – to an age when Triumph motorcycles ruled America.

Triumph Trophy 1200

The first of revitalised Triumph's modular superbikes caused a sensation when it was released in 1991. A big, four-cylinder machine designed to deliver both performance and comfort, the Trophy 1200 was fast, smooth, stable, sophisticated – a match in almost every department for the very best sports-tourers on the roads. So impressive was the British firm's debut model that it could have been built by one of the Japanese giants.

Instead it had been developed from scratch by the team led by John Bloor, the multi-millionaire builder who had bought bankrupt Triumph from the liquidator in 1983. Bloor then spent eight years secretly building an impressive new factory at Hinckley, not far from Triumph's old Meriden base, and planning a range of modular machines. Three- and four-cylinder engine layouts used alternative crankshafts to produce four different motors. These powered six initial models, the biggest of which was the four-cylinder Trophy.

Apart from its modular construction, which was unique in the bike world, the Trophy's 1180cc engine was conventional. The watercooled in-line four contained 16 valves, worked by twin overhead

camshafts, and produced a very respectable maximum of 125bhp at 9000rpm. More impressive still was its crisp carburation and outstanding supply of midrange torque, which made riding the big Triumph delightfully easy and relaxing.

Instant acceleration was available everywhere, from below 2000rpm to the redline at 9500rpm. Simply winding back the throttle sent the Trophy hurtling forward with a breathtaking mixture of power, tractability and smoothness. There were no power steps, just a steady stream of irrepressible torque that sent the Triumph surging towards a top-speed of just over 150mph and made its excellent six-speed gearbox almost redundant. Better still, efficient twin balancer shafts ensured that vibration was minimal at all engine speeds.

Triumph's modular approach was also employed in the chassis, notably the frame, shared

Arguably the most effortless powerplant in motorcycling, the Trophy's is precisely $1^{1}/_{3}$ Triumph triples. The extra cylinder gives lashings of additional torque to what was already a potent engine.

Trophy design has evolved to make it a high-speed mile-eater with few equals . . .

. . . yet it can still do this (left) with startling panache.

by all six models and based around a single large-diameter steel spine that incorporated the engine as a stressed member. The frame held 43mm forks and a vertical rear monoshock, both from Japanese specialists Kayaba. Brakes were also made in Japan, by Nissin. Twin-piston front calipers squeezed a pair of 296mm discs up front, giving braking that was adequate – but no more – in conjunction with the single rear disc.

Although the spine frame design appeared dated in comparison with the latest alloy twin-beam constructions, the Trophy handled very well. In a straight line it was totally stable at all speeds, and barely gave a twitch even in bumpy high-speed curves. Chassis geometry was fairly conservative, and at 529lbs the bike was no lightweight. But the Triumph's steering was neutral, suspension was good and the bike could be hustled along a twisty road at a very respectable rate.

The Trophy's efficient full fairing, large fuel tank and comfortable seat were also well designed. Along with the Triumph's impressive strength and reliability, they combined to create a superb sports-

tourer that was competitive with long-standing Japanese favourites such as Kawasaki's ZZ-R1100 and Yamaha's FJ1200. If the Trophy had a fault, it was simply that its four-cylinder engine layout and conservative styling were unexceptional.

Few riders complained after they'd tried the Trophy 1200, which became a long-standing success for the British firm. In subsequent years it was refined with features including uprated brakes, a lower seat, improved finish and a clock in the dashboard. All helped to make the first new-generation Triumph an even more competent all-round superbike than ever.

'The bike could be hustled along a twisty road at a very respectable rate.'

SPECIFICATION: TRIUMPH TROPHY 1200	
ENGINE	Water-cooled DOHC 16-valve in-line four
DISPLACEMENT	1180cc
HORSEPOWER	125bhp @ 9000rpm
CARBURETTORS	4 x 36mm Mikuni
GEAR BOX	Five speed
FRAME	Tubular steel spine
WHEELBASE	58.7ins
WEIGHT	528lbs dry
TOP SPEED	153mph

Yamaha FJ1200

....

*I*f the expression 'Superbike' sometimes encompasses ephemeral machines which fade as quickly out of the limelight as they flitted in, Yamaha's FJ1200 has proved to be one of the most enduring. A by-word for effortless long-distance work, it is comfortable, practical and fast. Very few bikes demolish miles quite so effortlessly. Until ousted by Triumph's 1200 Trophy (see page 82), it was the yardstick by which four-cylinder grunt was judged. Little wonder, then, that half the motorcycle press seem to have owned a FJ at one time or another.

Like good wine, the big Yamaha has improved progressively with the years. Initially launched in 1984 as the FJ1100, the machine was initially conceived as a sports bike, but soon came to be regarded as the definitive high-speed sports-tourer. In 1986, the engine was bored out from 1097 to 1188cc, adding to the air-cooled engine's already copious mid-range power. In '88 a 17in front wheel belatedly replaced the previous 16 incher, which both helped handling and reduced the front tyre's excessive wear. At the same time the brakes were uprated to four-piston calipers, and hydraulic anti-dive abandoned.

1991 saw the biggest redesign yet. ABS brakes were offered as an option (FJ1200A). A new, sturdier version of the original 'perimeter' frame with rubber-mounted engine replaced the previous chassis, in which the engine was solidly bolted as a stressed member. Throughout its long life the FJ has also received innumerable detail changes, notably to screen and seat, aimed at improving its long-distance capability. At one time a shaft-drive option, as fitted to Yamaha's equally venerable XJ900, was rumoured to be imminent. The 1200, however, steadfastly makes do with a chain.

The heart of the FJ is its engine. Although now dated in concept, it is supremely robust and works superbly on this class of bike – a real autobahn bruiser. Where many other Superbikes rocket to 160mph and well beyond, the FJ12 struggles to reach 150. Several sports 600s are as quick. Yet very few machines are this easy. Bottomless midrange power makes overtaking effortless, and the top gear take-up from 100mph can embarrass more powerful machines. Pre-'91 examples suffer from buzzy

vibration at certain revs; later, rubber-mounted models are silky-smooth throughout the range.

With this class of machine, stability and steering are far more important considerations than the ability to flick through chicanes like a Honda Fireblade. The FJ is a big, heavy bike, but carries its weight low. Handling is all-round competent, but marred by somewhat limited ground-clearance two-up. Fitted with the right tyres, it behaves well, but it is very tyre sensitive. Michelin radials seem to work best. The brakes are excellent on later models (the entire front end is the same as the FZR1000's), and the optional ABS anti-lock system is the best on the market.

Add an effective (but not over-large) fairing, a seat more than roomy enough for two, and the ability to lug huge amounts of luggage, and you begin to appreciate the FJ's real-world value. Perhaps its only serious flaw as the ultimate sports tourer is its limited tank range – at 37mpg, you can easily find yourself looking for petrol stations every 150 miles. But despite its age, the big FJ still represents a supremely practical package for the long-haul rider. It is not the quickest Superbike, and it is certainly not the sexiest, but year-in, year-out, it does what many do not: it really works.

'Very few bikes demolish miles quite so effortlessly.'

Compared to more recent superbikes, the FJ's handling is ponderous with a marked lack of ground clearance two-up. Comfort, though, is hard to beat.

SPECIFICATION: YAMAHA FJ1200	
ENGINE	Air-cooled DOHC 16-valve transverse four
DISPLACEMENT	1188cc
HORSEPOWER	125bhp @ 9000rpm
CARBURETTORS	4 x 36mm Mikuni CV
GEAR BOX	Five speed
FRAME	Square-section steel perimeter
WHEELBASE	58.9ins
WEIGHT	546lbs dry
TOP SPEED	146mph

Big air-cooled engine lacks the latest technology, but is a by-word for big-hearted power.

Yamaha YZF1000R Thunderace

....

'Thunderace is the Sensible Superbike.'

Subtle styling changes give the Thunderace a new look, notably at the front of its reshaped fairing. But the mighty YZF1000R has much in common with its FZR1000 predecessor — notably its ability to combine speed and fine handling with a reasonable degree of comfort.

Yamaha's aim with its YZF1000R Thunderace was simple: to build the best-performing superbike on the road. In designing a replacement for the long-successful FZR1000, the Japanese giant's intention was not to compete head-on with singleminded race-replicas such as Honda's Fireblade and Suzuki's GSX-R750, but to produce an ultra-powerful road rocket that could hold its own on the track too.

And that's exactly what the Thunderace is. Retaining the basic FZR1000 format of 20-valve, four-cylinder engine and twin-beam aluminium frame, the Thunderace features sharp styling, generous midrange power, superb handling and even a reasonable amount of comfort. By superbike standards it's almost an all-rounder – but that

versatility does not come at the expense of speed or sheer excitement.

Beneath the restyled bodywork, the Ace's watercooled, 1002cc motor is internally unchanged from its FZR predecessor apart from forged pistons – lighter and stronger than the previous cast variety – and a lighter crankshaft. A bank of 38mm downdraft Mikuni carbs helps boost midrange output on the way to an unchanged claimed peak of 145bhp at 10,000rpm.

The Thunderace's frame is borrowed not from the FZR1000 but from the YZF750. Its twin-spar aluminium construction is essentially similar, but the wheelbase is significantly shorter than the FZR's, aiding manoeuvrability. The frame holds a pair of conventional front forks of massive 48mm

diameter, and a single rear shock which, like the forks, is fully adjustable for damping.

The Ace's riding position is instantly familiar to anyone who's ridden a big FZR, and so is the engine's response to a handful of throttle. The revs rise with stunning speed towards the 11,000rpm redline as the Yamaha powers smoothly towards a top speed of around 170mph. Top-end performance is fearsome, but it's the Thunderace's storming midrange output that is much more useful on the road. The old FZR1000 was much-loved for its midrange grunt, and its successor has even more of the same thing.

The Ace's handling is equally impressive, managing to combine super-sports lightness and precision with a generous amount of stability. Despite its racy steering geometry and short wheelbase, the Thunderace doesn't quite have the razor-sharp steering feel of some sportsters – partly because, at 436lbs, it's slightly heavier.

But if the YZF loses out fractionally in its speed of steering, it's still a brilliantly agile, neutral-handling machine that would run rings round its FZR predecessor and most other bikes on the road. Suspension at both front and rear is excellent. And the Yamaha's front brakes, whose four-piston calipers have a one-piece construction instead of the normal bolted-together halves (increasing rigidity), are arguably the best in all motorcycling.

Other aspects of the Thunderace uphold the Yamaha tradition of building super-sports bikes that are tolerably comfortable over long distances. Its screen is too low for sustained high-speed use but gives reasonable protection. Switchgear and instrumentation are sensibly laid out, the fuel tank holds a reasonable 20 litres and the seat is broad – although a pillion has nothing solid to hold.

In many respects the YZF1000R Thunderace is the Sensible Superbike – if such a description could ever be used of a vehicle that accelerates from a

standstill to 150mph in about the time it takes to read this sentence. The Yamaha has neither the brute power of Honda's Super Blackbird nor the lightning reflexes of Suzuki's GSX-R750 – but in many situations it's faster than both. And the way the Thunderace combines its speed with all-round ability makes it a hugely impressive machine.

The Thunderace does not steer particularly quickly, but its high-speed stability is immense.

The Yamaha's front end is excellent, featuring hugely thick front forks and supremely powerful brakes.

SPECIFICATION: YAMAHA YZF1000R THUNDERACE	
ENGINE	Water-cooled DOHC 20-valve in-line four
DISPLACEMENT	1002cc
HORSEPOWER	145bhp @ 10,000rpm
CARBURETTORS	4 x 38mm Mikuni CV
GEAR BOX	Five speed
FRAME	Aluminium alloy beam
WHEELBASE	56.3ins
WEIGHT	436lbs dry
TOP SPEED	170mph

Yamaha GTS 1000

When it comes to bringing technological innovation to mass-produced motorcycles, Yamaha leads the way with its revolutionary GTS1000.

The GTS was the first mass-production superbike of the modern age to use a front suspension system that didn't employ a pair of telescopic forks and a chassis that doesn't run more or less in a straight line from the steering head to the swingarm pivot.

Motorcycle manufacturers have long searched for a method of suspending the front wheel of a motorcycle that doesn't rely on conventional telescopic forks. 'Teles' are unsatisfactory for several reasons – they are prone to flexing under braking and when cornering, and then cause the front end of the bike to 'dive' under braking. The search for a realistic alternative has been the Holy Grail of motorcycle engineering.

Yamaha's alternative front end, as featured on the GTS1000, is a single-sided front swingarm with hub-centre steering not unlike one front wheel of a car. Separating the steering function from the

Bold styling and high price of Yamaha's 'flagship' GTS has tempered sales, but expect to see more such technology on future models.

suspension should, in theory, produce a bike that steers, corners and brakes better than a bike with conventional forks.

The GTS's Omega chassis is different from that of a conventional bike because the front suspension removes the necessity for a headstock. The aluminium-alloy frame is a squat box-shaped affair which wraps around the engine, on to which are bolted the front and rear suspension systems, as well as the sub-frames necessary for the steering, seat and bodywork.

So how does this alternative front suspension system work? Basically it's in two parts. A single-sided swingarm attaches the front wheel to the chassis and a single shock-absorber bolts between the two. The steering is handled separately by a vertical cast aluminium-alloy spar that goes from the front axle to a steering box and thence to the handlebar crown.

The result is a bike that has one of the most sophisticated front suspension systems in production. The bad news is that, in the case of the GTS at least, this kind of suspension system offers no significant improvement over conventional telescopic forks. Being designed as a sports-touring

motorcycle the GTS is too long and carries too much weight to reap any benefits from hub-centre steering other than the elimination of front end dive under braking.

Indeed, the GTS is actually slower steering and more ponderous than many of its competitors, which surely isn't what Yamaha intended. Oddly enough, the harder the GTS is ridden the better it responds, which gives credence to claims that this is the way forward for sports bikes. It just doesn't seem to suit 550lb sports-tourers too well.

But what of the rest of the GTS? The engine is a state-of-the-art, 100bhp fuel-injected 1000cc in-line four with five valves per cylinder. The exhaust system features a three-way catalytic converter, and a tamper-proof ignition system. The front brake is also worthy of mention. The single-sided front swingarm means that only one disc brake can be fitted to the GTS, so Yamaha have equipped the GTS's single 320mm ventilated disc with a six-piston caliper for stupendous stopping power.

The GTS's performance is brisk rather than

exceptional, with a top-speed nudging 140mph. Although it shares the same basic layout as the Yamaha FZR1000, modifications to the valve timing and the fuel-injection system, ensure that the GTS only puts out 100bhp but with a substantial increase in mid-range power.

The GTS1000 is technologically very ambitious, and presents some interesting solutions to age-old problems. But ultimately it is an example of technology for technology's sake rather than a major step forward in motorcycle design.

Sure-footedness of the GTS's novel front suspension comes into its own on bumpy Lakeland back roads such as these.

'The result is a bike that has one of the most sophisticated front suspension systems in production.'

SPECIFICATION: YAMAHA GTS1000	
ENGINE	Liquid-cooled DOHC 20-valve in-line four
DISPLACEMENT	1002cc
HORSEPOWER	100bhp @ 9000rpm
CARBURETTORS	Electronic fuel injection
GEAR BOX	Five speed
FRAME	Aluminium-alloy Omega twin beam
WHEELBASE	58.8ins
WEIGHT	542lbs dry
TOP SPEED	140mph

Yamaha V-Max 1200

'Trying to go fast on a V-Max anywhere other than a straight line is not a relaxing experience!'

It's too big, too fat, too heavy, it won't stop and it doesn't handle. But — my! — is it *fast*.

By the mid-'eighties, motorcycle design had come a long way. From the early, over-powered and ill-handling Japanese superbikes, had evolved machines which took their cues from the racetrack and had tyres, suspension and steering to match. Suzuki's GSX-R750 and Yamaha's FZ750 typified the new breed.

But there will always be those who are less concerned with all-round performance than with sheer, brute power and the thrill of violent standing start acceleration. The Yamaha V-Max was designed just for them.

When it was first introduced in 1985, the V-Max caused a sensation, as much for its styling as its potential performance. The high-barred, low-slung look was based on the American cruiser style – bikes made for showing off in illegal sprints on impromptu drag strips on public roads. Real drag bikes had already evolved into long-wheelbased, front-heavy machines designed specifically for speed. Cruiser style puts the emphasis on *looking* fast – lots of noise and the ability to leave long strips of burnt rubber off the startline are more important than actual times.

And with a claimed 145bhp, the V-Max was capable of leaving a line of rubber all the way to the horizon – rear tyres on V-Maxes live short and tortured, but exciting lives.

The V-Max is completely dominated by its engine. At the time its V-four layout was a high-tech departure from the in-line fours that powered most Japanese motorcycles (only Honda built V-fours in any numbers). It featured a novel carburettor arrangement which meant each cyclinder was fed by two carburettors, then a gate moved to allow those same two carburettors to fill a different cylinder, thus eliminating the 'dead' time that usually occurs during a bike's combustion cycle. The result was midrange power that was literally like nothing any rider had experienced before, without sacrificing peak power. For a four cylinder engine it made its power at comparatively low revs – the red line was at just 8,500rpm. Visually, the massive black and silver V-four is the centrepiece of the bike's styling. And once on the move, the slightly lumpy power delivery – and the sheer amount of power it delivers – distract attention from the bike's handling.

It was the handling, more than the excess of power, that got the V-Max a reputation as a bike for would-be He-Men. It weaves, it wobbles, and it has so little ground clearance that a cornering V-Max strikes showers of sparks wherever it goes. The tyres are built for long life, not grip, and the brakes are only just about up to the job of hauling the V-Max's bulk down from speed. Trying to go fast on a V-Max anywhere other than a straight line is not a relaxing experience!

None of this matters to V-Max owners. Most don't even care that the top speed is 'only' 140mph. For a start, the lack of a fairing means hanging on at anything over 100mph is gruelling work. No, V-Max owners know that for that moment when the lights change to green (whether on the drag strip or the high street) what matters is how quickly and impressively the bike gets off the line.

In this, the V-Max is the motorcycling equivalent of the huge American muscle cars of the 'seventies – built for fun in a land where the speed limit is 55mph. It may not be the fastest or best-handling bike available, but it's become a modern classic for one reason – there is nothing else in Creation quite like a V-Max.

SPECIFICATION: YAMAHA V-MAX	
ENGINE	Water-cooled DOHC 16-valve V-four
DISPLACEMENT	1198cc
HORSEPOWER	145bhp @ 8000rpm
CARBURETTORS	4 x 35mm Mikuni
GEAR BOX	Five speed
FRAME	Steel cradle
WHEELBASE	62.6ins
WEIGHT	578lbs dry
TOP SPEED	140mph

Whether it's a standard V-Max (right) or a special such as the Egli (below), only the devastating punch of the imposing V-four engine really matters. UK versions, sadly, have their power restricted.

Yamaha XJR *1200*

....

'Acceleration
was fearsome
above
4000rpm.'

When Yamaha decided to enter the retro-bike market with a big, unfaired four-cylinder roadster, the perfect powerplant was already close to hand. The FJ1200 sports-tourer had been hugely popular for years due largely to its superbly tractable air cooled, 16-valve engine. This faithful brute of a motor was detuned, its cylinder fin-tips were polished, and it was put on display at the heart of a twin-shock musclebike called the XJR1200.

Yamaha lacked the four-stroke tradition of Kawasaki and Honda, whose Zephyr and CB1000 models the XJR was created to challenge. But the new bike's lines contained a hint of the 1978-model XS1100 four, and its all-black colour scheme echoed that of the later XS1100S Midnight Special. Maybe the lack of an illustrious predecessor was an advantage, because the clean, simply styled XJR was an undeniably good-looking machine.

The 1188cc motor was placed in a new round-tube steel frame which, like the square-section FJ frame, incorporated a bolt-on lower rail to allow engine removal. Forks were conventional 43mm units, while at the back the XJR had a pair of remote-reservoir shocks from Öhlins, the Swedish suspension specialist firm owned by Yamaha. A pair of broad 17-inch wheels, the front holding big 320mm front discs with four-piston calipers, completed a purposeful profile.

From the rider's conveniently low seat the Yamaha gave a view of slightly raised handlebars, and chrome-rimmed instruments with a central fuel gauge. The engine contained numerous internal modifications to bring peak power output down to 97bhp at 8000rpm, from the FJ1200's 123bhp, and developed even more of the addictive low-rev torque for which the big four had long been renowned. Not that the motor hinted at the power waiting within, as it fired up with a mechanical rustle and a restrained burble from short twin silencers.

The upright riding position and that big, lazy engine set the tone of the bike, encouraging gentle riding and minimal use of the smooth-shifting five-speed gearbox. The XJR responded crisply from as

FJ1200-based engine is the ideal candidate for a Retro musclebike. In XJR form, the air-cooled four puts out even more mid-range torque.

low as 2000rpm in top gear, which made for effortless overtaking, and remained impressively smooth at almost all engine speeds. Acceleration was fearsome above 4000rpm, the handlebars tugging hard at the rider's shoulders as the Yamaha surged smoothly forward. If you hung on and kept the throttle open, it kept pulling remorselessly all the way to 140mph.

Handling was competent for this class of machine and the XJR remained stable at speed, despite the forces being fed into it by the human parachute at the handlebars. The Yamaha always felt like a fairly big, heavy bike, but it changed direction without a great deal of effort. Suspension at both ends was compliant enough for a comfortable ride, but firm enough to allow reasonably spirited cornering. Dunlop's fat radial tyres gave more than enough grip to exploit all the available ground-clearance, and the big front disc brakes were superbly powerful.

Japanese riders were the first to discover this first-hand, as the XJR was introduced as a home-market bike in 1994, before being released elsewhere a year later. Most of those who rode it were impressed. Inevitably, the XJR1200 shared the limitations of every big naked bike, in that the exposed riding position soon made using the engine's top-end performance tiring. But the big four's flexible power delivery made up for that. And the Yamaha's solid handling, handsome looks and general feel of quality made the XJR many riders' choice as the best big retro-bike of all.

SPECIFICATION: YAMAHA XJR1200	
ENGINE	Air-cooled DOHC 16-valve in-line four
DISPLACEMENT	1188cc
HORSEPOWER	97bhp @ 8000rpm
CARBURETTORS	4 x 37mm Mikuni
GEAR BOX	Five speed
FRAME	Tubular steel
WHEELBASE	58.5ins
WEIGHT	488lbs dry
TOP SPEED	140mph

Yamaha were late to clamber on board the Retro bandwagon, but the brutally handsome XJR1200 hits the spot.

Wide 'bars and upright riding position make the big Yamaha surprisingly agile through the turns, but this is still a massive machine to throw around.

Yamaha YZF750

Yamaha's FZ750 had been one of the company's best-sellers in the mid-'eighties, but by the early 'nineties it was dated – outhandled and outpowered by a new generation of alloy-framed, fat-tyred race replicas. Rumours of a replacement had been rife since Kawasaki launched the ZXR750 in 1989. But at that time Yamaha's answer was to launch the OW01, (a limited edition – and extremely expensive – World Superbike contender), and let the FZ soldier on as a road bike.

But by late 1992, the OW01 had also reached the end of its potential in world-class competition – now it was time to build a bike for the racetrack as well as the road.

The YZF750 was launched at the beginning of 1993 and quickly got a name for itself as a nimble, quick-steering sportster that handled more like a 600 than a big 750. It was based on the well-proven OW01 design, but developed to the point where no parts are interchangeable between the two.

Importantly for road riders, the YZF's road manners didn't need to be compromised by its track aspirations. A limited-edition SP version was built for racing, with a close-ratio gearbox, stiffer, multi-adjustable suspension, a single race seat and huge carburettors. That left the standard YZF with more useable gear ratios, proper pillion accommodation and far better engine behaviour than the SP. In fact, only the SP's adjustable suspension made YZF owners jealous. Yamaha listened to them and the standard YZF soon sprouted fully-adjustable Öhlins suspension front and rear.

The new suspension helped to make an already quick-steering and sweet-handling bike into a real road weapon. Surprisingly for a 750, it's easy to handle on twisty backroads, and civilised enough to cover long distances in reasonable comfort. That's partly down to the quality of the suspension, which allows relatively soft springs without compromising control – bumpy bends don't throw the YZF off line, or throw the rider out of his seat. But if you really want to experience the YZF's mind-expanding limits safely you need smooth, open roads or the freedom of a race track.

Because the YZF is fast. Not just in terms of outright speed – Kawasaki's ZXR is a little faster in still conditions. What makes the YZF's engine

Better looking and far, far cheaper than the Yamaha OW01 from which it is derived, the YZF is the classiest transverse four in the 750cc division.

Despite its superb credentials as a road bike, the YZF has never quite had the development to deliver in world superbike competition. The potential, though, is certainly there.

'The new suspension helped to make an already quick-steering and sweet-handling bike into a real road weapon.'

special is its smooth, linear midrange power delivery. For this, we have to thank Yamaha's unique EXUP system. The EXUP (it stands for Exhaust Ultimate Powervalve) is a valve in the exhaust collector pipe that opens and closes at preset revs, and fools the engine into thinking it has an exhaust pipe specifically tuned for those revs. The result is apparent as soon as you ride the YZF – where its competitors have little low-down pull, followed by peak power coming in with a bang, the YZF just pulls, and pulls, and pulls, from 3,000rpm all the way to the 13,000rpm redline.

Slowing the YZF down from its 160mph+ top speed are some of the most powerful front brakes fitted to any road bike. Twin discs are gripped so hard by six-piston calipers it's not unknown for the discs to warp under the strain. Other bikes now wear six-piston brakes (including some Triumphs and Suzukis), but the YZF was the first production bike to boast them as standard.

But its instant success as a road bike wasn't to be mirrored on the track. It was to be late 1994 before the YZF proved its worth and achieved its first serious international success – victory at the Bol d'Or 24-hour race in the hands of brothers and ex-GP racers Christian and Dominique Sarron. The race bike had finally caught up with the road bike.

SPECIFICATION: YAMAHA YZF750	
ENGINE	Water-cooled DOHC 20-valve in-line four
DISPLACEMENT	749cc
HORSEPOWER	122bhp @ 12,000rpm
CARBURETTORS	4 x 38mm Mikuni
GEAR BOX	Six speed
FRAME	Deltabox aluminium twin beam
WHEELBASE	55.9ins
WEIGHT	432lbs
TOP SPEED	160mph

YZF's 'Fox-eye' headlamps and superb six-piston front brakes set a trend. Its performance simply sets the pulse racing.

MAC MᶜDIARMID ●

Classic
Super BIKES

FROM AROUND THE WORLD

Contents – Classic Superbikes

Opposite – The ultimate Bonnie – 1965 Thruxton model.

Below – Honda CB750: perhaps the most revolutionary machine of a revolutionary era. Once, only factory racers were built like this.

Introduction

·····························

Only two things are common to the motorcycles on the following pages. Most obviously of all, they each have two wheels. And, with rare exceptions, they have telescopic forks and paired rear shock absorbers. This was, in essence, the twin-shock era, bounded fore and aft by plunger and monoshock rear ends.

Yet it is engines which most distinguish the period. As befitted the austerity of the post-war years, the 'fifties began with the single – four-stroke or two-, as the people's engine. Although there were what we might call 'bespoke singles' (like Velocettes and Norton's Inter), riders of greater means or ambition sought four-stroke twins. Most were parallel, the descendants of Alfred Turner's 1937 Triumph Speed Twin. A few, notably Harley-Davidson and the Vincent in their very different ways, were in Vee configuration. Others, even more rarely, were opposed.

Multis barely got a look-in. The Danish Nimbus, the last surviving relic of countless car-type longitudinal fours, failed to survive the decade. Ariel's Square Four was an heroic, imposing, but largely irrelevant cul-de-sac. Indeed, it was the commercial failure of machines like the Square Four which did much to dissuade the British motorcycle industry from further such enterprise.

Meanwhile the two-stroke, DKW's valiant efforts aside, was effectively confined to the role of humble commuter. Most were smoky, slow, and – even by the standards of the time – unreliable. In 1950 they were certainly not the sort of fare to justify inclusion in any catalogue of 'Classic Superbikes'.

Three revolutions in three countries changed all this. Italy (with a little help from West Germany's NSU) turned the concept of high-revving, multi-cylinder four-strokes into screaming metal – but

Series C Vincent Rapide: rare, expensive and fast. These attributes made it definitely a Superbike long before the expression was coined.

exclusively on the race track. Meanwhile a comparable transformation was set in motion when East Germany's MZ utterly transformed ideas of two-stroke capabilities. Again, this revolution was confined to competition. But it redefined human ideas of what was possible. And it is people, let us not forget, who create motorcycles.

It was left to the Japanese, who entered the 'fifties as motorcycling nonentities, and the 'sixties as a two-wheeled joke, to put both sets of ideas onto the street. The 'sixties was the decade in which Japanese manufacturers stole a little, borrowed a lot, and innovated massively, to transform the face of motorcycling. By design they proved that complexity could go hand-in-hand with reliability; and by the third of our revolutions – in manufacturing – they proved that both could be achieved at an affordable price. In 1969, the transverse multi and the high-performance two-stroke twin were exotic. Just six years later they had begun to establish themselves as the norm.

A few manufacturers copied the Japanese approach with, at best, transient success (although others, notably in Italy, have since succeeded). Of the rest, most who ploughed their own furrow dwindled or died. BMW's opposed twins continue

to survive in their iconoclastic way, yet even they have resorted to multis, albeit of an independent bent. Moto Guzzi's Vee twins hang on to life rather more grimly. Harley-Davidson have 're-invented' the past, and sell hugely on an anti high-tech ticket. Ducati continue to create two-wheeled Ferraris to evocative, if relatively small-scale, effect. And the British motorcycle industry disappeared. Of all the manufacturers on the following pages, only nine, at most, continue as producers of 'superbikes'.

Since our quarter century ended in 1975 the two-stroke twin has effectively been sidelined by emissions legislation. Strokers survive on the street either as slightly delinquent sports machines, or – echoes of the 'fifties – as utilitarian lightweights. In competition they remain supreme – an anachronism the racing authorities must surely soon address.

On the dominant, four-stroke front, much of what has happened since has been in the detail – four (even five or eight) valves per cylinder; the almost universal adoption of water-cooling; fuel injection (but surprisingly rarely); and above all a transformation in the quality of chassis, suspension and brakes. But the foundations for all of this were laid here, 1950 to 1975; twenty-five years that changed the face of motorcycling.

Ducati 750SS factory racer: Fogarty's 916 is a direct descendant. Liquid-cooling, multi-valves, fuel injection and – above all – chassis refinements would come later.

Harley-Davidson WL45

It's fitting that the first 'Classic Superbike' should wear the tank badge of the world's oldest surviving motorcycle manufacturer. Since their foundation in 1903, Harley-Davidson have been doing things resolutely the American way – or perhaps 'Milwaukee way' is more apt.

Harley-Davidson, of course, is synonymous with the Vee-twin, a layout they first adopted in 1909. That first twin, with the now-familiar 45 degree included angle, displaced 61cu.in (999.6cc) and was said to be capable of almost 60mph from its 7bhp. It was a notable success, and the company grew rapidly. By 1914 the factory had mushroomed to 297,000 square feet, and during World War I no less than 20,000 Harleys saw military duty.

But in 1995 Harley-Davidson are the iconoclasts of world motorcycling – a situation little different from the '50s. This particular model, the WL45,

began life in 1929, continuing in production with only relatively minor modifications until the arrival of the 'K' Model in 1952. For an entire generation, this was *the* Harley-Davidson, as American as apple pie.

In 1929, the WL was the first of a new generation of side-valve 'flathead' Vee-twins. The '45' denotes the capacity in cubic inches, equivalent to 739cc. In 1930 it was joined by a sister model, the 74-inch VL. Almost on their own, this duo saw Harley through The Depression, for no significant new models were to be developed during six years of economic strife. Of literally hundreds of American bike manufacturers, only Harley and Indian survived, as industry-wide production dropped from 32,000 to 6000 units by 1933. One Harley response was the three-wheeled 'Servi-Car' a cheap delivery and police vehicle powered by the WL engine, which lasted until the mid-'70s.

In 1936 new models began to emerge, with an

SPECIFICATION: HARLEY-DAVIDSON WL45	
ENGINE	739cc side-valve Vee-twin
HORSEPOWER	24.5bhp @ 4600rpm
TRANSMISSION	3-speed
FRAME	tubular single cradle, rigid rear end
BRAKES	drum/drum
TOP SPEED	68mph

'For an entire generation, this was <u>the</u> Harley-Davidson, as American as apple pie.'

80-inch (1310cc) side-valve twin and the legendary 61-inch ohv Knucklehead. But the WL, along with Indian's side-valve 750, remained the Harley mainstay, an increasingly integral part of American culture. (And elsewhere – WLs were actually manufactured in Japan under licence, bearing the Rikuo name). Not surprisingly it was to the WL (suffixed 'A' for Army) that the American military turned during World War II. Of 90,000 Harleys 'enlisted' almost 89,000 were good ol' 45-inch WLA V-twins. It was a long way from 1903, when William S Harley, Arthur Davidson and two other Davidson brothers produced just three motorcycles in a shed measuring 10 foot by 15.

Hostilities over, Harley set about uprating their range, first with the 74-inch, alloy-headed Panhead, complete with hydraulic lifters; then with the first of the Glides, the Hydra Glide. Yet still the WL plodded on, its girder forks, side-valve engine and rigid rear end a growing anachronism but its sheer indestructibility continuing to be prized. Eventually, in 1952, it was replaced by another machine which was to become an American legend. For the K-model not only featured hydraulically damped suspension at both ends, but was later to become the XL Sportster.

The WL is – and was for most of its life – a crude, heavy machine better suited to the American Prairies than any road with bends. Cruising all day at 60mph on a long, straight road, it is in its element. But with 550lbs of momentum, poor brakes, minimal suspension and a wide gap between its three gear ratios, anything else is hard work. Even setting off is a knack, thanks to the WL's foot-operated 'suicide' clutch.

The WL was, even in 1950, a motorcycling dinosaur. But if it was slow, outdated and cumbersome, it was also strong as an ox and almost indestructible; a tough old workhorse that delivered the bacon. The superbikes that were to come would be something else altogether.

Thundering along the straightaways has been the Harley forte since long before the invention of recreational 'cruising'.

Never powerful and certainly not very fast, the side-valve 45-inch 'flathead' Harley, with girder forks and rigid rear end, helped keep America mobile for a generation.

Nimbus 750-Four

· · · · · · · · · · · · · · · · · ·

Fours are nothing new. Since the early years of the century, a host of manufacturers have shoe-horned four-cylinder engines into road-going motorcycles; FN in Belgium, Henderson in the USA, countless others around the world, and even, briefly, Brough in the UK. And the most enduring of these was a small company from Copenhagen, Denmark – Nimbus.

In 1918 the company's founder, Peder Fisker, launched his first production machine, the 'Stovepipe' Nimbus. Loosely based on the FN, it was exquisitely made, with swing arm rear suspension only one of several innovative features. Although the years brought a few diversions, the basic layout was to remain until the very last Nimbus; four cylinders longitudinally in-line, with shaft final drive.

Reminiscent of the Austin Seven car engine, the softly-tuned Nimbus was the opposite of the fours which would later dominate the Superbike era.

The early Nimbus was very expensive to produce, and the onset of the Depression demanded that economies be made. The MkII, introduced in 1934, was much more utilitarian. Gone was the rear suspension, and the brazed tubular backbone frame gave way to a curious affair of riveted steel strip. The MkII had Fisker's own telescopic forks, however, several months ahead of BMW's and probably the first on any motorcycle.

The new 750cc engine, too, was advanced: a SOHC four, with inclined valves and hemispherical combustion chambers. The camshaft was bevel driven, whilst the crankshaft ran in just two huge ball bearings. The big-ends were shell-type. A three-speed gearbox transmitted the Nimbus' modest power by shaft to the rear wheel.

This was never likely to amount to a performance machine. Cooling, with four close-set cast-iron cylinders each heating the other's air, was always poor. The valvegear is open to the elements. The two-bearing crank would flex if revved hard. And the single 26mm Nimbus carburettor is probably the smallest ever fitted to a four. Power in standard trim (and the Nimbus was never much tuned) was 22bhp at a leisurely 4500rpm. Whilst this was good for brief bursts up to 60mph, sustained flat-out cruising evidently warped the cylinder head 'like a banana'.

The Nimbus was the last of the in-line fours which graced the early years of motorcycle development. By the 'fifties, it had become an anachronism.

'This was a machine for riding with dignity, never panache.'

But 1934? Yes, and not really. Fisker was, as a matter of policy and temperament, opposed to change for change's sake. So the MkII continued in production, in much its original form, until 1958. Any part from a 1956 Nimbus will almost certainly fit one 20 years older, and vice versa. Such changes as were made were minor, mainly to instruments, brakes and other ancillaries.

To the end of its life, the MkII retained its rigid rear end. In solo use the ride, like almost everything about the machine, was deeply idiosyncratic. This was a machine for riding with dignity, never panache.

Yet it was, in Denmark at least, a moderately successful motorcycle. In all, something like 12,000 MkIIs were produced. It was rugged, economical (60-plus mpg), maintenance was simple, and it hauled a sidecar with ease. The MkII became popular with Danish tradesmen and military alike.

Even after motorcycle production ceased in 1958, the factory continued to manufacture spares. Although this was mainly to honour its obligations to the military, even in the late 'sixties it was possible to have a Nimbus built from new parts to special order.

But was it a superbike? Not really. Sure, it was a four, which might otherwise mark it as special. But everything about the Nimbus, far from looking forward to the days of high-revving sports bikes, harked back to an age of motorised gentlemen's carriages. It was an utter anachronism, surviving into the Space Age but almost Edwardian in character. Yet, if nothing else, it shows that there is nothing innately sophisticated about multis. As such, it is a useful book-end to an era that ended with fours of an altogether different ilk.

SPECIFICATION: NIMBUS 750-FOUR	
ENGINE	air-cooled 746cc SOHC longitudinal four
HORSEPOWER	22bhp @ 4500rpm
TRANSMISSION	3-speed
FRAME	Riveted steel strip
BRAKES	drum/drum
TOP SPEED	60mph

Scott Squirrel

....

'The lightness and simplicity of the two-stroke twin were potent features.'

The Scott Squirrel only just creeps into this volume's frame of reference, but its background warrants mention in any book on motorcycling. Alfred Angas Scott, founder of the Scott motorcycle company, was one of the great innovators of motorcycling's early years. It was Scott who patented a form of caliper brake as early as 1897, a fully triangulated frame, rotary induction valves, unit construction, the first motorcycle kick-start and much, much more.

Most of all, Scott pioneered the liquid-cooled two-stroke parallel twin with which the Scott name will forever be associated. Yet for all this ingenuity, once Scott had hit on their favoured engine layout, they stuck to it through thick and thin until the company collapsed almost half a century later.

The epitome of Edwardian endeavour, as well as being a gifted inventor and engineer, Scott was an accomplished artist and painter. As early as 1904 he patented his first engine, a vertical twin two-stroke, inevitably – which he fitted onto his Premier bicycle (and occasionally into a small boat, the Petrel).

In 1908 he began motorcycle production, initially using the Bradford facilities of the Jowett brothers, later famous for their cars. The first Scotts used a patented frame which was to survive substantially unchanged until 1930; and a new 333cc liquid-cooled engine.

Although the engine shortly grew to 450cc, with later versions displacing 498 or 596cc, all were of the 'classic' Scott design; two-stroke, using overhung two-bearing crankshafts with the drive taken from a central flywheel. This layout allowed for a large diameter flywheel which was effective without excessive weight. Coolant was circulated through the large honeycomb radiator (another Scott patent) by natural thermo-syphon effect, rather than pumped.

By the time the company moved into new premises at Shipley in 1912, the 'yowling two-strokes' had a string of competition successes behind them. Scott's twins had proved, 55 years before the Japanese demonstrated it again, that the lightness and simplicity of the two-stroke twin were

potent features. As well as innumerable wins in trials and hill-climbs, Scott machines won the Senior TT in 1912 and 1913.

Early Scotts used a simple, but effective, two-speed transmission. The first three-speeder, the legendary Flying Squirrel, appeared in 1926. This was produced in both 498 and 596cc forms. However, four years earlier Alfred Scott himself had died at the age of just 48, from pneumonia contracted after a pot-holing trip. With his departure much of the initiative went out of the company, which was having increasing difficulty competing with the ever-more powerful four-strokes. In 1931 the official receiver was called in.

A Liverpudlian, Albert Reynolds stepped in to save Scott, but the under-capitalised company never fully recovered. Plans for a 650cc twin never

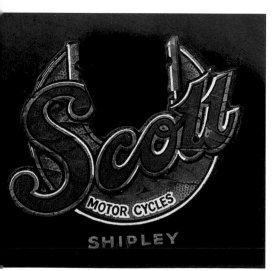

By the 'fifties, Scott's once-revolutionary design was as quaint — and dated — as the Shipley factory's logo.

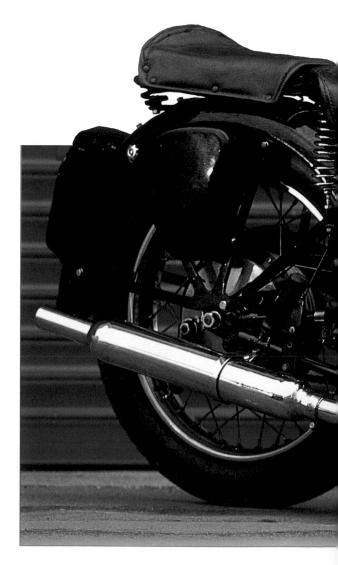

SPECIFICATION: SCOTT SQUIRREL

ENGINE	liquid-cooled 596cc two-stroke twin
HORSEPOWER	30bhp @ 5000rpm
TRANSMISSION	3-speed
FRAME	tubular steel triangulated twin cradle
BRAKES	drum/drum
TOP SPEED	85mph

Production of the 596cc rigid framed Flying Squirrel continued after the war, initially with girder forks and later with Dowty telescopics. In 1949 coil ignition replaced the more familiar Lucas Magdyno. However, sales were poor and production ceased less than 12 months later. The example pictured is from 1950, one of the very last machines to leave Scott's Shipley works.

However, the story did not quite end there. In 1956 a new generation of Scotts were built in small numbers, basically Flying Squirrel engines in a contemporary swing-arm frame. Sadly the project was short-lived, as was the later Silk, essentially a Scott in a sophisticated racing-type Spondon chassis. Exquisite though it was, it was underpowered and expensive, and flickered only briefly.

reached fruition. An even more exciting prospect, Bill Cull's three-cylinder two-stroke design, originally of 747, later 986cc, was shown at the 1934 Olympia Show but never reached production. 1938 brought a 596cc Clubman's Special whose 90mph-plus top speed aroused considerable interest, but the war intervened.

In the 'twenties, thanks to the energy and imagination of Alfred Scott, liquid-cooled two-stroke twins such as this were the machines to have. But the last Squirrels were little more advanced than those of a generation earlier.

Indian Chief

For many years the Indian name evoked American motorcycling quite as vividly as Harley-Davidson does today. Founded by George Hendee and Oscar Hedstrom in 1901 – even earlier than Harley – the Springfield, Massachusetts company's first model was a 1³/4 horsepower single. Yet just a decade later an Indian ridden by OC Godfrey became the first overseas machine to win the Isle of Man TT. Numerous other competition successes followed, particularly in the uniquely American sports of flat-track and board racing. There were laurels, too, in long-distance ordeals, where men like Erwin 'Cannonball' Baker achieved almost legendary status.

Nor were Indian averse to novelty. They offered early forms of electric start and rear suspension before World War I. They even built engines with four valves per cylinder – although the 'Big Valve' two-valve 1000 of 1919 proved to be faster. In the early 'twenties they built an experimental overhead camshaft 500, although this never raced and it was on a sidevalve Indian that Freddie Dixon placed third in the 1923 TT. The last racer to come out of the factory, a 1948 'Big Base' 750 V-twin, was still going strong on American half miles into the late '60s. More remarkable still, the same Indian Scout that had set a speed record in 1931 was last seen racing at Sacramento in 1968.

Despite this endeavour, Indian fell into the first of many financial crises as early as 1919. The machine which rescued them then was to form the backbone of their range for decades. The 600cc Scout stood out in a market dominated by heavyweight 1000cc machines (although a 1000cc Indian Chief followed). It was light (300lbs), smooth and agile, with a full electrical system, all-chain drive and three-speed gearbox. Nonetheless the Scout retained the traditional 'suicide' foot clutch and hand-operated gearchange. And although it wore two brakes, both acted on the rear wheel. It wasn't until 1928 that a Harley became the first American motorcycle to 'pioneer' the front brake.

On acquiring the Ace motorcycle company in 1927, Indian began production of a range of in-line fours which were to become almost as uniquely Indian as its twins. Although the Vee-twin is now thought of as the definitive American engine configuration, for many years a host of US manufacturers, notably Henderson, produced such behemoths. Paradoxically, the Danish Nimbus featured on page 10 was the last of this breed.

In 1940 both the twins and the fours gained sprung rear ends, nine years before Harley were to follow suit with the Hydra-Glide. Yet the 'forties also saw an ill-advised attempt to build vertical twins in the Triumph mould. Indian's elderly designs certainly needed modernising, but this was not the way. The vertical twins proved to be unreliable and unpopular, imposing a huge financial strain on the troubled Indian company.

If it looks like a Harley, that's because it did a similar job over the same terrain. The 1308cc side-valve engine was as rugged as it was crude, but failed to meet the performance expectations of the post-war generation.

'The same Indian Scout that had set a speed record in 1931 was last seen racing at Sacramento in 1968.'

Early Indians toyed with overhead cams and four valves-per-cylinder. But by the 'twenties, let alone the 'fifties, Indian's early taste for novelty and experiment had long worn off. Ironically, Harley now prosper recreating the same 'iron horse' image.

In 1949 the 1200cc Chief was enlarged to become the 1300cc juggernaut pictured. However, quality was poor and sales sluggish, and in August 1953 the once-mighty company ceased motorcycle production. Instead, the Indian name degenerated into a sales device for re-badged British machines. At one time or another, AJS, Douglas, Excelsior, Matchless, Norton, Royal Enfield, Velocette and Vincents have all worn the familiar Indian Chief tank badge. Indeed, the engine of the Rickman Interceptor featured on page 64 had originally been destined to wear an Indian timing cover in the USA.

At the end of the 'seventies, yet another tribe of 'Indians' appeared. Assembled at the Italian Italjet factory, using Italian cycle parts but British Velocette Venom engines, these were the brainchild of Floyd Clymer, of Clymer workshop manual fame. When this venture folded after Clymer's (and Velocette's) death, the Indian rights passed to a Los Angeles company who embarked on the first of two failed attempts to sell Taiwanese mopeds under the old Springfield name. Yet for all these undignified failures, the Indian name continues to hold a resonant attraction to motorcyclists. It is currently being linked to a Vee-twin machine being designed for Indian by John Britten in New Zealand.

SPECIFICATION: INDIAN CHIEF	
ENGINE	air-cooled 1308cc OHV Vee-twin
HORSEPOWER	50bhp @ 4800rpm
TRANSMISSION	3-speed, hand change
FRAME	duplex tubular steel cradle
BRAKES	drum/drum
TOP SPEED	90mph

Norton International

....

*I*f the Manx Norton was one of the most famous racing motorcycles of all time, then the International must be one of the most legendary roadsters. In fact, they were substantially the same machine, differentiated at the factory by the name scribbled on the job-card. 'Manx' simply meant racing specification, whilst 'Inter' referred to a roadster with lights. Nonetheless, many Inters found themselves stripped down for racing. Over half a century before Suzuki's GSX-R750 re-worked the theme, these were the 'race replicas' of their day.

The precursor of both was the Norton CS1, a 490cc 'fast tourer' which itself derived from the works machine on which Stanley Woods had emphatically led the 1927 TT until retiring with clutch failure. Fortunately for Norton, Alec Bennett

A bevel-driven overhead camshaft (the works racers later had two) was the most exotic touch to the 500cc Inter engine. The system demanded far more expert setting-up than chain-driven valvegear designs.

rode a second machine rather more circumspectly, winning at an average speed of 68.41mph.

Overhead camshafts were new to Norton, whose previous racing success was achieved with pushrod engines. But the success of overhead camshaft designs from Velocette and Blackburne spurred Walter Moore to design the classy 'cammy' Norton single. When a production version was unveiled at the 1927 motorcycle show, the 'CS' of the name stood for 'camshaft' for, like the Inter and Manx which were to succeed it, the CS1 boasted an overhead camshaft driven by shaft and bevel gears.

However, by 1929 the new Norton racer was already being eclipsed, and Arthur Carroll set about the redesign which was to create the immortal Manx. A road-going version was first offered to the public in 1932, and the Inter was born. Almost at once it was tested at 100mph, an astonishing speed for a half litre machine at the time. Buoyed by the continued track success of its factory racing siblings, the International became the definitive sporting machine of its era.

'The
International
became the
definitive
sporting
machine of its
era.'

The example pictured is an unrestored 1952 'Garden Gate' International, one of the last before the legendary Featherbed chassis gave the cammy single a brief new lease of life.

Factory versions of the cammy Norton engine went on to win no less than seven Senior TTs in the 'thirties, raising the lap record from 76 to over 90mph in the process. 350cc versions of the same engine were no less successful. Yet perhaps the biggest accolade for the roadster came in 1939. With the factory pre-occupied with military affairs, Norton's TT effort centred around six privateers riding – what else? – stripped-down Internationals.

The 'thirties, undoubtedly, was the Inter's heyday. But just as the factory Norton racers had to fight hard to remain competitive after 1950, so the Inter felt the weight of competition from a new generation of machines. Not the least of these came from Norton itself. The 497cc Dominator launched in 1948 offered a comparable level of performance in a machine that was far cleaner, easier to maintain, and cheaper to produce. Of all the methods of driving overhead camshafts, bevel gears are the most intricate, which is why belt or chain drive is preferred today. Inters, moreover, retained their messy exposed valve springs to the end.

The Inter, along with the rest of the Norton range, had acquired telescopic forks from 1948. The next development came in 1953 with the introduction of an alloy cylinder barrel, improved gearbox, better brakes and – above all – the renowned Featherbed frame. Whilst this marked a quantum leap in the Inter's roadholding, the same was true of Norton's sporting twins. Nonetheless, stripped-down Inters were still popular amongst racing privateers, but even here a threat was looming. 1952 had brought Clubman's TT victories for BSA's emerging Gold Star in both 350 and 500cc classes. Although the Featherbed Inter resumed it's rightful place in claiming the 1953 500cc Clubman's TT, the Gold Star went on to sweep all before it. From then on, the Norton International faded quietly away, last being listed in the 1958 Norton catalogue at £303.2.10d.

More than any other design, Norton were associated with highly-tuned overhead cam singles. The 'Inter' was a rare chance to use one on the road.

SPECIFICATION: NORTON INTERNATIONAL	
ENGINE	air-cooled 497cc OHC single
HORSEPOWER	up to 46bhp
TRANSMISSION	4-speed
FRAME	'Garden Gate' tubular steel cradle
BRAKES	drum/drum
TOP SPEED	up to 120mph in racing trim

Sunbeam S7/S8

....

'This 'magnificent' creation was overweight, slow, fairly thirsty, looked weird, didn't handle and soon attracted a reputation for unreliability.'

This was to be the jewel in the crown of post-war British motorcycling, and it had the full weight of the giant BSA Group behind it. During the war years, BSA acquired two things; the Sunbeam name, and a captured German BMW R75 outfit. As the war was coming to a conclusion, BSA recognised that they needed a flagship model, and set about creating one under the Sunbeam banner, which had always been associated with 'gentlemen's conveyances'

Erling Poppe, essentially a car man, was the project's chief designer, and the resulting machine adopted much from automotive technology. It borrowed even more from the BMW – frame and running gear layout, dynamo, brakes, wheels and tyre sizes, and the concept of a shaft-drive twin with the gearbox behind the engine. Unfortunately the one vital German piece that was not purloined turned out to be the Sunbeam's downfall.

BSA might also have pinched BMW's flat-twin engine, but that would have been a little too obvious. Instead, Poppe designed a new powerplant, still a twin with the crankshaft fore-and-aft, but now with cylinders in-line astern rather than opposed. Astonishingly, this was the only new overhead cam motorcycle engine to go into production in post-war Britain until the (even more ill-fated) Hesketh in 1981.

Poppe also designed a new four-speed gearbox with bevels allowing the kick-start to be sited much less awkwardly than the Bee-eM's. Unfortunately this meant ditching the proven crown-and-pinion final drive in favour of an underslung worm gear. Apparently the choice was made because the BSA Group, which also produced Daimler and Lanchester cars, was familiar with making this type of drive!

BSA leaked details of the new machine liberally, as well as presenting one to Field Marshal 'Monty' Montgomery of Alamein. Such was the sense of anticipation, and so great the curious crowd, that at the 1948 Motor Cycle Show the Sunbeam stand collapsed under the weight!

Yet this excitement was sadly misplaced. Early prototypes of what was actually a fairly free-breathing and potent engine had already shown that final drive worm gears lasted no more than 5000 miles. Rather than address the real problem, Sunbeam designed an entirely new cylinder head to reduce power. The resulting 23.6bhp, allied to a dry weight of 435lb, left the S7 serious under-motivated.

There was more. An early batch of S7s rushed out to South Africa had to be recalled when vibration proved too severe. Later examples had rubber-mounted engines (and a corrosion-prone

SPECIFICATION: SUNBEAM S7/S8

ENGINE	air-cooled 487cc OHC tandem twin
HORSEPOWER	26bhp @ 5800rpm (S8)
TRANSMISSION	4-speed
FRAME	tubular twin loop
BRAKES	drum/drum
TOP SPEED	80mph

flexible exhaust section) – and the handling, on those fat 4.75 x 16 tyres, was distinctly odd (and gave the S7 the look, according to a contemporary report, of 'a motor trapped between two doughnuts').

Billed as 'The world's most magnificent motor cycle', the S7 went on sale in 1947 at the very high price of £222. This 'magnificent' creation was overweight, slow, fairly thirsty, looked weird, didn't handle and soon attracted a reputation for unreliability. Only around 2000 S7s were made before 1949 when the heavily reworked 'sports' S8 and S7 De Luxe were introduced.

Both received numerous engine changes (notably a bigger oil capacity), and the S8 adopted BSA A10 wheels and forks but retained plunger rear suspension. The S8 was about 5mph quicker and

30lb lighter than its predecessor. Ridden prudently, it proved reliable, but pedestrian – that flawed final drive was more dependable, but it still soaked up power. Arguably it is the 'dignity' of its performance (and the snootiness of Sunbeam dealers), as much as anything aristocratic in its design, that gave the Sunbeam the aura of gentleman's carriage.

Still, the 'Beam began to sell, and by December 1952, 10,000 had been built. From then on sales steadily declined, and the range was dropped when BSA and Triumph merged in late '56. The attempt to produce the first post-war superbike had failed.

Quiet, smooth and clean, the shaft-drive S8 'gentleman's carriage' was the nearest thing to a British BMW.

Although the only British overhead cam roadster to go into production between the war and 1981, the Sunbeam's development – and its potential – was fudged.

Vincent 1000 Series C

'Every red-blooded motorcyclist aspired to owning one, yet very few could.'

They still speak of the ghosts of Vincent Vee-twins thundering down the Stevenage by-pass. Long before the expression was coined, 'the world's fastest standard production machine' was in every way a superbike; fast, technically advanced and brutally good-looking.

Although now associated most of all with *that* engine, Vincent had originally used proprietary power plants from the likes of Blackburne and JAP. After a duff batch of JAP engines was foisted on him at the 1934 TT, Phil Vincent resolved never to be dependent on outside engine suppliers again.

Although Vincent was himself a brilliant and innovative designer, the resulting engines were the work of the ingenious Australian, Phil Irving. Irving first produced the Meteor, a high-camshaft 499cc single capable of 90mph in sports 'Comet' form. Then came the big 'un, essentially a brace of 499cc Meteor top-ends arranged in a 47 degree Vee on a common crankcase. This became the Series A, dubbed the 'plumber's nightmare' due to an abundance of external oil pipes.

Breathtaking though it was, the Series A had several problems – the wheelbase, at 59 inches, was ponderously long; and, worst of all, no proprietory clutch or gearbox could handle its prodigious torque.

The result was the post-war Series B Rapide. The transmission was uprated by the use of an ingenious self servo clutch, and a new gearbox was designed in-unit with the engine. The latter was not only sturdier than its predecessor, but shorter. A radical new 'frame' – basically a box joining steering head and rear sub-frame, with the engine as a stressed member – allowed Vincent to dispense with

Vincent horsepower tested the technology of the time – in transmissions, brakes, tyres and suspension – to the absolute limit. Maintenance had to be similarly painstaking.

DCH 412

VINCENT

front downtubes, further shortening the wheelbase. When the Rapide arrived in 1946, this stood at a relatively nimble 56 inches.

Meanwhile the Vee was increased to 50 degrees, allowing both the use of a standard Lucas magneto, and better location for the carburettor float bowls.

The Rapide was better in every way than the Series A, and with 45bhp and 110mph, at least as rapid. The first Black Shadow, in 1948, claimed 55bhp on 'pool' petrol – or a staggering 100bhp on racing methanol. In 1949 the Series C arrived, with Vincent Girdraulic forks in place of Brampton girders (but retaining Vincent's novel Series A triangulated rear suspension), and began re-writing the record books the world over.

Irving's post-war engine design survived the next nine years, from Series B to Series D, fundamentally unchanged. Produced in touring, sports and racing guises as the Rapide, Black Shadow and Black Lightning respectively, its performance remained unequalled by any production motorcycle until well into the 'seventies. Every red-blooded motorcyclist aspired to owning

one, yet very few could; the hand-crafted Vincent was always prohibitively expensive.

Times became particularly hard in 1954. Vincent's response, on the one hand, was to manufacture NSU mopeds and commuter machines under licence at the Stevenage factory. More humiliating still, these were marketed under the Vincent name.

His other response was to ask his customers, the Vincent Owners' Club, what they wanted from the forthcoming Series D. For any manufacturer this is always a risky practice, and so it proved. Series D duly arrived in the form of the Black Knight and Black Prince, successors to the Rapide and Shadow respectively. Some details, notably coil ignition, were better. But both models were fully enclosed, like giant black scooters. The public was horrified.

Series D was quickly reintroduced with 'proper' naked Vincents, and almost everyone was happy. But this costly U-turn was the factory's last major act. Sales were tumbling and costs rising, and in 1955 Vincent closed their gates for the last time. The big black Vee-twins are no more. But the legend lives on.

A top speed of 125mph made the Black Shadow comfortably the fastest machine of its age – indeed, nothing very much faster would appear for 20 years.

SPECIFICATION: VINCENT 1000 SERIES C	
ENGINE	air-cooled 998cc OHV Vee-twin
HORSEPOWER	55bhp @ 5500rpm
TRANSMISSION	4-speed
FRAME	backbone box-section, engine as stressed member
BRAKES	Double drum/double drum
TOP SPEED	125mph

Moto Guzzi Falcone Sport

Like Triumph's twins, in one form or another this quintessential Moto Guzzi single spanned the entire 25-year range of this book. Yet even when the 'fifties began, it was not essentially new. The Italian company's very first prototype machine, in the days when they were known as Guzzi and Parodi, was a horizontal single not a great deal different from the Falcone. The year was 1920.

For its time, the single was very advanced. It used a short-stroke engine of 498.4cc, with a single overhead cam driven by bevel gears in the manner of later Manx Nortons. Most radical of all was its four-valve head. However, by the time production versions were announced in December 1920, both the company name had changed – to the familiar Moto Guzzi – and the machine's specification had been downgraded. It now used push-rod operation of just two valves, and went on sale in 1921 as the Moto Guzzi *Tipo Normale* – Standard Model.

The original four-valve design later appeared as a racing machine, winning first time out in the 1924 *Circuit del Lario*. Thus began a long tradition of Moto Guzzi track success, mostly based on light, aerodynamic singles. From 1947 until the rise of NSU in 1954, their 250 single was well-nigh

unbeatable; and in taking the world title from 1953–57, their 350 single showed the virtue of simplicity in defying the mighty MV and Gilera fours. Yet at the other extreme, there was the awesome 500cc Vee-8, a supercharged transverse four as early as 1930, and numerous other twins, triples and fours.

Guzzi's roadsters, however, took the simple route. When the Falcone was first introduced in 1950, it was little more than a tuned version of the 1949 Astore tourer, which itself had much in common with the original *Normale* of 1921. A flat single with the same 88 x 82mm short-stroke layout, compared to the Astore, the Falcone had a bigger carburettor, higher compression ratio, hotter camshaft and lighter con rod. Power had risen from 19bhp at 4300rpm to 23bhp at 4500. A characteristic of both engines was their large external flywheel, a means of achieving considerable flywheel effect (necessary in a single), without an equally considerable weight penalty.

The Falcone dispensed with the Astore's legshields, also adopting flatter handlebars and more rear-set footrests. In keeping with its sporting pretensions, the rear springs were both shorter and stiffer than before. Although the rear suspension

If it doesn't move, paint it scarlet! Falcone was an antique, even in the 'fifties, but a glorious one. Note the low engine, reminiscent of later Aermacchis, and the 'upside down' front forks: very few motorcycling novelties are actually new.

The Mandello eagle has probably graced a greater variety of engine layouts than any other European logo.

used a triangulated swing-arm, the general design dated from 1928 and employed a crude friction damping system. The springs, four in all, live in a box under the engine – not unlike Harley-Davidson's current Softail 'retro' design.

Equally 'modern but dated' were the telescopic front forks. These were of the 'upside-down' type, adjustable – yet first appeared on the 250cc Airone of 1947. Meanwhile the frame, an odd collection of steel tube and plate, splits in two in the manner of several much later Bimotas.

In 1953, when the Falcone Turismo replaced the Astore, Guzzi officially christened the existing model the Falcone Sport. Of all the many versions of the post-1950 single, a genuine Sport is the rarest, most prized – and most imitated. Collectors beware!

For all its ancient origins, the Falcone went well for an early 'fifties machine. Quicker than all but a handful of the most raucous British sports singles, it was smooth, comfortable, with a plush and well-damped ride which belied its dated suspension.

Yet as the years passed, Guzzi singles changed little. Increasingly old-fashioned, they were mainly bought by civil and military authorities in their native Italy. A new, but broadly similar, Nuovo Falcone was launched for police and military use in 1969, and offered to the public two years later. It sold poorly and was dropped in 1976.

SPECIFICATION: MOTO GUZZI FALCONE	
ENGINE	air-cooled 498cc OHV flat single
HORSEPOWER	23bhp @ 4500rpm
TRANSMISSION	4-speed
FRAME	tubular/plate, twin downtubes
BRAKES	drum/drum
TOP SPEED	85mph

Ubiquitous Guzzi outside flywheel design allowed considerable flywheel effect without the penalty of heavy internal flywheels.

'For all its ancient origins, the Falcone went well for an early 'fifties machine.'

Ariel Square Four

*I*n the days before Italy, and then Japan proved otherwise, mounting an in-line four cylinder engine in anything but a touring motorcycle posed an insurmountable problem: mount it longitudinally, and the bike was too long; transversely, and it was unacceptably wide. So any four with sporting pretensions required a different layout.

This was the thinking of a young engineer in a small machine shop in Dulwich, South London. His response? A 497cc overhead cam square four. His name? Edward Turner, later to find fame as the designer of Triumph's immortal Speed Twin.

Turner hawked his engine around several manufacturers until Jack Sangster of Ariel decided to give it a chance. The resulting prototype, housed (with room to spare) in a 500 'sloper' frame, was the sensation of the Olympia motor cycle show. The year was just 1930.

The 497cc engine, essentially two vertical twins on a common crankcase, comprised paired transverse crankshafts, geared together at their centres. A chain on the right side of the engine drove both a magdyno and the single overhead camshaft. The wet-sump crankcases split horizontally. It was an astonishingly light and compact design which delivered most of what Turner had set out to achieve. The whole machine weighed only 330lbs.

Throughout its life, however, the 'Squariel' had one major weakness. The cylinder head was prone to distortion, as the rear cylinders sat in the heat shadow of the front ones, and the provision of cooling air around the head was always marginal. On early examples this was exacerbated by inadequate lubrication. Early attempts to race the

Undoubtedly still a Superbike in the 'fifties, the 1000cc Squariel was even more so when this girder-forked example was built in 1937. Post-war changes, including telescopic front suspension and plunger rear, were insufficient to keep the big four competitive.

Rear cylinders of the Square four engine (above) tended to run hot, so it was only suited to low-stressed touring use, for which its top gear pulling power was ideal.
The Squariels pictured left are a rigid-framed 1946 4G model and a 1957 4G MkII with plunger rear end.

four, albeit in supercharged form, were plagued by problems of heads warping. Although a normally-aspirated version managed to take the coveted Maudes Trophy by covering 700 miles in 668 minutes, overheating and the inefficient 'cruciform' inlet tract would always impose a limit on the Squariel's performance.

When the machine went on sale it cost £70. A year later, a bored 597cc version was displayed at Olympia, but shortly afterwards the Depression hit the British economy. In 1937 a less ambitious range of fours was launched. Available in both 597 (the 4F) and 997cc (4G) form, these featured push-rod valve actuation, vertically-split crankcases and, partly to suit sidecar use, very much heavier flywheels. The 4G produced 38bhp at 5500rpm. In 1939, a clever form of plunger rear suspension was added.

After the war the 600cc Squariel was dropped, and by 1948 the 1000 had developed telescopic forks. Thanks largely to a new light alloy cylinder head and block, weight was down by some 33lb, but this was still a 500lb machine – and it still ran very hot.

1954 brought the final Square Four, the MkII 'four-piper'. Power had risen to 42bhp, but plunger rear suspension was retained in an age when

swinging forks were becoming commonplace on machines of this price. In 1958, the last Squariel rolled off the Selly Oak production line. To remain competitive the four would have needed expensive and radical surgery, and the money was needed for a new generation of mould-breaking Ariels, the Leader range of two-stroke twins.

Ariel's Square Four, like the Sunbeam twin produced down the road at Redditch, was another case of 'Nice try, but no cigar'. Both were clever and advanced designs, yet both were fatally flawed. Of the two, perhaps the Ariel best deserves the epithet 'superbike'. It was smooth, effortless and, above all, imposing. It attracted a certain mystique (so much so that a much revised Square Four, the Healy 1000, was produced in limited numbers in the mid-'seventies). Yet in the end, far from liberating British motorcycle manufacturers from the yoke of the vertical twin, it probably deterred them from departing from what they knew best. It is surely the ultimate irony that one man, Edward Turner, was responsible for both.

SPECIFICATION: ARIEL SQUARE FOUR	
ENGINE	air-cooled 997cc OHV square four
HORSEPOWER	42bhp @ 5800rpm
TRANSMISSION	4-speed
FRAME	tubular single loop
BRAKES	drum/drum
TOP SPEED	100mph

Douglas Dragonfly

'In many ways it was a sophisticated yet rugged design.'

The Dragonfly was the final model produced during the chequered and diverse history of the Douglas factory. As well as producing motorcycles, the Kingswood, Bristol company built aero and stationery engines, Vespa scooters, trucks and even dabbled with cars.

Douglas, despite their rather staid reputation, began their days with competition success. Within three years of producing their first motorcycle in 1907, they took the coveted team prize in the International Six Days Trial. Two years later, WH Bashall brought them their first TT win, the 1912 Junior. Such triumphs paved the way to making the company a major manufacturer during World War I, supplying the army with some 70,000 machines.

Further successes followed – first 500cc machine to lap Brooklands at 100mph in 1921; Senior TT victory in 1923 (with a form of disc brake); Sidecar TT laurels the same year. 'Duggies' had become so established that even King George VI acquired one. Whatever else they might offer, 'the best twins' always exuded an aura of class.

Throughout these years, until the end of production in 1957, Douglas championed opposed twin engine layouts, either transverse (like BMW) or, in the early years, fore-and-aft. But the post-war years hit Douglas severely, and in 1948 the receiver was called in, forcing the company to 'rationalise' with a line of models all based on the same 350cc flat twin. At the time, the decision seemed sound. The 1949 'Sports' model was timed at 84mph, allowing Douglas to dub it the world's 'fastest 350 roadster'. But by the time the Dragonfly succeeded the 'Mark' series in 1954, things were very different.

The Dragonfly featured horizontally opposed cylinders and a car-type single plate clutch, but chain final drive. Earles-type Reynolds front forks complemented swing-arm rear suspension, and the novel styling included a headlamp faired into the large petrol tank.

In many ways it was a sophisticated yet rugged design. Cooling was good, the gear cam drive robust, and clutch action uncharacteristically light for the period. Handling and steering was light yet precise, it toured well, and the brakes were good for the time. And, gentlemanly though they were, they also revved, at least in race trim; the last-ever official Douglas TT entry was by a special 90 Plus model in 1954. This spun to 11,000rpm, developed 31bhp, and was timed at 108mph. But, although Duggies had been highly competitive in production-based clubman's racing in the immediate post-war years, by now they had been comprehensively eclipsed. The new clubman's king was BSA's Gold Star.

This was the problem – the Dragonfly was an expensive machine, but it was heavy (365lb), no faster than the MkV it replaced, and failed to satisfy an increasing yearning for performance. Paupers could certainly not afford them, and princes were no longer interested.

Unmistakably Douglas: smooth, refined and idiosyncratic.

At the 1951 Motorcycle Show, Douglas had responded with a 500cc prototype, but even this was not quick and never went into production. However, certain elements – enclosed engine styling, in the manner of BMW, along with a stiffer crankshaft and crankcases and improved lubrication – found a home on the Dragonfly. But, handsome and civilised though it was, the public was unimpressed. Sales were poor, and the Dragonfly was now the only egg in the company's motorcycle basket. Indeed, Douglas' new owners, Westinghouse, seemed more interested in the

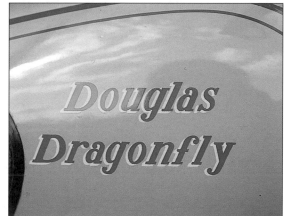

Once the choice of kings, but as the horsepower race gathered momentum in the 'fifties, the 350cc boxer became unable to compete with much faster vertical twins.

production of Vespa scooters than the regeneration of the motorcycle range, and by the time motorcycle production ceased in 1957, only 1570 Dragonflies had been built. What was left of the company, Douglas (Sales and Service) Ltd., continued to import and assemble Vespa scooters and later Gilera motorcycles.

SPECIFICATION: DOUGLAS DRAGONFLY	
ENGINE	air-cooled OHV 348cc flat twin
HORSEPOWER	17bhp @ 5500rpm
TRANSMISSION	4-speed
FRAME	tubular double cradle
BRAKES	drum/drum
TOP SPEED	72mph

Triumph 650 6T Thunderbird

Triumph's 650 Thunderbird, first launched in 1949, is probably the single machine best known to the post-war generation. For this was the bike ridden so defiantly by Marlon Brando in the 1952 film *The Wild One* ('What are you rebelling against, Johnny?' 'Whaddya got?').

The T-bird also linked two eras. Its engine was the first substantial development of Edward Turner's famous Speed Twin design of 1937 – the machine which was to make parallel twins the mainstay of motorcycle design for over 30 years. Later, even Japan's first attempts at entering the big bike market aped the British layout; Kawasaki's 650cc twin was a near-copy of BSA's A65, although Yamaha's XS1 boasted one

overhead camshaft, whilst Honda's CB450 was the first roadster with two.

Yet in pumping out the twin from 500 to 650cc, Turner believed this to be the limit for the design if vibration was not to become excessive. Later 750cc versions (not to mention Norton's 850 Commando), would probably have surprised him. Most riders agree, however, that 650cc was the ideal compromise between smoothness and power.

Although nominally a post-war machine, the T-bird arrived at a time of austerity in Britain, with rationing still in force. The same constraints affected motorcycle manufacturing, although Triumph began the period with a TT victory for Ernie Lyons on a Tiger 100, the sports version of the 500cc Speed Twin. The Thunderbird itself was launched with an impressive publicity stunt. Three machines were ridden to the French race track at Montlhéry, put through 500 laps at an average of

SPECIFICATION: TRIUMPH 650 6T THUNDERBIRD	
ENGINE	air-cooled 649cc parallel twin
HORSEPOWER	34bhp @ 6300rpm
TRANSMISSION	4-speed
FRAME	tubular twin cradle
BRAKES	drum/drum
TOP SPEED	103mph

The Thunderbird – this is a 1956 example – was a response to American demand for more capacity and performance. The result put genuine 'ton-up' potential within reach of the ordinary working man for perhaps the first time.

1950 500cc Triumph Speed Twin (far left), precursor of the T'bird. Telescopic forks aside, this is essentially the machine with which Edward Turner launched a generation of British vertical twins.

90mph (with flying laps at over 100mph), then ridden home again. One such machine resides in the Beaulieu motorcycle museum.

In essence the early T-bird was identical to the contemporary Speed Twin, itself substantially a pre-war design, other than the extra 150cc and a change of colour. The air-cooled engine is separate from the gearbox, linked by an enclosed single-row chain. Valve actuation is by push rods from paired camshafts fore and aft of the crankcase mouth.

Rear suspension was by Triumph's ubiquitous sprung hub, for the rear swinging fork had barely arrived. Oil-damped telescopic forks of Triumph design had first replaced girder suspension on the 1946 Speed Twin. Overall, the Thunderbird was a lighter machine than most in its class, with the lively acceleration typical of the marque.

The extra capacity, though, was vital. Consumers, particularly in America, were increasingly demanding more power, and the 650 supplied it in becoming perhaps the first affordable 'ton up' machine. For Triumph, additional costs were modest, and even in the shops the difference between 500 and 650cc was a mere £10, the T-bird costing just £194 when introduced. Other British manufacturers soon followed suit.

When launched, the T-bird was almost in a performance class of its own, and certainly nothing could come near it at the price. In the USA, this frightened Harley-Davidson so much they went to astonishing (but unsuccessful) lengths to thwart Triumph sales. Yet just as the Tiger 100 had evolved as the high-performance version of the Speed Twin, so the need was clear for an even hotter version of the T-bird.

The result was first the Tiger 110 of 1954, then the legendary Bonneville 120, dealt with in a later

It looks sedate now, but in the 'fifties the Triumph's acceleration, handling and brakes were in a different league from Stateside competition, precipitating some underhand tactics from Harley-Davidson.

chapter. Development of the T-bird continued, adding swing-arm rear suspension, light alloy cylinder heads, more power (37bhp by 1960), better brakes and, in 1963, unit construction. By then the controversial 'bathtub' rear bodywork had been largely accepted, as the original concept gave way to a handsome, more civilised touring design. But even 46 years on, the evocative legacy of the Thunderbird name lingers on, in the 900cc triple of born-again Triumph.

'When launched, the T'bird was almost in a performance class of its own.'

Gilera 500-4 Racer

....

'Part of the machine's continued competitiveness lay in its aerodynamics.'

Gilera, like their Italian competitors MV Agusta, had aristocratic beginnings. In 1909 the Arcore company was founded by Count Giuseppe Gilera, rapidly making its mark as a producer of high-quality singles. But it was for high-revving racing fours that the company is best remembered.

Between the start of the world championship in 1949, and 1957 when they pulled out of racing, Gilera won a remarkable 33 *grands prix*, three manufacturers' championships and six world titles.

The basis for the success was Count Gilera's 1936 acquisition of the Rondine four-cylinder engine, which was itself based on the 1926 OPRA push-rod design. The supercharged Rondine featured double overhead camshafts and liquid

cooling. A year later a development of this engine brought Gilera a world speed record of 170mph at the hands of development engineer Piero Taruffi – a success a certain Mr Mussolini was not slow to exploit. In 1939 Dorino Serafini won the 500cc European championship on a similar machine.

Despite inferior handling, the post-war ban on supercharging theoretically favoured Gilera's multi against the opposition singles and twins. Pietro Remor was responsible for redesigning the four into air-cooled, normally-aspirated form. In 1949, two *grand prix* wins brought Nello Pagani and Gilera second place in the inaugural championship. A year later Umberto Masetti went one better, but in 1951 the irrepressible Geoff Duke brought Norton's 500 single their first title. Masetti won again in '52, but for the following year Gilera covered all bases by recruiting Duke to ride the 500. The Englishman took the title in each of the next three years. The 1956 crown went to another British legend, John Surtees, on another Italian four, the MV, before Libero Liberati brought Gilera their last title in

Perhaps the most influential post-war four-stroke engine: from this original Gilera racer can be traced a line via MV, Benelli and Honda to the multi-cylinder Superbikes of today.

1957. In the same year, Bob McIntyre made history when his 500 Gilera became the first machine to lap the Isle of Man TT course at 100mph.

Gilera returned to racing with much the same machinery in 1963, under Duke's *Scuderia Duke* banner. The venture lasted only one season, but it was a measure of the bike's prowess that John Hartle, Phil Read and Derek Minter brought the six year-old hardware to second place in the manufacturers' championship.

Part of the machine's continued competitiveness lay in its aerodynamics. Although the same Pietro Remor was responsible for both engines, the Gilera enjoyed a considerably more compact engine than the MV four, with more efficient and stable streamlining. The Gilera is a mere 15 1/2 inches wide at the crankcases, which split horizontally and contain a built-up roller bearing crankshaft running on six main bearings. The lower left frame rail demounts for engine removal, again permitting a more compact overall design. Each of the cylinder barrels is a separate casting. Its twin overhead camshafts were driven by a central train of gears from the crankshaft.

Although this was a long-stroke design, less revvy and more driveable than later MV and Benelli fours,

its four small cylinders allowed a compression ratio of 11:1 and maximum revs around 11,000. Four 28mm carbs were employed, with four crackling megaphone exhausts at the rear. The Gilera pictured is a 1957 five-speed machine, although an experimental seven-speeder later followed.

Gilera was taken over by Piaggio in 1970, concentrating on small capacity commuter and off-road machines. The early '90s saw an abortive return to 250cc *grand prix* racing. Then, in 1994, the parent company allowed this once great name to die in the name of 'rationalisation'.

As the first of the post-war fours to achieve racing success, the Gilera enjoys a special place in racing history. It would be the Japanese who first put a comparable machine into large scale production, and today the transverse four is by far the most common high-performance format. But it was those fiery Italians who first showed the way.

Remor's masterpiece splits horizontally like later MV-four, with six main bearings carried in magnesium upper crankcase half. The MV was some 1 1/4 inches wider.

SPECIFICATION: GILERA 500-4 RACER	
ENGINE	air-cooled 499cc DOHC four
HORSEPOWER	70bhp @ 10,500rpm
TRANSMISSION	5- or 7-speed
FRAME	tubular steel twin cradle
BRAKES	double drum/drum
TOP SPEED	155mph (over 165mph with dustbin fairing)

Compact Gilera four is astonishingly small, with efficient aerodynamics and a top speed close to 170mph. Weight is around 330lbs.

BMW R69

Of all the 1950s motorcycles in this book, BMW's is the one most readily identifiable today. The Bavarian company has been inextricably associated with horizontally-opposed, shaft-drive twins since Max Friz' original design of 1923. They have equally been associated with high prices and top-quality engineering.

In the late 'fifties, this was almost to prove BMW's downfall. With motorcycle sales plummeting at home, and burdened with the cost of development of a range of small cars, Bee-eM was practically bankrupt. Fortunately the banks bailed them out long enough for the four-wheelers to begin to make their mark – and marks – and the future began to look rosier.

The R69 produced throughout this difficult period was a descendant of the 1951 R67, the company's first 600cc overhead valve twin. Producing 26bhp, the R67 boasted telescopic forks (which, with the 750cc R12 of 1935, BMW had been the first major manufacturer to fit) but rather dated plunger rear suspension.

With the arrival of the R69 in 1955, the teles gave way to pivoted 'Earles-type' front suspension which was then becoming fashionable. At the rear, a new swing-arm set-up was adopted, although at first glance the frame looked like the old plunger trellis. The rebuildable shock absorbers mounted on horns rising up from the main frame rails, which itself swept down close to the rear spindle as before. A rubber sprung saddle mounted airily behind the classic black tank, adding to the dated appearance. A sports version, the R69S, was added in 1960.

Compared to the R67, the 69 had a hotter cam, higher compression pistons, larger carbs and valves, a sports gearbox and nine more horsepower, but was still essentially the same design. Although extremely well-built, with a sturdy pressed-up crank with roller-bearing big-end and main bearings, lubrication is crude and frequent oil-changes essential. The main bearings, which tolerated some whip in the crankshaft, were of a type later to appear as 'Superblend' bearings on later 750cc Norton Commandos. Looked after, the R69 could, like most of its successors, offer prodigious trouble-free mileages.

The R69, with full swing-arm rear suspension and Earles-type forks, was the first 'modern' Beemer twin. Its high price and sheer build quality did much to create BMW's reputation as builders of 'bespoke' motorcycles. This is a 1966 R69S.

Some idea of the painstaking production process is hinted by the availability of cam drive gears in a wide range of sizes to ensure perfect meshing. Not surprisingly, later Bee-eMs adopted chain driven camshafts.

Mechanically, with its heavy cast iron cylinders and needle-roller rockers, the R69 is commendably smooth and quiet. Power, even in 'sport' guise was modest, making the Bee-eM a far more pedestrian

machine than contemporary British hot twins. The Earles-type forks, too, were more suited to sidecar than solo use, where they give a vagueness that good teles avoid.

It was, however, a comfortable machine ideally suited to long-distance work on its native autobahns. Despite its weight (445lb ready to roll), it was low and manageable. Above all, it was civilised and, in that uniquely BMW manner, at the same time conservative and defiantly odd. And its price tag was definitely in the superbike league.

As the 'sixties began, the R69 gave way to the /2 twins, which featured detail revisions but were still very much in the same 'fifties mould. Major changes had to wait until 1969 and the R60/5. This, along with its 5-series siblings the 500cc 50/5 and 750cc R75/5, was an altogether more modern-looking machine, with more power, electric start and styling which would last into the eighties. For 1974 the /5 gave way to the five-speed 6 series, now in 600, 750 and 900cc, the latter the 'ultimate' R90S featured on page 84. The last of BMW's 600s was the R60/7 of 1978.

This R60/2 succeeded the 69-series in 1967, but is just as unmistakably BMW. The simple Boxer engine offers a low centre of gravity, shaft final drive and a brand image even Coca-Cola must envy. More Bavarian than *lederhosen*, and probably a great deal more practical.

'It was, however, a comfortable machine ideally suited to long-distance work on its native autobahns.'

SPECIFICATION: BMW R69	
ENGINE	air-cooled 594cc OHV opposed twin
HORSEPOWER	35bhp @ 6800rpm
TRANSMISSION	4-speed, shaft final drive
FRAME	tubular twin cradle
BRAKES	2LS drum/drum
TOP SPEED	102mph

Harley-Davidson Duo-Glide

'It didn't much like corners, and was woefully under-braked.'

Few makes of motorcycle arouse such conflicting emotions as Harley-Davidson. To lovers of fast, nimble sports machines in the European tradition, they're slow, heavy and primitive. Others define the same characteristics as laid-back, solid and traditional, and are equally committed to motorcycling as conceived in Milwaukee. As one of the few manufacturers in this book to have been in volume motorcycle production in every one of the 25 years in question, clearly the American way has something going for it.

The Duo-Glide is a case in point. By the time it appeared in 1958, pretty well everything it offered had already been done – and done better – by every other major manufacturer. It didn't much like corners, and was woefully under-braked. But, with its big, slow-revving engine, it was indisputably a Harley. And it was beautiful.

Its roots went back at least to 1922 and the arrival of Harley's first 74 cubic inch (1200cc) Vee-twin model, the 'F-head' JD. In 1930 this became the VL which regressed from inlet-over-exhaust to full side-valve layout – hardly a go-ahead step. Another 11 years produced the Big Twin, now with overhead valves.

In 1948 another engine redesign saw the iron-headed 'Knucklehead' replaced by the 'Panhead', so-called because its rocker covers resembled upturned skillets. The alloy-headed Panhead unit was some eight pounds lighter than before, ran cooler and used hydraulic valve 'lifters' instead of conventional push-rods. Bore and stroke remained the 'traditional' 87 by 101mm (or rather, as Americans still prefer it, 3⁷/16 x 4 inches). 1947 also – whisper it quietly – marked the debut of a range of budget Harley two-strokes that refused to go away for almost 20 years.

However the big event came a year later with the arrival of the first of Milwaukee's 'Glide' models.

Although retaining a rigid rear end, the Hydra-Glide broke with the Harley reliance on leading-link forks. Instead, here was a Hog with a modern telescopic front-end. As if to compensate for this fit of novelty, the Hydra persevered with a uniquely American hand-change gearbox until 1952, and even later as a die-hard option.

The Duo-Glide was the logical next step. As well as real front suspension, the Duo floated on a swinging-arm rear end, hence the name. The hydraulic rear brake was a gimmicky novelty, since both hubs contain tiny six inch single-leading shoe drums which struggle to haul down the 'Glide's substantial bulk.

Harley have always encouraged customising and tuning of their machinery, which invariably comes in a very low state of tune as standard. The example pictured is a 1961 FLH model. The 'H' denotes 'hot' – the engine has an optional high-lift camshaft and higher compression pistons. Even so, power is modest, with a comfortable cruising speed not

SPECIFICATION: HARLEY-DAVIDSON DUO-GLIDE	
ENGINE	air-cooled OHV 1212cc V-twin
HORSEPOWER	54bhp
TRANSMISSION	4-speed
FRAME	tubular steel cradle, single front downtube
BRAKES	drum/drum
TOP SPEED	80mph

much more than 65mph. A 'King of the Road' package includes front and rear nudge bars, twin rear lights and a dual exhaust system.

When Duo-Glide production ceased in 1964, its successor was to become another American legend – the Electra-Glide. The name, and the spirit, endures today. Indeed, current Harley styling, far from modernising the big Vee-twins, has sought to emulate the look of the 'fifties.

Along the way there have been major upheavals. Financial difficulties in the late 'sixties led to an ill-starred merger with AMF, intense competition from Japan, and a disastrous decline in production quality. The 'eighties was to see a management buy-out which initially failed to halt further decline. In the nick of time a new, more reliable range of models, backed by a government tariff on imported models over 700cc, allowed Harley to turn the tide. Today the world's oldest surviving motorcycle manufacturer is in good shape. No other marque is quite like it, and few now command the same passionate loyalty. But for a while, it was touch and go.

Descended from the Hydra-Glide, the Duo was later to evolve into the quintessential Harley — the Electra-Glide of 1964.

Harleys make a virtue of putting their mechanical parts on display. These days the same classic Milwaukee lines can be seen in 'Retro-tech' machines like the Heritage Softail.

MZ: The Racers

Picture shows (left to right) a 1969 liquid-cooled RZ250, 1970 RZ125 tandem twin, 1960 RZ250 and 1960 RE125. During the 'sixties the power of the 125 rose from 22 to 34bhp, while the 250's output climbed from 42 to 58bhp.

Mention the expressions 'MZ' and 'super-bike' in the same breath, and the most likely reaction will be incredulous laughter. From its foundation in 1945 until very recently, the former East German company has produced nothing but single-cylinder two-strokes. MZ motorcycles were cheap and cheerful, certainly, but scarcely exotic.

Well yes, and no. MZ roadsters, true, have always been humble machines. But, during the 'fifties and 'sixties, the company produced a range of competition machines that revolutionised two-strokes both on the track and off. Every *grand prix* victory since 1970 (with the exception of MV's swan-song wins), is the legacy of MZ's work.

The company was founded in 1907 by a Dane, Jurgen Rasmussen, initially making parts for textile machinery. In 1915, spurred by wartime petrol shortages, they built a steam-engined car, *Dampf*

Kraft Wagen, which gave the company the name – DKW – it was to carry until the end of World War II. After World War I, the Zschopau-based concern developed a proprietory two-stroke engine, *Das Kleine Wunder* (DKW, again, now meaning 'The Little Marvel').

DKW built its first complete motorcycle in 1922, and by 1928 was using advanced manufacturing methods to build 100,000 units per year, making them the world's largest manufacturer of motorcycles. In 1932 they merged with Audi, Horsch and Wanderer to form Auto Union – a foursome now represented in the four rings worn by Audi motor cars.

DKW soon became prominent in racing, Edwald Kluge bringing them a Lightweight TT victory in 1938. After the war, the rights to the DKW name passed to the West, with a new company, Motorradwerke Zschopau, occupying the

old site. For the next 45 years, their principal concern would be to mass produce two-wheelers for the Communist Bloc, with some going for export to earn foreign currency.

There was, however, a competition department – small and under-resourced, but possessing one of the most remarkable minds in the history of motorcycling. When Walter Kaaden took over in 1953, two-strokes had been rendered almost obsolete by the post-war ban on supercharging, on which machines like the pre-war *Ladepumpe* DKWs had depended.

Kaaden's gift to motorcycling was his development of rotary disc induction and tuned expansion chamber exhaust systems, which was to hurl MZ to the forefront of racing development. In 1958, Horst Fügner rode a 250 MZ to the company's first GP win, going on to place second in the world championship. 13 more *grands prix* wins were to follow, a number which would undoubtedly have been far greater had MZ not been so strapped for funds. Ancillary parts for their racing bikes were commonly scrounged or bartered at race meetings.

By 1961, Kaaden had taken the power of MZ's 125cc racer from eight to 25bhp the first normally-aspirated engine ever to develop 200bhp/litre. These engines, models of elegant simplicity, have since become the building blocks of every successful *grand prix* powerplant of modern times. Indeed, 14 years later the first of Barry Sheene's RG500 Suzukis – unashamedly four

MZ125s in a square box – could boast only 180bhp/litre. In motocross the story is the same.

The early 'sixties, of course, was the time when the Japanese were putting huge sums and effort into *grand prix* racing. And whilst Honda ran four-strokes, Suzuki and Yamaha envied MZ know-how. In 1961, whilst leading the 125cc world championship for MZ, development rider Ernst Degner defected to the West, joining Suzuki. One year later the previously uncompetitive 50cc Suzuki became the first two-stroke to win a world road race championship. Ernst Degner was the rider.

If the impact of Kaaden's work was revolutionary, it was also a triumph for inspired endeavour over the throw-money-at-it approach prevalent elsewhere. Kaaden elevated MZs from paddock curiosities to the fastest racing motorcycles in the world. The MZ riders' list reads like a *Who's Who* of road racing – and all of them did it for nothing, or close to it. The only fee MZ could offer was the privilege of riding one of the master's creations. There were plenty of takers.

1960 MZ RE125, the very machine on which Ernst Degner came so close to winning the 1961 world title, before defecting and handing the crown to Honda (and MZ's technology to Suzuki).

Walter Kaaden (left) photographed in 1993. His genius elevated two-strokes from propelling budget commuter bikes to powering the fastest racing machines in the world.

BSA Gold Star

'Boy racers,

after all, will

be boys . . .'

The one and only DBD34 'Goldie' was both the ultimate clubmans production racer and *the* single-cylinder street racer of the 'fifties. Yet its origins could not have been more humble, nor more different. For not only was the 500cc Gold Star basically a souped-up B31, but in 1949 it actually began its competitive life on dirt.

The name, of course, was much older. In 1937 the great Wal Handley won at Brooklands on a works-prepared BSA M20 Empire Star, averaging 102.27mph and earning himself a coveted Brooklands gold star medal. Had war not intervened, the Gold Star name was to have been applied to a new sports 500 BSA, the M24 'Handley replica'.

In 1946 the sports mantle passed instead to a tuned version of the unpretentious B31 350cc push-rod single, the B32. In even more highly-tuned form this became the 350cc Gold Star which won the 1949 Clubmans TT at an average speed of over 75mph – on 73-octane 'pool' petrol.

The 500cc B34 version arrived in September of the same year, taking no less than eleven gold medals at the ISDT. In 1950 it acquired swing-arm rear suspension, and in a few short years had achieved such utter domination of the Clubmans TT that the races themselves were threatened. The Goldie was becoming too fast for its own good. Of 37 Junior entries in 1955, for instance, no less than 33 were Gold Stars.

But our interest lies with 500cc street versions of what has been described as the 'most anti-social roadster ever made'. The reason for this was simple; the Goldie wasn't really a roadster at all, but a thinly-disguised track machine taking cynical advantage of 'production' racing regulations.

With those compact, elegant lines, the definitive DBD34 Gold Star certainly looks the part. Less apparent is its highly-strung nature, its often

temperamental starting and erratic running. With the Amal GP carburettor normally fitted to competition versions, there is little or no drive below 3000rpm, and the high compression engine declines to run at all below 2000. Road versions came equipped with more civilised Amal Monobloc carbs, but didn't always keep them. Boy racers, after all, will be boys . . .

The lack of slow-running is made worse by the Goldie's gearing. The RRT2 competition gearbox was ridiculously tall for street use, necessitating violent clutch slipping from low speed. Silencing was strictly nominal, in either track or street guise, but did produce the Gold Star's famously evocative

The Gold Star name came from the Brooklands Gold Star awarded for lapping the famed banked circuit at over 100mph. From the very beginning, the Goldie had that sort of pedigree.

'twitter' on the over-run. To appreciate the Goldie you had to take it into its element – if not the race track, then at least the open road. But even the Gold Star's biggest fan would admit that, with its clip-on 'bars and rear-set footrests, it's an uncomfortable machine.

Housing this uncompromising engine was a very ordinary frame almost identical to the 'cooking' B31. This is nonetheless a fairly rigid structure with the quick steering demanded for racing use. The damping, however, is poor and even the Goldie's brakes are nothing special.

What the 500cc Gold Star did have was around 43bhp in race trim, five bhp less for roadsters, both impressive figures for a push-rod two-valve single. This was all the more surprising because the Gold Star's valves were unfashionably small for a performance engine, yet it clearly breathed well.

The secret lay in painstaking detailed refinement of port shapes – and perhaps a little good luck.

Gold Star production ceased in 1962 when BSA declared their highly-strung hooligan single uneconomic to produce. Instead they set about developing a modest 250cc single, the C15, for trials and scrambles. This grew by degrees to 250, 440 and 500cc, gave Jeff Smith two world motocross titles, and transformed off-road sport. From humble beginnings . . .

SPECIFICATION: BSA GOLD STAR	
ENGINE	air-cooled 499cc OHV single
HORSEPOWER	38bhp @ 7000rpm
TRANSMISSION	4-speed
FRAME	tubular double cradle
BRAKES	drum/drum
TOP SPEED	100mph

Elegant yet raw, with no superfluous details, the Goldie was everyone's idea of the classic British single. Although the highly-tuned engine could be a temperamental nightmare, the B31-based chassis proved remarkably able.

Royal Enfield Constellation

....

'Where Triumphs tended to do it on revs, the 'Conny' offered sheer punch.'

'There is nothing', Americans are fond of saying, 'like cubes'. The US market for both two- and four-wheelers has always had an enduring love affair with cubic capacity for its own sake, a lust that Royal Enfield amongst British motorcycle manufacturers most attempted to satisfy.

Like most other major British factories, Royal Enfield's post war programme was yet another tribute to Alfred Turner's 1937 Triumph Speed Twin design. Royal Enfield saw, as BSA, AMC and Norton also concluded, that their flagship model had to be a four-stroke vertical twin. The layout was compact, relatively easy to manufacturer, fitted readily into a conventional motorcycle chassis and developed a particularly punchy brand of power. So a twin it had to be. But those produced in Redditch would be bigger, and bigger – in America, at least – was best.

Enfield's first post-war vertical twin, the 500cc Meteor, was launched in 1948. This set the pattern for later twins, using a one-piece iron crankshaft, separate heads and barrels, and dry-sump oiling but with the oil neatly held in a reservoir cast integrally with the crankcases. Along with the 350cc Bullet, the Meteor also featured swing-arm rear suspension whilst BSA, Norton and Triumph were still persevering with plunger rear ends.

In the USA, Enfields were sold under the otherwise largely defunct Indian name. Feedback from the States soon prompted the development of a larger machine, and in 1953 the 692cc Meteor was the result (known as the Indian Trailblazer in the US). From the Meteor was derived the Super Meteor, then in 1958 the Constellation – basically a sports version of its predecessor.

692cc was a good deal larger than any other vertical twin on the market. Not surprisingly the

Solid and imposing as it was, the Constellation never quite captured the aura enjoyed by Norton and Triumph twins, although a good one was just as fast.

Constellation, and its 736cc successor, the Interceptor, have always been associated with prodigious bottom-end and mid-range power. This is partly due to sheer capacity, partly to the Constellation's long-stroke (70 x 90mm) cylinder dimensions. Where Triumphs tended to do it on revs, the 'Conny' offered sheer punch.

Royal Enfield claimed 51bhp at 6250rpm for the Constellation. At 425lb, weight was relatively modest, and acceleration brisk. In 1960 a Conny was independently timed at 112mph, faster than any other British big twin other than a sports version of the Triumph Bonneville. The down-side ought to have been vibration, to which any such twin is prone, and a big one even more. Enfield substantially reduced this by dynamic balancing of their crankshafts during assembly – the only major manufacturer to do so.

Despite this, Enfield big twins were never so popular as twins from Norton, BSA and Triumph. The engine was regarded as strong, but somewhat staid – often being associated with pulling sidecars, for which it was eminently suited. The gearbox, too – made by Enfield's sister company, Albion – was heavy and slow. Worst of all, they gained a reputation for leaking oil – 'Royal Oilfields' – and for leaky cylinder head joints. Enfield twins also suffered several high-profile breakdowns in major production races. And they simply lacked the cachet enjoyed by many of their rivals.

Constellation production continued until 1962 and the introduction of the 736cc Interceptor, another long-stroke engine with similar characteristics – and shortcomings. A substantially revised Mk2 Interceptor followed, but neither was conspicuously successful and the company sold its last bikes in 1968. Ironically this collapse stranded a shipment of engines en route to Indian in the USA, which subsequently (see page 64) found homes in the Rickman Interceptor. The other Indian connection is that the Enfield name survives in Madras, where 350 and 500cc Bullets continue to be produced.

SPECIFICATION: ROYAL ENFIELD CONSTELLATION	
ENGINE	air-cooled 692cc OHV vertical twin
HORSEPOWER	51bhp @ 6250rpm
TRANSMISSION	4-speed
FRAME	tubular steel cradle, single front downtube
BRAKES	drum/drum
TOP SPEED	112mph

The big Enfields enjoyed dynamically balanced cranks, prodigious torque — and a thoroughly British reputation for leaking oil.

Triumph T120 Bonneville

'Even standing still, it looked 20mph faster than just about any other machine on the road.'

Whatever shortcomings Triumph may have had, struggling to find just the right name for their models wasn't one of them. And if 'Thunderbird' went right to the heart of the American psyche (so much so that Ford later 'borrowed' the name), the legendary Bonneville struck a similar chord.

A development of the Tiger 110, the 'Bonnie' was Triumph's first twin-carb engine since the legendary *Grand Prix* model. The name, of course, came from the famous Bonneville salt flats in Utah, where in 1956 Johnny Allan's streamlined T110 Triumph had clocked the sensational speed of 214mph. The record wasn't accepted by the FIM, but the the reputation stuck – the speed was all that mattered.

For all this pedigree, the T120's start was surprisingly uncertain. The first attempt, in 1959, was a comparatively staid affair, with touring-type mudguards and an ungainly headlamp nacelle. Subsequent versions were altogether leaner and more purposeful-looking. By 1960, even standing still, it *looked* 20mph faster than just about any other machine on the road.

The vertical twin engine produced 46bhp at 6500rpm, fully 12 more than the original Thunderbird. Dry weight was 393lb, 18 more than the T'bird but still light for the class. From the start the Bonnie enjoyed the much stronger one-piece crankshaft introduced in 1959, but other improvements followed year-on-year: twin downtube frame in 1960; unit construction in 1963; 12-volt electrics one year later. Perhaps most important of all was the arrival of Doug Hele at Triumph in 1962. The former Norton man was

Probably the most desirable 'Bonnie' of them all, a 1965 Thruxton model, of which only 64 were built. Distinguished by a heavily tuned engine, competition wheels, brakes and suspension, it took the Bonneville hallmarks of leanness and purpose to their ultimate extremes.

later to find fame as the inspiration behind the success of the 750cc three-cylinder racers, but his first job at Meriden was to improve the geometry and front suspension of Triumph's premier twin.

1962 also saw another shortcoming remedied, at Bonneville itself, when Bill Johnson's Triumph *did* take the speed record on a similar machine at 224.57mph. Two years later Bob Leppan rode another 'Bonnie' streamliner, Gyronaut X-1, to 245.557mph. Although the factory itself was not particularly racing-minded, in 1969 another Bonnie became the first production motorcycle to lap the Isle of Man at 100mph (thus christening Dunlop's TT100 tyre) when Malcolm Uphill took the 'proddy' race with a fastest lap of 100.37mph. Bonnevilles also won the Thruxton 500 mile race, the Le Mans 24-hour races, and many more.

But the Bonnie's real home was on the street, where a 1961 road test described it as 'perhaps the fastest point-to-point roadster produced in Britain today'. Later in the year Triumph offered a carburettor kit offering 117mph, close to the notional '120' of which its name bragged. The

Not Malcolm Uphill, and not a 100mph TT lap, but any biker can dream . . .

T120 was not only the machine to have amongst 'ton-up' kids of the day, but it developed a rare reputation for speed *and* reliability and, at a shade over £284, was actually affordable.

In 1969, and not before time, the Bonnie received the twin leading shoe front brake developed for the new Triumph triples. In 1972 a 52bhp 750cc version, the T140, was added. Yet many riders still consider the 650 the ideal capacity, because vibration made the 750 a painful thing to put through its paces for any length of time.

By now competition from Japanese multis was becoming intense, with the venerable Bonnie increasingly appealing to a niche market. Scarcely had a five-speed T120 been introduced in 1973 than the Triumph/BSA group went bankrupt. With government support, production of Triumph twins eventually passed to the Meriden workers co-operative after a

. . . for if ever a bike awaited the invention of the by-pass to thrash along, the legendary Bonneville was it.

long and rancorous 'sit-in'. 750cc twins, including the £1149 limited edition 'Silver Jubilee' T140V, continued to be built until the collapse of the experiment in 1983. By a matter of months, the Bonnie had failed to reach its own silver jubilee, but the reign had been glorious, all the same.

SPECIFICATION: TRIUMPH T120 BONNEVILLE	
ENGINE	air-cooled 649cc parallel twin
HORSEPOWER	46bhp @ 6500rpm (later 51bhp @ 7100rpm)
TRANSMISSION	4-speed (later 120V: 5 speed)
FRAME	tubular twin cradle
BRAKES	drum/drum
TOP SPEED	110mph

Velocette Venom Thruxton

Gaping Amal GP carb gulping unfiltered air did nothing for engine longevity, but for Thruxton owners performance was far more important. Example pictured dates from 1965.

Veloce Ltd., despite occasional and usually blighted adventures with twins, scooters and oddball two strokes, will always be associated with pedigree four-stroke singles. Although a small manufacturer, in the years preceding this book's period they were a potent force in racing – Velocettes took eight Junior TT wins between 1926 and '49, and the inaugural 350cc world championship in 1949, and again when our era began in 1950.

Their road bikes, too, were equally prized – and potent. The company was founded in 1913, and as early as 1921 Velocette were habitual record-breakers with modified roadster machines. Precisely 40 years later they claimed a further fistful of records, included the first 350 to average 100mph for 24 hours (a record which still stands).

From the outset they were an independent-minded company, often producing designs of great technical novelty. But it is singles for which they are best remembered, usually in classy gloss black, picked out with gold pin-striping. Indeed, throughout the 'sixties they made what became the epitome of British road-going singles; the 350cc Viper and 500cc Venom. And most celebrated of all was the 'Thruxton' Venom, the ultimate street-racing single.

This was more than a cosmetic exercise. In 1964 a Venom tricked-out by Reg Orpin of Velocette dealers L Stevens had won the prestigious 500 mile race at Hampshire's Thruxton circuit. From mid-'65 limited numbers of 'replica' Thruxton's were built at the Hall Green factory. Over the next five years, only about 1000 were built, at a retail price of £400 – ten per cent *more* than a Triumph Bonneville twin.

Powering the Thruxton was a hotted-up version of the standard 499cc Venom overhead valve engine. Engine modifications included a 1⅜ inch Amal GP5 racing carburettor. Special cylinder heads were also used, with huge inlet valves, revised porting, one-piece push-rods and sharper-acting cam-followers.

Before the Thruxton, the Venom Clubman was the hot 500cc Velo. This handsome device is a 1961 model, in more traditional all-black livery.

Equipped with clip-on handlebars, rear-set footrests, a humped seat and long-distance fuel tank, the Thruxton was a factory version of the then-popular 'café racer'. In standard form it wore a Mitchenall full fairing, but many owners dispensed with the lower half, or removed the streamlining altogether.

With or without, it was a wildly impractical machine, demanding considerable mechanical sympathy and a useful touch with the tool kit. Starting any Velocette is tricky, requiring a technique which has become legendary. With 9:1 compression, racing carb and manual-advance magneto ignition, the Thruxton was more pernickety still. Even when running, the 'Thrucky' could be just as contrary. Tuning the engine had made it hesitant at low revs – and the GP5 carb had no idle provision. On later versions an Amal Concentric carb and coil ignition gave better starting and low-speed running.

Maintenance, too, was time-consuming, with the tappets and clutch, in particular, demanding regular attention. Although the engine, with its short, stiff crankshaft, was fundamentally sturdy,

getting it running 'just so' was both a delight and a rarity. But when it did go, it went well, winning the first 500cc Production TT in 1967, at an average speed of 89.89mph. A good Thruxton was capable of 120mph in race tune, well up with the fastest twins.

Even more than its occasional triumphs, the Thruxton attracted the sort of mystique which the motorcycling fraternity reserves for something special. Vincents had it, as Ducatis do today. Velocettes such as this had it in abundance. Sadly others did not. When the company finally went into liquidation on 4 February 1971, what brought them down was the tooling and development costs of, of all things, the Viceroy scooter. Like much that Veloce produced, the little two-stroke twin with reed valve induction was way ahead of its time. But classic machines such as the Thruxton are a far more fitting memorial.

'A good Thruxton was capable of 120mph in race tune.'

SPECIFICATION: VELOCETTE VENOM	
ENGINE	air-cooled 499cc OHV single
HORSEPOWER	41bhp @ 6500rpm
TRANSMISSION	4-speed
FRAME	twin loop with single front downtube
BRAKES	2LS drum/drum
TOP SPEED	120mph (in race trim)

Norton 650SS

· ·

Designed, like BSA's A10 twin, by Bert Hopwood, the single-camshaft Norton was produced in 500, 600, 650 and later 750 and 850cc form. Of all these the 650SS is the rarest and most desirable.

Ever since their racing exploits of the early 'fifties, Norton were chiefly associated with two things – arguably the best-handling machinery in motorcycling; and the frame which was held responsible, the legendary 'Featherbed'.

In the later 'forties, spurred by the prowess of Alfred Turner's Triumph Speed Twin, Norton (and almost everyone else) sought a twin of their own. Their first design, an in-line twin in the Sunbeam pattern, was rejected as being too unconventional. Jack Moore then drew up a parallel twin, but the model was not built. In 1947 Bert Hopwood arrived and designed what was, in later years, to become Norton's only engine. Not surprisingly, it was similar to the BSA A10 design for which Hopwood was also responsible, but unusual in having a single camshaft across the front of the crankcases. The engine went into production as the 'Dominator' in 1948, but was not available on the home market until late the following year.

Meanwhile the Featherbed frame, designed by the McCandless brothers of Belfast, comprised a bronze-welded duplex cradle with swinging fork rear suspension. Coupled with the 'Roadholder' front forks first introduced in 1948, this conferred an unprecedented level of handling on Norton's racing machines. It first appeared in 1950, replacing the 'Garden Gate' frame on the Manx Norton racer, when its handling was described as 'like a feather bed'. The name stuck.

Although the public was also clamouring for 'proper' rear suspension – and preferably Featherbed frames – their introduction into the Norton range was slow. The problem was that Featherbeds were manufactured for Norton by Reynolds Tubes Ltd., and they could make only 70

per week. So the Featherbed-equipped Dominator 88 de Luxe first shown at Earls Court in 1951, was for export only. As an interim measure, Bob Collier worked out a way of grafting swinging-arm rear ends onto their old lugged frames, which were rushed into the range for 1953.

Eventually the Featherbed became Norton's standard frame, and remained the yardstick by which the handling of other machinery was judged long after production ceased in the late 'sixties. Indeed the Japanese were to imitate the design for a further 20 years. But in the 'fifties, if Norton had a problem, it was in developing an engine worthy of the Roadholder/Featherbed package.

In late 1955 the 600cc Dominator 99 was added to its 500cc stablemate. The bigger engine was, like all subsequent Nortons, non-unit (a Hopwood-led unit-construction project begun in the late 'fifties was later abandoned). It developed 31bhp at 5750rpm – an improvement, but significantly less

than Triumph's sporting twin. In 1960 a revised Featherbed, the 'Slimline' was introduced. Then, in 1961, came the 650SS, initially for export only.

With comparable products already available from BSA, Royal Enfield, AJS/Matchless and Triumph (the Bonneville first appeared in '59), the SS had to be good – and it was. Early versions suffered some failures – notably burst cylinder barrels and fatigue fractures of various fittings – but through it all shone that pedigree handling package. Ridden to the limit, no other production machine could come close. And with a top speed comfortably over 110mph, the new Norton was no slouch on the straights. Not surprisingly, the 650SS went on to win production races by the score.

Yet for all this success, these were troubled times for Norton. In 1962 they amalgamated with the AMC Group. The 750cc Norton Atlas appeared on the home market two years later, the same engine appearing as the Matchless G15 under the AMC flag. Four years later still, the 650SS was succeeded by the single-carburettor Mercury, and in the same year AMC themselves collapsed into liquidation. Norton Villiers arose from that

particular pile of ashes, and with them, the next generation of Norton vertical twins – the Commando.

On any half-interesting road, all you'd see of a well-ridden SS was this badge disappearing into the distance.

SPECIFICATION: NORTON 650SS	
ENGINE	air-cooled 647cc OHV vertical twin
HORSEPOWER	49bhp @ 6800rpm
TRANSMISSION	4-speed
FRAME	'Featherbed' duplex steel cradle
BRAKES	drum/drum
TOP SPEED	115mph

'Ridden to the limit, no other production machine could come close.'

The 650SS added serious horsepower to the already 'unapproachable' Norton chassis. Almost out of the crate, the newcomer was capable of winning races.

Honda RC165 250-6 Racer

·····························

'With Hailwood on board, the six began to fly.'

By any standards the Honda story is remarkable. From the time Soichiro Honda sold his first motorcycle in 1948, it was to be barely 20 years before his dream of providing motorcycles for the masses established his company as the world's largest producer of two-wheelers. This explosive growth was built on a rush of technology which was equally staggering. And in the minds of the motorcycling public no machine epitomised it quite so vividly as the six-cylinder 250cc racer.

The year was 1964, just five short years after Honda's debut at the Isle of Man TT. Yet by 1961 Honda had taken their first world championship crown, two times over – Mike Hailwood taking the 250cc title, Rob Phillis the 125.

Although Honda went on to become the dominant force in 125, 250 and 350cc *grands prix*, their Japanese rivals were also making spectacular progress with two-strokes of ever-increasing power and complexity. Of this 'new wave', only Honda were committed to four-stroke engines, and the two-strokes were intrinsically more powerful.

When Phil Read handed Yamaha the prized 250cc title in 1964 and again in 1965, Honda had to do something dramatic. The result, in this crazy, helter-skelter decade, was

Never has so much technology been packed into a mere quarter litre. Six cylinders, six carbs, 24 valves and 18,000rpm made the 250-6 perhaps the most sensational device in the history of *grands prix*.

the unforgettable 250-6 taken by Soichiro Irimajiri's design team from drawing board to prototype in just two months. Although debuted by Jim Redman in a desperate attempt to stem the Yamaha challenge at Monza late in 1964, the six's first full season was a disappointment. Handling and reliability problems, and Redman's loss of form, handed the '65 title to an irrepressible Read. Then, at the last *grand prix* of the season, the Japanese, one of racing's great partnerships began: Hailwood, still riding MVs in the larger classes, climbed aboard the Honda six.

Hailwood won, but his outspoken criticism of the machine's handling caused headlines in a country more accustomed to dignified restraint. Yet when Honda signed him for the 1966 season, they gained not only his unparalleled riding ability, but his diagnostic experience as well. With Hailwood on board, the six began to fly, winning no less than ten of the 12 *grands prix*. For good measure he took the 350cc world title with a 297cc machine, the RC174, which was essentially a bored and stroked 250-six.

For Honda nothing less would have done, for this was the season in which they attempted an unprecedented piece of audacity; to win all five solo

championship classes. They were partly successful, in that they took the manufacturers' title in each, but provided champions in 'only' three – Agostini took the 500 title for MV, Anscheidt winning on the 50cc Suzuki. In all, Honda scored 29 *grands prix* wins in this single season.

The rationale for the six was that if a four-stroke was to compete with the strokers, it had to compensate for having only half as many firing strokes by breathing better and spinning faster. This meant smaller cylinders with a very short stroke and, inevitably, lots of them. The 250's cylinders were just 39mm across, with a stroke of 34.5mm. It meant four valves per cylinder – 24 in all – and double overhead camshafts. It meant no less than six 17mm flat-slide Keihin carburettors. Most of all, it meant revs; the six eventually produced its peak power of 60bhp at a giddy 18,000rpm (the even more outrageous 125-five revved well beyond 19,000rpm).

Placing six cylinders in-line across the frame was not the obvious choice, yet this miracle of miniaturisation was no wider across the fairing than a contemporary racing single. The 150mph machine weighed just 260lbs.

In 1967, Honda pulled out of *grand prix* racing. But no-one who saw – or heard – the six will ever forget it.

A masterpiece of miniaturisation, the 250's six cylinders – count 'em – made it no wider across the fairing than many a single.

SPECIFICATION: HONDA RC165 250-6 RACER	
ENGINE	air-cooled 247cc DOHC transverse six
HORSEPOWER	60bhp @ 18,000rpm
TRANSMISSION	7-speed
FRAME	tubular steel open cradle
BRAKES	double drum/drum
TOP SPEED	153mph

Suzuki T20 'Super Six'

Suzuki's T20 set the world back on it heels in producing 500cc performance from such a tiny package. Inside, the engine was even more impressive.

This was the machine that first put the writing on the wall for the British motorcycle industry. In 1966, when Suzuki's 'Super Six' was introduced, multi-cylindered Oriental behemoths were still but a distant dream. Yet if Honda's CB750 was to be dubbed the first 'superbike', the little Suzuki was the first roadster to reveal the awesome potential of the emerging Japanese giants.

During its first six months on sale, over a thousand Super Sixes were sold in the UK alone. More ominously still, in December 1966 it became the first Oriental motorcycle to be voted 'Machine of the Year' by readers of *MotorCycle News*. One year later it retained the title.

The attraction, of course, lay in the numbers. The 'six' that were 'super' were gears, an unprecedented number for a roadster. (They were also an insult – two years previously, Royal Enfield's first five-speed 250 sports bike was named the

Super Five.) Then there was 100, the top speed alleged in T20 marketing hype. The Super Six was capable of nothing like that in neutral conditions, of course. But even a genuine 90mph was enough to shame many a 500, and thoroughly see off any European 250 foolish enough to give chase.

Also unprecedented was the Suzuki's level of technical sophistication, detailing and reliability – in a truly sporting package at an affordable price. When introduced, the machine cost less than £2 more than the comparable, but much slower, Enfield Continental GT.

To fully appreciate a Super Six, however, you need to strip it. Invert the engine, lift off the bottom crankcase half (the cases split horizontally, unlike Suzuki's previous 250, the T10) and a design of surpassing elegance lies before you.

There are three main shafts – crank-, lay- and mainshaft, with a final train of gears driving the Suzuki's novel Posi-Force oil pump (which

Still dominant in modern classic racing, here British champion Bob Jackson powers round Brands Hatch on Peter Berwick's Super Six.

dispensed with the messy job of mixing oil and fuel). The crank runs on three main bearings, the outer two being lubricated directly by the oil pump, the centre one by gearbox oil. One-piece steel connecting rods run on the pressed-up crank, their roller big-ends receiving oil from the outer mains. Small ends are needle roller, supporting cast, two-ring pistons with a shallow dome. Primary drive is by gear.

Each cylinder has its own head and iron-sleeved barrel, the latter sporting 'classic' 54x54mm dimensions. Porting was conservative by modern standards, with the inlet port bridged to give the piston rings an easier life. It was an exquisite, seminal design, barely distinguishable in principle from racing Yamahas of 20 years later. It was light (297lb), reliable, and started easily. But most of all – although the claimed 29bhp is optimistic – it was fast.

The T20 was regarded in its time as a good handler, with damping 'superior to any [other] Japanese machine'. In truth, the suspension was harsh, and the brakes no better than adequate. It has a general air of flimsiness which was largely overcome with the introduction of the much sturdier T250 Hustler in 1969.

Not surprisingly Super Sixes found their way onto the tracks in large numbers, both in standard guise and as the 'kitted' TR250. On a good day the TR250 was a match for Yamaha's contemporary TD1C. As well as race wins – notably in the '67 Manx Grand Prix – modified Eddie Crooks T20s broke world records over six hours, 1000km, 12 hours and 24 hours (the latter in 256cc '350' form, at 91.055mph). They were even modified for off-road competition.

Thirty years on, the Super Six inevitably feels dated. Its power is around half that of a modern sports 250, and the chassis and cycle parts come from a different planet. Yet despite that, it was a revelation in its day and has an unmistakable feel of modern-ness about it. And, above all, it set in train a revolution that is still winning races today. With the Super Six, less truly was more.

SPECIFICATION: SUZUKI T20 'SUPER SIX,	
ENGINE	247cc two-stroke parallel twin
HORSEPOWER	29bhp @ 7500rpm
TRANSMISSION	6-speed
FRAME	tubular double cradle
BRAKES	drum/drum
TOP SPEED	90mph

'It was an exquisite, seminal design, barely distinguishable from racing Yamahas of 20 years later.'

Honda CB450 'Black Bomber'

....

'Despite its chequered history, the Bomber was undoubtedly a major breakthrough.'

In 1965, a large-capacity Japanese vertical twin represented a frontal attack on the entire British motorcycle industry. The advanced but flawed CB450 failed to win the battle, but Honda unquestionably won the war.

Although Honda's CB750-four was the more awe-inspiring machine, the CB450 twin introduced in 1965 was in many ways more technologically advanced. Perhaps more crucially still, it was also the bike the British motorcycle industry deluded themselves into thinking Japan couldn't build; a large capacity, high performance four-stroke. The CB450 put the writing graphically on the wall.

By the time the 'Black Bomber' arrived, Honda four-stroke roadsters were already achieving remarkable speeds and healthy sales in the smaller classes. The largest previous model was the 305cc CB77, a sports twin derived from the 250cc CB72, and capable of over 95mph. Yet both Soichiro Honda's technology-driven philosophy of constant development, and the aspirations of marketing chief, Fujisawa, demanded more. The result, ready to cash in on the American preoccupation with large-capacity machines, was the CB450.

Although the vertical twin engine layout was conservative, the Bomber's internals were not. Rather than follow the British practice whereby the pistons rise and fall together, the CB450 featured crank throws 180 degrees out of phase, substantially reducing primary imbalance and vibration.

Instead of conventional coil springs, the Honda's valves were closed by torsion bars. But most dramatic of all was the use of twin overhead camshafts, a system previously confined to exotic racing machines. Bore and stroke were substantially oversquare at 70 x 57.8mm, allowing the engine to fully exploit the valvegear's capacity for revs. An electric starter was also fitted.

The result was a motorcycle that was not only as civilised and convenient as its Japanese predecessors, but as fast as many a British 650. Early versions, finished in black and chrome (hence the affectionate 'Black Bomber' tag) produced 43bhp.

Sales of the CB450 were quite good in the UK, but not where it counted; the USA. For Honda's first large capacity machine turned out to be as flawed as it was innovative. Maintenance, especially valve-lash adjustment, was laborious. Cylinder head removal required the splitting and re-rivetting of the cam chain. The handling, particularly at low speed, was peculiar. And the original tyres did more to protect the rims than offer grip.

Perhaps worst of all, the Bomber wasn't notably reliable, and it *did* vibrate. The uneven firing intervals of 180 degree crank manifested themselves in snatchy low-speed running which the relatively small flywheels were unable to overcome. This was made all the more intrusive by the widely-spaced ratios of a gearbox with just four speeds. At high revs, however, it was uncannily smooth for a parallel twin.

In 1967 an improved model was developed, with five speeds, different carburettors, a claimed 45bhp, and a top speed of around 104mph. Chassis modifications also improved the handling, but the die had been cast; the CB450 was not the success that Honda had hoped for.

Despite its chequered history, the Bomber was undoubtedly a major breakthrough. A double overhead camshaft engine had previously been considered far too expensive to produce for an ordinary roadster, yet Honda managed to build one, ship it halfway around the world, and still make a handsome profit. Their solution was to use a simple, single roller-less chain where expensive spur-gears or bevels were conventionally used. Such chains were cheap, and dispensing with rollers eliminated the possibility of one breaking and wrecking the engine. The inherent noise of the system was reduced by cunning use of guides, rollers and quietening rubbers.

However, novelty has a price. The first batch of Bombers were embarrassingly recalled due to top-end wear – caused by rubber quietening inserts in the timing gear breaking up and finding their way into the oil pump. More dramatic still was a tendency for a cam chain idler gear to fall into the crankcases, and the early constant velocity carburettors' habit of sticking wide open.

Yet the CB450 set a trend: almost every overhead camshaft Honda motorcycle engine produced since has employed a broadly similar set-up. Whilst it must be said that Honda have sometimes got their cam-drives embarrassingly wrong, the CB450 set them along the right path.

Before the CB450, twin overhead camshafts had been the exclusive preserve of exotic factory racers.

SPECIFICATION: HONDA CB450 'BLACK BOMBER'	
ENGINE	air-cooled 444cc DOHC vertical twin
HORSEPOWER	43-45bhp @ 9000rpm
TRANSMISSION	4-speed (later 5-speed)
FRAME	tubular steel single cradle
BRAKES	drum/drum
TOP SPEED	104mph

Bridgestone 350 GTR

'The GTR was also the smoothest in its class.'

Bridgestone's foray into motorcycle production was brief, but memorable. With disc-valve induction, six speeds, chrome bores and a 'piggy-back' alternator, the GTR anticipated many of the advances of the following decade.

If Suzuki's Super Six was the people's two-stroke screamer back in the late 'sixties, the 350GTR was the connoisseur's. Never had any stroker featured such a level of specification, not to mention acceleration capable of humbling many a 650 twin.

Bridgestone began making motorcycles in 1952, the same year Suzuki's production began. Although the GTR was essentially similar in design to the Super Six which had appeared a year earlier, it was awash with even more advanced touches. Like the Suzuki (and contemporary Yamahas and Kawasakis), the Bridgestone's crankcases split horizontally to reveal crank-, lay- and main-shafts laid out neatly for inspection. Also like the Suzuki, it featured six-speed transmission.

Where the GTR differed most was in its use of disc valve induction. A 'normal' two-stroke uses the rise and fall of the piston to control the flow of incoming and exhaust gases through ports in the cylinder walls. Because this inevitably gives symmetrical port timing, it can lead to poor running and spitting back through the carb, particularly at lower revs.

By offering asymmetric timing, rotary disc valves – basically cutaway discs mounted on the crankshaft – can overcome this problem. The system was perfected by MZ's race engineer, Walter Kaaden, before the technology was stolen – by Suzuki – in 1961. The Bridgestone wears two such disc valves – one per cylinder – keyed to each end of the crankshaft. A 26mm Mikuni carb sits outboard of each of these.

There was more. Since the side-mounted carbs make the powerplant quite broad enough, a 'piggy-back' alternator kept engine width within acceptable limits. The cylinder bores, rather than being of iron, are hard chrome, allowing tighter piston clearances. A dry, racing-style clutch is fitted. Not new, but welcome, is 'Jet Lube' positive oiling (driven by a pump under the right-hand carb), a version of the system first introduced on Yamaha's 1964 YA6. The 2.5 litre oil tank features an inspection window, with another allowing riders to check gearbox oil level; both commonplace later, but huge refinements at the time.

In the 'sixties, of course, half the world was changing gear with its right foot, the other half with its left. The GTR accommodated both; gearchange and rear brake pedals could be swapped. Less intelligent was the positioning of neutral above sixth gear in the down-for-up gearbox. Another 'modern' touch was that the 350 could be kick-started in gear, although the left-side kick start was rather less convenient.

More fashionable were the inflated performance claims made for the GTR – anything between 100 and 110mph. The reality, despite a speedo calibrated to 140, was around 93mph. In 1967 this nonetheless made the bike probably the quickest two-stroke roadster ever built.

Thanks to its rubber-mounted engine, the GTR was also the smoothest in its class. 37bhp (40bhp

was also claimed) offered searing acceleration with that exhilarating rush typical of performance two-strokes. The 330lb machine handled well on suspension that was more supple than most, and the drum brakes were equally impressive.

Not only was this specification impressive, but the build quality of the Bridgestone was also exceptional. Unfortunately, so, too, was the price. In 1968 a GTR retailed at £340, about £60 more than a Super Six and only £29 less than a Triumph 650 Bonneville. This, and widespread doubts about the durability of such 'buzz boxes', severely restricted sales. Just 33 GTRs were imported to the UK before Bridgestone abruptly ceased motorcycle production in late 1968 to concentrate on its core tyre-making business. The 350 GTR may not have lasted long, but it was certainly memorable.

Advanced disc-valve induction (above right) put the Bridgestone one jump ahead. Like other Japanese machines of the period, the GTR's engine was way ahead of its chassis.

SPECIFICATION: BRIDGESTONE 350 GTR	
ENGINE	air-cooled 345cc disc-valve two-stroke twin
HORSEPOWER	37bhp @ 7500rpm
TRANSMISSION	6-speed
FRAME	tubular double cradle
BRAKES	2LS drum/drum
TOP SPEED	93mph

Suzuki RS67 Racer

·····················

This is a tale of a headlong technological onslaught such as we may never see again. If Europeans were inclined to laugh at Japan's early forays into *grand prix* racing, it was Suzuki who gave them the most opportunities. When Suzuki entered the world championship in 1960, the unreliability of their machinery was only equalled by its slowness. Their 125, for instance, developed a mere 13bhp, substantially less than Honda's RC142 and about *ten horsepower* fewer than Ernst Degner's East German MZ RE125.

Even in 1961, when Honda were winning their first TT, the Suzukis were woefully uncompetitive. Yet just 12 months later a 50cc Suzuki became the first two-stroke ever to win a world championship. A year later still, Hugh Anderson gave Suzuki their first 125cc world title. Suzuki had arrived.

The difference was largely due to one man; that same Ernst Degner, who had defected to the West

in 1961 whilst leading the 125cc championship. His escape was 'sponsored' by Suzuki, for whom Degner was soon working under an assumed name. At the time, thanks to the genius of Walter Kaaden, MZ were masters of the two-stroke technology to which Suzuki aspired. Degner was the means of obtaining it.

For the most part, it worked. But, such was Anderson's success that Suzuki grew bold. For 1964, they decided to aim for the 250cc title as well. The result, the RZ64 liquid-cooled 'double 125' square four, has been described as 'one of the most embarrassing flops in *grand prix* history'. In two years of GP racing, it never finished higher than third. Even to this day, Suzuki has never won a 250c world road race title.

Although Suzuki continued to win the 50cc title, the major titles eluded them other than Anderson's repeat 125cc win in 1965. Honda had leap-frogged

Despite a lightweight aluminium frame, the RS67's chassis parts were primitive. What mattered most was cramming maximum technology into minimum volume, at which the V4 excelled. Sadly, Suzuki withdrew from racing before it was fully developed.

to the 1964 125cc championship with an eight-speed transverse four. In 1966 they responded just as emphatically with their miraculous 125cc-five, effectively 2^1/$_2$ 50cc twins. Thus equipped, Taveri won again, although harried all the way by Bill Ivy's V4 Yamaha.

Against this relentless development, when even the most sophisticated machine could be rendered obsolete in less than 12 months, Suzuki needed something far more potent than the ageing 35bhp RT67 twin with which they contested most of the 1967 series. After just four frantic months of development the V4 was ready to race at the last *grand prix* of the year, the Japanese, in October.

The RS67 is a still-incredible machine which must have been mind-blowing at the time; four tiny cylinders in 90 degree vee formation, four 24mm carbs, four geared cranks, 12 gears, liquid-cooled, with positive oil lubrication and disc-valve induction.

Peak power was 42bhp – over *three times* greater than Suzuki's 125 of a mere seven years earlier – at a dizzy 16,500rpm. Top speed was 136mph. To

reduce friction losses, the gearbox was dry sump, with forced lubrication from a trochoidal pump. Yet for all this complexity, extensive use of titanium and aluminium alloys (even the frame was aluminium), kept weight down to just 95kg – only 6kg more than the twin.

When Stuart Graham placed second to Bill Ivy at the Fuji circuit, the signs were encouraging. Yamaha may have taken the championship, but the new Suzuki was clearly a force to be reckoned with. By February 1968, power had improved to 43.8bhp. Suzuki were also developing the astonishing RP68, a 50cc Vee-3 which reportedly produced 19.8bhp at 19,000rpm – the highest specific output ever recorded by a normally-aspirated internal combustion engine. It was so peaky that its 14 gears were insufficient.

Yet time was running out for the multi-cylinder factory specials. 125s were soon to be limited to two cylinders and six speeds. When Suzuki, along with Honda, withdrew from world championship competition, the days of the most exotic generation of machines in racing history were over.

The product of Japanese engineering enterprise and East German genius, the V4's disc valves and screaming expansion chambers produced an astonishing 340bhp/litre.

SPECIFICATION: SUZUKI RS67 RACER	
ENGINE	liquid-cooled 124cc two-stroke V4
HORSEPOWER	42bhp @ 16,500rpm
TRANSMISSION	12-speed
FRAME	aluminium twin cradle
BRAKES	drum/drum
TOP SPEED	136mph

'The new Suzuki was clearly a force to be reckoned with.'

BSA Spitfire

They didn't know it at the time, but when the Spitfire arrived, BSA had a distinctly chequered future.

Understated but potent, the Spitfire was too little, too late to reverse the decline in BSA's fortunes. By the time the MkIV arrived in 1968, Honda's CB750 was just around the corner.

BSA's first post-war big twin, the 500cc Model A7, first came under public gaze at the Paris Motorcycle Show of 1946. Public reaction was favourable, but the bike's wasn't: performance proved to be disappointing, with a tendency to 'run-on' through self-ignition.

Cue Bert Hopwood, one of the most creative spirits in post-war British motorcycle design and the man also responsible for Norton's enduring Dominator. These days he might easily be described as 'Twins-R-Us'. Hopwood redesigned the 500cc BSA twin into the 650cc A10 Golden Flash. This in turn generated a better A7, plus a sports 500 known as the Star Twin.

In 1952 the Star Twin made one of the most impressive attempts on the Maudes Trophy, awarded for feats of exceptional motorcycle endurance. Three Star Twins were ridden 1000 miles to the ISDT in Austria, competed (earning gold medals apiece), then continued until each machine had completed 4900 miles. Not surprisingly, this earned BSA the coveted trophy, and a reputation for mechanical strength.

The unit construction BSA A50/A65 series followed early in 1962, prompted by Triumph's similar move. As well as eliminating the primary chain adjustment, the new twins had better electrics, weighed some 30lbs less than their predecessors, and were significantly less expensive than their Triumph competitors. They had clean, neat lines – perhaps too neat, because many considered the styling bland. But the first A65 claimed only 38bhp, and there was soon some concern about main bearing and oil pump failures. For whatever reason, the public wasn't impressed.

The performance benchmark during the early 'sixties was of course Triumph's T120 Bonneville, whilst Norton set the yardstick for handling. BSA twins, on the other hand, were ideal sidecar hacks with a reputation for robustness rather than sparkling looks or performance.

True, BSA had created some worthy contenders, notably the A10RGS Rocket Gold Star twin. But these were specialised machines produced in relatively small numbers. It wasn't until the arrival of the Spitfire in 1965 that BSA truly entered

the fray (British bikers had to wait until 1966). Although basically a development of the twin-carb A65L Lightning, this was a much more single-minded beast. With vibrant red paintwork, alloy wheel rims, close-ratio gears, high-compression pistons and substantially less weight, this was the Beezer they'd been waiting for.

The first Spitfire, with racing-style Amal GP carburettors and hot camshafts, claimed a potent 55bhp. Later examples were slightly de-tuned, if less raucous, with Concentric carbs and slightly less compression. The chassis, on the other hand, was only slightly different from 'cooking' BSA twins. And, worst of all, the short-stroke twin vibrated savagely at high revs.

1968 brought the last of the Spitfires, the MkIV, with a twin leading shoe front brake and audacious 150mph speedometer. More pointedly still, it brought the first public showing for Honda's CB750. BSA actually did the right thing in buying a Honda four for evaluation. Astonishingly, when its chain snapped after less than 100 miles and wrecked the crankcases, they felt able to dismiss the growing hurricane from the East as an inconsequential breeze.

Although a revised range of twins with oil-bearing frames appeared in 1970, these were unattractively styled and increasingly dated in overall design. Ironically, during this period BSA boasted a highly sophisticated development department at 'space age' Umberslade Hall, and perhaps the most automated motorcycle production line outside Japan. Yet for all this potential the company flapped around like a headless chicken, producing a succession of misbegotten models in search of a replacement for the venerable Bantam. These included the Dandy and Beagle commuter bikes, a 250cc scooter and the catastrophic Ariel-3 tricycle. Perhaps the most promising project, the 350cc ohc Fury twin, never reached production. In 1973, this one-time giant gently subsided, its remaining assets passing to the Norton-Villiers group.

This particular MkIV Spitfire is still going strong despatch riding around London. The Spit's always-considerable punch has been made even stronger by a 834cc top-end, although the brakes struggle to cope with modern traffic conditions.

SPECIFICATION: BSA SPITFIRE	
ENGINE	air-cooled 654cc OHV vertical twin
HORSEPOWER	up to 55bhp @ 7000rpm
TRANSMISSION	4-speed
FRAME	tubular steel twin cradle
BRAKES	drum/drum
TOP SPEED	110mph

'This was a much more single-minded beast.'

Triumph Trident 750

For once, advertising told the truth. When the BSA/Triumph triple was launched in 1968, the advertising insisted that 'After today, the motorcycle world will never be the same'. It wasn't, but it was Honda, rather than BSA/Triumph, who prospered. The triple was in some ways a better machine than the shattering CB750 launched one year later. It certainly handled far better, yet somehow it never quite cut it against the sophistication and sheer flamboyance of the four.

Originally the BSA Group (which had acquired Triumph/Ariel in 1951) produced two versions, the Triumph Trident T150 and the BSA Rocket-3. The latter used forward-inclined cylinders in a tubular twin cradle, compared to the Triumph's upright powerplant in a single-downtube 650-type frame.

But the powerplant, imposing as it was, was little more than a stop-gap measure, proposed by two of the rare forward-thinkers in the British industry at the time. Designers Bert Hopwood and Doug Hele had proposed such an engine, essentially 1½ Triumph Tigers on a common crankcase, some years earlier. In the longer term Hopwood favoured a modular engine system, not unlike that adopted by the Bloor/Triumph company 20 years later.

In the meantime, the Trident would have to suffice against the multis known to be coming from Japan, and it did so pretty well. A good one was at least as fast as the Honda (the first press test Trident, possibly a 'special', clocked almost 130mph; others struggled to reach 118mph). The handling, though good, was undoubtedly

Virtually 1½ 500cc Triumph twins on a common crankcase, the triple wasn't quite sophisticated enough to exploit the multi-cylinder era it anticipated.

'The handling, though good, was undoubtedly compromised by the sheer mass of the beast.'

Although now much sought-after, the striking Craig Vetter-designed X-75 Hurricane version of the triple (below and left) was not the sales success BSA/Triumph hoped. If only the same flair had been allowed in R&D . . .

compromised by the sheer mass of the beast. Nonetheless, it could leave the Honda for dead through the turns.

Mechanically, though, this was the triple that Edward Turner might have designed in 1937. Push-rods opened the valves, at a time when overhead camshafts were becoming commonplace. The crankcases split vertically, like the twin's, and primary drive was by chain. A diaphragm clutch was more up-to-date, but the original four-speed gearbox was not. Overall, despite Ogle Design's styling of the BSA (with 'Ray-gun' silencers and 'Bread-bin' fuel tank), the bike was more a child of the 'sixties than the imminent 'seventies.

Where the triple scored its biggest success was on the track, where anyone who heard it still shivers from that haunting wail. For British race fans of the 'seventies, the Rob North-framed triple was the 'feel-good' factor on two wheels – first, second and third at Daytona in 1971; countless other short-circuit victories, and a succession of production TT wins for the legendary 'Slippery Sam'.

On early versions the equipment, too, was less than state-of-the-art. Triumph's twin leading shoe drum front brake was never very potent; on the 460lb triple it was downright embarrassing. Starting, unlike the Honda's, was by kick.

(Ironically, BSA bought an early CB750 for evaluation. When its drive chain broke after less than 100 miles, they dismissed the entire machine as 'no threat'). Despite a higher selling price, it simply wasn't as refined as the Honda.

When it finally arrived, the Triumph-Lockheed disc front brake was good, but by then the triple had been five years in production. Also in 1973, attempts to improve sales resulted in the X-75 Hurricane, one of the most eye-catching roadsters ever produced; it flopped. Two years later still the Triumph T160 electric start version appeared, now with more power from an engine leaning forward in the old Rocket-3 manner.

It was all too little, and too late. In 1973 the bankrupt BSA Group amalgamated with Norton-Villiers, planning closure of the Triumph factory at Meriden. This provoked the famous workers' sit-in which, after the election of a Labour government in February 1974, established Meriden as an independent cooperative. Henceforth, however, it would produce only twins.

SPECIFICATION: TRIUMPH TRIDENT 750	
ENGINE	air-cooled 740cc OHV transverse triple
HORSEPOWER	58bhp @ 7500rpm
TRANSMISSION	5-speed
FRAME	tubular twin cradle with single front downtube
BRAKES	2LS drum/drum (1972-on: disc/drum)
TOP SPEED	120mph

Honda CB750

∙∙∙∙∙∙∙∙∙∙∙∙∙∙∙∙∙∙∙∙∙∙∙∙∙∙

'Fastidious little cable guides abound, and the instruments are elegant in their one-piece neatness.'

Prior to 1969, the word 'Superbike' simply didn't exist. Then Honda's seminal 750-four came along, opening up a whole new lexicon of jargon, and a revolution in motorcycle design. Almost every Japanese superbike – and many not so super – can trace its ancestry back to this one machine.

Honda's *coup* – even more than winning Daytona with the four in 1970 – was in putting such a device into mass production. Engine technology, far from being at the cutting edge, was fairly old hat. Honda already made twin-cam roadsters (CB450), but the 750 made do with one. They were at the sharp end of pent-roof combustion chamber development, but the 750 used hemispherical heads. They pioneered four valves per cylinder, but the 750 had just two. To an engineer, there was really nothing remarkable about the CB750 – except that it was a four, and it was in the shops.

No, what you got was a neat and surprisingly compact transverse four, with eight valves, one chain-driven overhead camshaft and – unlike most of its descendants – dry sump lubrication. Bore and stroke were slightly undersquare at 61 x 63mm. Primary drive was by duplex chain, and a five speed gearbox fed a peak of 67bhp to the rear wheel. It had four 28mm Keihin carbs and – above all – four brilliant chrome exhaust pipes. 'Look at me', it screamed at the world.

25 years ago, the turbine-like acceleration was a sensation. It's smooth and tractable, happy to pull away at just 1000rpm, and whirr seamless up to 9000. The effect is utterly civilised and totally anodyne, and it set the bench mark for at least two decades.

Like all performance machines, exaggerated claims were made for the Honda's performance. 115mph was the true potential. A good Norton twin was its equal, and a decent Triumph or BSA triple its better – especially when the bends arrived. What the Honda had was gentility in abundance; scarcely a single rough edge had made it into production.

With minimal vibration, no oil leaks, reliability and super-light throttle and clutch actions, the Honda mollycoddled anyone fortunate enough to step on board. On the other hand, the hydraulic disc front brake – the first on a production

motorcycle – requires considerable pressure to underwhelming effect.

The handling is mixed. Early examples, in particular, topple into corners at town speeds – in contrast to the sublime neutrality of the best of British. Otherwise, it offers impeccable walking-pace balance, and effortless 40 to 80mph cruising. Press it some more, however, and it weaves and wobbles like no British bike with sporting pretensions.

None of the CB750's handling deficiencies are primarily due to a lack of frame stiffness, although if the chassis could boast half as many tubes as the exhaust, it might handle better. The problem is distinctly limp damping mated to stiffish springing and skinny forks. The truth was that in Honda's principal market – the USA – pedigree handling was not a selling point. So why waste money designing it in?

But this is carping. The CB750 was as much a corporate vehicle as a production motorcycle; living, revving, weaving proof that a cammy four need cost little more than the price of a traditional twin (£680

Curiously understated '750' didn't say the half of it. But four pipes and silencers did the Honda's talking with chrome-plated eloquence.

in 1970). It was awesome, even to look at. Strewth, we'd never seen four silencers on *anything* before.

The other revolution was in the detailing – or sanitising – that practically everyone has since taken on board. Parts fit, precisely. Fastidious little cable guides abound, and the instruments are elegant in their one-piece neatness.

And, boy, did it sell! In the decade it was in production, from the K0 of 1969 to the last four-piper, the K7 of 1977/78, almost one million CB750s were made. *Motorcycle Sport* summed it all up at the time: 'In years to come, when historians look back on . . . motorcycling in the '70s, one of the turning points will be seen as the day when Honda made one of the most sophisticated, supposedly complicated and certainly potent motorcycles available to the public at a price it could afford.' They were right. This was, after all, the first superbike.

Blue bike is the original 750-4 K0 of 1969. Golden K2 model of 1974 was re-styled but went and handled substantially the same. Almost one million were produced.

In 1968 there wasn't a word to describe it, so they invented one: 'Superbike'. Motorcycling has never been the same.

SPECIFICATION: HONDA CB750

ENGINE	4-cylinder 736cc SOHC
HORSEPOWER	67bhp @ 8000rpm
TRANSMISSION	5-speed
FRAME	tubular steel twin cradle
BRAKES	single disc/drum
TOP SPEED	115mph

Rickman Interceptor

For an accidental marriage, Rickman's Interceptor worked well. The Metisse chassis was later to prove itself capable of handling even CB750 and Z1 horsepower.

It's a stunner – a screaming eyeful of nickel, chrome and orange, subtle as a Hawaiian sunset and twice as blinding.'

It began, to cut a long story short, as one of those accidents of history. 'When Royal Enfield went out of business in 1969 and left 200-odd Series II Constellation engines stranded at the docks en route to Indian in the States, someone had a brain-wave', recalls a former Rickman employee. The brain-wave was to become the Interceptor, an amalgam of Rickman's acknowledged chassis know-how and Enfield's biggest twin.

On the face of it, it's a winning combination. Visually, certainly, it's a stunner – a screaming eyeful of nickel, chrome and orange, subtle as a Hawaiian sunset and twice as blinding.

Colour aside, this was precisely the philosophy behind the Rickman brothers' – Derek and Don's – approach. The 'sixties, to quote another employee, was a time when there were 'plenty of good engines and good frames about, but it wasn't often that you got the two together'. The Rickman answer was the Metisse chassis – the name is French for mongrel bitch – to fit a variety of mainly racing engines.

To meet the Rickman maxim of 'extreme rigidity with minimum weight', the frame features a bronze-welded double cradle of $1^{1}/_{4}$ in 16-gauge Reynolds 531 steel. Eccentric chain adjusters preclude Rickman's other pet hate – inaccurate wheel alignment. The execution, as always, is superb. Even more compelling, the finished machine tips the scales at just 353lb, an astonishing 95lb less than a standard Constellation.

The first of 'around 205' Interceptors left the Rickman factory in 1970. All wore glass fibre tanks and dual seats, Borrani rims, and motocross-derived

Apart from their exquisite nickel-plated frames, Rickman also developed disc brakes and their own large-diameter telescopic forks. The machine would originally have been a more muted mustard colour.

Rickman forks of a diameter – 15/8 in (41mm) – sturdier by far than the standards of the time. Braking is taken care of by a single AP Racing caliper up front, and a rear disc of Rickman design – both ahead of their time. Indeed, the high specification of the Interceptor's standard equipment had stirred a contemporary French magazine to call it 'the Rolls-Royce of motorcycles'.

Its engine, despite Enfield's demise, was quite new. The 736cc high-cam Constellation engine had been substantially revised to become the Series II model in 1969, with twin 30mm Amal Concentric carburettors, 8.5:1 compression and higher-lift cams. The dry-sump lubrication of the Series I was superseded by wet-sump oiling, with a much-enhanced flow-rate. In typical Enfield fashion, the powerplant sat 'semi-unit' with its gearbox, the two bolting rigidly together across flat mating faces, and keeping in touch via duplex chain to a wet multiplate clutch.

Power was variously quoted as 52 or 56bhp at 6750rpm, good for a top speed of around 115mph. Best of all, the long-stroke engine is hugely tractable, with ready power from below 2000rpm. It makes even a Triumph twin feel peaky, as well as vibrating a good deal less.

The ride is light, low and agile, yet stable, precise and predictable – a rare enough combination of virtues for machines of any vintage. On the other hand, the Metisse chassis isn't altogether happy about being plucked from the race-track and plunged into duty as a sit-up-and-beg roadster. There's next-to-no steering lock, the handlebars are uncomfortably wide and the girth across the footrests simply doesn't mesh with the narrowness of the tank. For all its high-class constituent parts, the Interceptor feels slightly makeshift.

What it really begs is rear-sets and clip-ons. As a café racer, it could be peerless. As a gentleman's carriage, it affects too many compromises. Yet the build quality and redoubtable chassis of the Metisse shine through, and perhaps as small an outfit as Rickman can be forgiven for the compromises they had to make. In the overall scheme of things, outfits such as Rickman meant little, but in showing that even big bikes could handle, they paved the way for the rest.

SPECIFICATION: RICKMAN INTERCEPTOR	
ENGINE	736cc OHV parallel twin
HORSEPOWER	56bhp @ 6750rpm
TRANSMISSION	4-speed
FRAME	Metisse twin cradle
BRAKES	disc/disc
TOP SPEED	115mph

Yamaha XS-1

....

'It's a big softie which, despite the brash claims made for it, makes little attempt to out-perform the Bonneville.'

'It's as near as you'll get to a Triumph without pushing it home every night', said the owner of this particular XS-1. Heresy? Maybe, but no more blasphemous than Yamaha's creation of the XS range of 650cc twins in the first place. Four-stroke fours and two-stroke triples were one thing, but in 1970 a machine such as this was a frontal assault on 33 years of Britishness in engine design. Vertical twins were ours, as English as eel pie, waxed cotton jackets and – yes – the Triumph Bonneville.

Indeed, the engine is what Triumph themselves might have designed if they'd had any money in 1969. Inevitably, it is in-unit, wet sump and the crankcases split horizontally. A single overhead camshaft, with the ignition points at its right end, is chain-driven from the centre of the crankshaft. Breathing was in the hands of two 38mm 'constant velocity' carbs, one of CV's earliest appearances on a production motorcycle.

Yamaha, of course, were pretty new to four-strokes at the time. The result is a sprinkling of components which look less like four-stroke parts than big RD250 bits, like the roller-bearing crank, with distinctly two-stroke-ish con-rods, running on roller big-ends. The earliest XS-1s even had needle-roller small ends.

Yamaha claimed 53bhp and 110-plus mph from the XS-1 (115mph for the later XS-2). True top speed in neutral conditions was about 105mph. Revealingly, the Bonneville, with supposedly two horsepower less, was capable of maybe 5mph *more*.

Surprisingly, considering it first appeared at the same time as Honda's CB750, the XS series did not adopt electric start until the XS-2 of 1972, which has completely reworked crankcases to accommodate the starter motor under the sump.

On the road, the engine is a delight: flexible, responsive and, thanks to rubber mounting, fairly smooth. It's a big softie which, despite the brash claims made for it, makes little attempt to out-perform the Bonneville.

Anyone expecting the best of British handling and steering, however, was in for a big disappointment. The frame, and particularly the swing-arm, probably aren't the stiffest in the world. The skinny 34mm forks and twin rear shock absorbers are patently underdamped. So, above 80mph the steering becomes vague. Throw in a few bends, bumps and cambers, and it's positively random even at speeds well below that figure. And ground clearance is poor. On the other hand it's small, not too heavy (439lb), and is manageable enough to be chucked around despite its deficiencies.

The 'Hamamatsu Bonneville' became the most successful of Japanese attempts to re-create the British vertical twin. It was ultimately bound by the same limitations inherent in the layout which confronted Triumph and BSA.

In 1970 the substantially identical similar XS-1B appeared. The first major revision was the XS-2, with a twin-piston single front disc and electric start (operated from a two-stage decompressor/starter lever on the right hand handlebar).

In 1975 the XS-650 arrived in Britain. European versions wore twin front discs, whilst the rest of the world made do with one. Frame and suspension modifications (under the guidance of British racer, Percy Tait) much improved the handling, at the expense of considerable weight. Other variants followed, until the final version was produced in 1982.

Although outwardly unremarkable compared with the likes of Honda's 750-four, the XS-1's strength was undoubtedly its engine. The 650 twin earned a reputation for rugged reliability which even big-bore sidecar motocross use couldn't dent. Neither the engine nor chassis were as sports-oriented as the best British vertical twins, nor did they possess the same pedigree. But, for all that, the XS-1 worked well in a lazy sort of way, managing to combine some of the better aspects of Japanese design with patently un-Japanese lashings of character. Heresy, perhaps – but nice.

SPECIFICATION: YAMAHA XS-1	
ENGINE	654cc air-cooled OHC parallel twin
HORSEPOWER	53 bhp @ 7000rpm
TRANSMISSION	5-speed
FRAME	Tubular twin cradle
BRAKES	drum/drum
TOP SPEED	105mph

The scene – Shaftsbury's 'Hovis Hill' – is as British as the Bonneville. The XS-1 was a comparable piece of impertinence and probably the least 'super' of the Japanese Superbikes – its frame and cycle parts were inferior to the Triumph's, whilst its engine offered only slightly more.

Laverda 750 SFC

....

This, more than any machine of its time, was a racer built for the street. Laverda's SFC was a raw, uncompromising beast of a machine, which even by the time it went on sale had an enviable reputation.

The Laverda factory raced only rarely. Yet in 1968 an early version of what was to become the SFC won the *Giro d'Italia* long-distance race. Three years later, an even bigger and more comprehensive triumph came Laverda's way: at the 1971 Barcelona 24-hour race, SFCs placed first, third and fourth. Not a bad weekend's work for a company which began by making tractors.

The 750 from which the SF and later the SFC was developed certainly didn't go like a tractor, but its engine was built like one. The crankshaft ran in no less than five main bearings; drive to the single overhead camshaft was by a double-row chain; and the 13-plate clutch, very heavy in operation, had its own outrigger bearing. The gearbox was similarly robust.

Although the basic configuration was much like many British parallel twins, the Laverda was thoroughly modern. As well as being overhead cam, its wet-sump crankcases split horizontally. There was electric start (a kick-start wasn't even fitted), and it didn't leak oil. And the engine's close-pitched finning, not unlike Honda's CB72, was strikingly modern. Mindful of the dodgy reputation of Italian electrical equipment, Laverda also sourced much of their components in Germany and even, later, Japan. The 36mm carburettors, though, were Spanish Amals, whilst the Italian CEV switchgear is pretty horrible.

The engine hangs from a backbone comprising four huge rails, two of which dip down to the swing-arm pivot, whilst the other two support the seat assembly and rear suspension. The engine bolts rigidly to the frame by its cam box and crankcase rear, further strengthening the design. The same overkill extends to the swing-arm which, rare for the period, is cross-braced.

Topping this off was a bright orange half-fairing and race-style 'bum-stop' seat, the latter with room for a racing number. Despite the massive engine, the silver-painted spine frame gave an impression of lightness which wasn't entirely illusory. The SFC weighed-in at 420lb, 60lb less than the SF.

SPECIFICATION: LAVERDA 750 SFC

ENGINE	744cc SOHC parallel twin
HORSEPOWER	70bhp @ 7500rpm
TRANSMISSION	5-speed
FRAME	tubular spine type
BRAKES	double drum/drum (later double disc/disc)
TOP SPEED	130mph

Although a later 500cc twin would bear the name of Barcelona's Montjuich circuit, the SFC's pedigree derived from the gruelling Spanish 24-hour race.

Early SFCs wore 230mm Laverda twin leading shoe brakes (double-sided at the front), later graduating to triple 280mm Brembo discs. Suspension, with 38mm forks from 1974, is by Ceriani. Later versions also had lighter bodywork and a magnesium rear hub, whilst their engines benefited from higher compression ratios, lighter crankshafts and a hotter 6C cam.

Although they had else little in common, the SFC was to the 'seventies what the Velocette Thruxton had been to the previous decade. Yet in contrast to the highly-strung single, the intervening years allowed the Italian machine to be both raucous and civilized (if only slightly). The SFC certainly thrives on revs – real power begins at around 6000rpm – but it is genuinely flexible and happy to dawdle at much lower speeds. Relatively smooth for a parallel twin, it is also very, very fast.

The chassis is rather less accommodating. The suspension might be fine on a smooth, purpose-built race track, but on a bumpy road any SFC is a spine-jarring experience. Clip-ons and rear-sets demand a racing crouch which soon becomes uncomfortable.

But so what? This is manifestly not a tourer. It steers accurately (and much lighter than Ducati's 750SS), handles well (far better than any contemporary Japanese superbike), and has more ground clearance than any road tyre of its vintage could exploit. It sounded like a million dollars, and looked like ten million. It wasn't for the faint-hearted, but it was special.

Just how special can easily be quantified. Of 19,000 750 Laverdas built between 1971 and 1976, only 549 were SFCs. Lucky owners.

Uncomfortable race-style riding position made hard riding almost second nature.

'It sounded like a million dollars, and looked like ten million.'

Red 1972 SFC wears large Grimeca drum brakes and Amal carbs. By 1975 (orange machine) triple Brembo discs and Dell'Orto carbs were standard.

Kawasaki 750H2

. . . .

In *Bike* magazine of November 1984, Mark Williams wrote of the H2 Kawasaki that 'here is a machine so utterly and completely dedicated to completing the distance from A to B in the fastest possible time . . . such acceleration will satisfy even the most mind-wrenched adrenalin addict'.

It was true. Here was the first mass-produced motorcycle aimed squarely at the world's nutters. These things were *ferocious*; 748cc of pure exhilaration. They'd never made two-strokes that big before. In an age still reeling from the potency of the latest quarter-litre strokers, one three times the size, in much the same state of tune, was simply – although the word wasn't so fashionable at the time – awesome.

Originally introduced as the 74bhp 750 H2 Mach IV in 1972, the H2A was, believe it or not, a refinement. The Mach IV was smoky, thirsty, peaky, wheelie-prone and evil-handling. The H2, with three horsepower less, more fork trail and a longer wheelbase, was all of the above but merely handled badly. Despite sharing the same basic engine layout, it was everything Suzuki's portly and staid GT750 was not.

Mechanically, the H2 was deceptively simple; three 250cc singles strung across the frame. Three slide-type carburettors fed in copious quantities of petrol, whilst three exhausts (one on the left, two on the right) dispensed with the proceeds and made a modest effort to quieten the ensuing racket. Almost as radical was the styling, mean and lean, with a low tank and kicked-up 'duck tail' seat, belying the machine's 450lb weight.

Everything about the machine was uncompromising. Power came in hard at 4500rpm, giving a demented surge all the way to 7000, when power trailed off abruptly. Vibration was severe at high revs. The seat was comfortable, but the high-bars and upright riding position were not. In this

respect appalling fuel consumption, as low as 22mpg, was a blessing; stopping to fill up was a relief.

All large Japanese bikes of the period had engines which far outstripped their chassis. In the H2's case, the shortfall was extreme. The skinny frame and swing-arm flexed appallingly under load. Even the brakes could be felt bending the forks under hard braking. Kawasaki progressively extended the wheelbase between each of the three models, but never got the H2 to handle.

It was another age, another world. Kawasaki's brochure for the Mach IV heralded the triple as having 'only one purpose in life; to give you the most exciting and exhilarating performance . . .

For all the menace beneath, the H2 was a handsome piece of kit. Admiring it from a distance was safer than climbing aboard.

demands the razor-sharp reactions of an experienced rider . . . a machine you must take seriously.' Try getting away with such a sales pitch these days.

By the time of the H2B of 1974, the world was no place for gas-guzzlers such as these. In three short years, the big-bore two-stroke delinquent had risen, frightened an unsuspecting world half to death, and died. We shall never see quite the like of it again.

SPECIFICATION: KAWASAKI 750H2

ENGINE	748cc air-cooled transverse two-stroke triple
HORSEPOWER	74/71bhp @ 6800rpm.
TRANSMISSION	5-speed
FRAME	Tubular twin cradle
BRAKES	disc/drum
TOP SPEED	120mph

74bhp, a wild powerband and a chassis which would have been hard-pressed on a moped . . . only a brave man would try to use all the H2's performance. In the 'seventies, there were plenty of takers.

'The world was no place for gas-guzzlers such as these.'

The big Kawasaki triple's uncompromising nature would quite possibly be outlawed today — reason enough, perhaps, for preserving one of the most awesome chapters in motorcycling history.

Münch Mammoth

....

Take one NSU car engine, add two wheels and stir the imagination . . .

Pretty, it was not. But as an exercise in technical overkill, Friedl Münch's monstrous creation held the motorcycling world in awe.

ong before Spielberg made his film, the cast list for *Jurassic Park* had already begun. The Münch Mammut (Mammoth) was quite simply the most monstrous motorcycle of the post-war years.

This Leviathan was the creation of a German, Friedl Münch, dubbed 'the Sorcerer of Ossenheim'. In the early '60s, Münch had a dream of building the most fantastic motorcycle in the world. No proprietory motorcycle engine was suitable, so Münch turned to the car world. He selected the air-cooled 1000cc unit which normally powered the NSU Prinz, enjoying considerable rally success at the time. Later versions employed a tuned 1177cc derivative of the same powerplant, and there was even a brief diversion with a three cylinder two-stroke engine.

Although an all-alloy engine, the NSU was both big and heavy. Münch's original choice of frame, a Norton Featherbed, proved too small, so he constructed a larger, beefier copy.

By then the real work had only just started. Münch made a primary drive and four-speed gearbox, both in purpose-built casings. The NSU's standard wet-sump lubrication was retained.

No ordinary cycle parts could cope with the Münch's sheer weight, so new ones had to be created. To forks of his own design Münch laced a massive 250mm twin-leading-shoe front brake which, big as it was, had trouble coping with the momentum of the 550lb machine. Much of the rest of the machine was also designed from scratch.

Like many more modern monsters – Honda Gold Wings spring to mind – the Mammoth is surprisingly well balanced once on the move. The four-cylinder engine is sublimely smooth, with a huge spread of irrepressible power which makes the four-speed gearbox almost redundant. 120mph comes easily (for the bike; with no fairing to hide behind, the rider gets a fearful battering). Claims of close to 150mph have been made for the 1177cc Mammoth Sport, but it would take a brave man to prove it.

If the Mammoth roadster was absurd, the racing version was even more bizarre. As well as a short-lived competition programme with sidecar aces Helmut Fath and Horst Owesle, in 1978 Münch attempted to beat the world one-hour record, set in 1964 by Mike Hailwood on a 500 MV.

Cornering was never the
Münch's strength, although one
125 horsepower example was
raced at Daytona. The tyres,
inevitably, couldn't cope.

'Claims of close to 150mph have been made for the 1177cc Mammoth Sport, but it would take a brave man to prove it.'

car engine during the period. Several road-going specials appeared, most using either the NSU unit, or the one-litre Hillman Imp engine. Both were also used in racing sidecar outfits. Some years later one bold individual even created a two-wheeler powered by a 3.5 litre Rover Vee-8 housed, oddly enough, in a standard-sized Norton Featherbed frame. More recently still, the gargantuan 'Boss Hoss' special crammed a full-blown Chevrolet Vee-8 into a motorcycle frame.

In 1972 the Münch commanded a mammoth price tag of £2500, over three times the cost of Honda's CB750. (Today, you'd need to pay perhaps eight times that for a good example). Nonetheless, about 450 were made over a period of about 15 years. The small company initially enjoyed the backing of the American motorcycle publisher, Floyd Clymer, and later from Heinz Henke. In 1977 Münch left to manufacture parts for yet another monster, the 1300cc TTS/E. But his legacy continues; the Mammoth remains the most colossal production motor-cycle ever offered for sale.

The attempt took place around the banked Daytona Speedway, using a 1370cc NSU engine with four 35mm Dell'Orto carbs and an estimated 125bhp at 8600rpm. Rider Ferdinand Kaczor had no trouble hurtling this missile through the speed trap at 178mph. However, contemporary tyre technology was simply not equal to the power and weight of the machine, nicknamed the 'Daytona Bomb', which shredded its rear cover after just three laps. A further attempt was thwarted when an American court awarded the machine to one of Münch's American backers in lieu of outstanding debts.

Nor was Münch's the only motorcycle to use a

SPECIFICATION: MÜNCH MAMMOTH	
ENGINE	air-cooled 1177cc OHC transverse four
HORSEPOWER	90bhp @ 6000rpm
TRANSMISSION	4-speed
FRAME	tubular twin cradle
BRAKES	drum/drum
TOP SPEED	125mph-plus

Kawasaki Z1

In 1972, a *grand prix* MV 500 produced around 80bhp. Then came Z1, and almost anybody could ride one on the street.

'Shutting the throttle mid-corner produced a series of violent weaves.'

efore 1972, when Kawasaki's legendary Z1 was launched, you had to be a works MV Grand Prix racer to know what 80-plus horsepower felt like on two wheels. Then Kawasaki launched the Z1, and almost anyone with £1284 to spare could share an experience only the likes of Agostini had known before.

Unlike the wild two-stroke triples which had preceded it, there was nothing particularly novel about the Z1. It wasn't the first 'modern' four (Honda's CB750 beat it to that), nor was it the first to put double overhead cams into mass production (Honda again, with the CB450). No, what the big Kawasaki did was give you more of everything, in one awesome package.

At its heart was a transverse four-cylinder engine of 903cc, fed by four 28mm Mikuni carburettors, blowing in turn into the swoopiest four-pipe exhaust system ever to pass through a chrome plater's tanks. A huge clutch housing spoke implicitly of the prodigious torque this animal could unleash.

Typical of the time, the cycle parts were less impressive. Attempting to keep the Z1 on the straight and narrow was a simple mild steel twin cradle frame which was essentially a bad copy of the Norton Featherbed of 20 years earlier. Nor was the suspension any more robust; skinny 36mm telescopic forks up front, and twin shock absorbers of doubtful damping capacity at the rear. It wasn't to be until Suzuki's GS750 of 1978 that the Japanese began to pay real heed to handling.

In the meantime the Z1 was fast – a genuine 134mph – and flawed. Ridden gently, the bike is fairly stable, with a slight tendency to understeer. Dial-in all that power, however, and Dr. Jekyll reveals Mr Hyde. You are no longer completely in control. Shutting the throttle mid-corner produced a series of violent weaves as the slack in the chassis unwound. It took a very committed rider to get the best out of the Kawasaki.

But the first impression is one of smallness for, US-style handlebars excepted, this is a low and compact device. Hit the starter, and the exhaust baffles chatter encouragingly over the breathy roar of the airbox. When the baffles quieten down, you know she's warm.

Apart from the noise and the firmness of the controls – far stiffer than the CB750, for example – there isn't as much as you'd expect to distinguish the Z1 from, say, a modern 750 Zephyr. That's how revolutionary it felt 23 years ago. Stiffest of all is the front brake, which needs a hell of a squeeze to haul down the Z1 from speed.

Tests of the time marvelled at the Z1's 'immensely strong bottom-end power', the engine's sheer durability and its reluctance to leak any oil. Above all they marvelled at top speeds well over

SPECIFICATION: KAWASAKI Z1	
ENGINE	4-cylinder 903cc DOHC
HORSEPOWER	82bhp @ 8500rpm
TRANSMISSION	5-speed
FRAME	tubular steel twin cradle
BRAKES	single disc/drum
TOP SPEED	134mph

130mph, with giddy revs and blistering acceleration, albeit only on roads with soft hedges. Even in 1995, when 82bhp is commonplace, the Z1 feels strong, eager – civilised, but with a satisfyingly raw edge that no modern retro could tolerate.

The 'true' Z1 was produced only for 1973. Rumour has it that this is the quickest example, and although its cams and exhaust are slightly noisier, this is more myth than substance. The Z1 was followed in successive years by the Z1A, Z1B and finally the much-revised Z900, before giving way to the Z1000 in 1977. In the process the machine earned a reputation for bullet-proof dependability. The fact was that the powerplant was over-engineered, for the top-end of even a 1986 GPz1100R will drop straight on to a set of Z1 crankcases. This legend was built to live on.

Over 20 years on, the Z1 remains one of the most striking superbikes to come from Japan. In contrast, all modern-day 'retros' are bland — especially when you wind open the throttle

Although Honda's CB750-4 comfortably beat it into the showrooms, Kawasaki's brutal musclebike is the one everyone remembers. Originally designed as a 750, it was punched out to 903 unforgettable cee-cee when the Honda was unveiled

Ducati 750SS

Not quite the real thing, but wickedly handsome and affordable: the 750 Sport.

The one that started it all: Paul Smart's Imola-winning factory 750SS. Any true 'Ducatisti', would rob banks to own it.

Whatever heroics Carl Fogarty, Doug Polen and the rest have achieved in recent years on their blood-red Italian twins, this is the one the connoisseurs remember. For an entire generation of bikers, this single machine launched a life-long love affair with Ducati.

Like most affairs of the heart, these ones rarely ran smooth. Twenty years ago Ducati's were cantankerous beasts with laughable electrics, fragile engines, flakey chrome and dodgy paint. 'Character', they certainly had. They also had soul.

The original soul child is Paul Smart's 750SS racer. In 1972, with no track record to speak of, this machine took on the best in the world and thrashed it hollow. The deed was done at the Imola 200-miler, just down the road from the Ducati factory in Bologna, in front of the wildly partisan *tifosi*. It was an unlikely dream come true.

In the early '70s, Ducati were known as manufacturers of lightweight racing machines – technically intriguing but well to the rear of the large-capacity horsepower race then blooming.

Then, in 1970, the Bolognese factory announced an official return to racing, with a desmodromic 500cc Vee-twin. Alongside the Colin Seeley-framed 500, Ducati developed a 750cc Vee-twin, first seen as a road-going prototype in 1970. A year later, at the Silverstone F750 round, Mike Hailwood practiced on a racing derivative of this. The bike was not competitive, and Hailwood elected instead to race a TZ350 Yamaha.

After a comprehensive winter redesign, Ducati set their sights on the 1972 Imola 200 miler, then being built up as 'Europe's Daytona'. Success would promote their new range of 750cc road bikes, but the race would be tough. No less than nine official or semi-official works teams would take part, including the brutal Kawasaki triples and Agostini on a very special 750cc MV. Briton Paul Smart, and Ducati development rider Bruno Spaggiari would pilot the machines.

Although 'very long and unwieldy', the 750 was ideally suited to Imola's fast sweeping bends. Unlike Hailwood's machine, it used standard roadster

crankcases, with a wet clutch and five-speed transmission. But unlike production versions, it was pared-down for lightness, with wafer-thin bodywork, and even more fragile. Power was around 85bhp at 8800rpm.

After five laps of the 200 mile race, Smart overhauled early leader Agostini, going on to hold off Spaggiari's challenge for a sensational Ducati 1-2. At a time when Japan was obsessed with horsepower above all, victory vindicated the European approach of mechanical simplicity married to pedigree handling and a slim, wind-cheating profile, always a Ducati hallmark. Yet engineer Fabio Taglioni's development programme had touched on many forms of novelty. Fuel injection was tried, but rejected. A triple camshaft version of Ducati's unique desmodromic valve system (an additional cam lobe, rather than a spring, closes the valve), succumbed to the accountant's knife.

The big Vee-twin had first appeared as a 'street' motorcycle at the Milan Show in November 1970. By the time of the Imola victory, two production versions were available, the 50bhp 750GT, and its 'café racer' variant, the bright orange 750 Sport. With 56bhp at 8200rpm, the Sport could comfortably exceed 120mph.

The 200-miler triumph, however, spawned *the* Ducati, the 'Imola Replica' 750SS. Essentially a works racer with lights, and a great many hand-finished engine parts, only 200 were built, during 1973 and '74. (The later square-case version, built for the Italian market, is a poor relation.) Of all the Ducati roadsters ever built, this is the most prized.

Yet even as the 750SS assembly line was rolling, events were consigning it to history. The 1973 Barcelona 24-hour race brought victory for yet another prototype Duke, this time an 864cc Vee-twin. The first 860 roadster was introduced at the Milan Show, going on sale in 1975 as the 860GT. Fans of booming race replicas were not disappointed, for a few months later another Ducati classic, the 900SS, was introduced. The legacy continues today with the mouth-watering 916.

Bright orange colour scheme aside, the 120mph-plus 750 Sport was almost indistinguishable from the SS. Valves were closed by springs, however, rather than Taglioni's desmodromics.

SPECIFICATION: DUCATI 750SS	
ENGINE	748cc OHC desmodromic Vee-twin
HORSEPOWER	65bhp @ 8500rpm
TRANSMISSION	5-speed
FRAME	tubular steel backbone with engine as stressed member
BRAKES	twin disc/disc
TOP SPEED	135mph

'For an entire generation of bikers, this single machine launched a life-long love affair with Ducati.'

Yamaha RD350

....

This is less about one particular model, than an enduring dynasty of Yamaha two-stroke twins. For 25 years from the mid-sixties, such machines captivated a generation of street riders, as well as winning more *Grands Prix* than any other manufacturer (350 from 1963 to 1990).

It wasn't always like that. In 1887 the company began making reed organs (hence their logo of three crossed tuning forks, which later became an apt metaphor for two-stroke tuning). In the 1920s they branched out into aircraft components, yet it was not until 1954 that they produced their first motorcycle. The 125cc YA1 'Red Dragonfly' was a near-copy of the same German DKW design which had spawned the BSA Bantam. In 1975 the Yamaha Motor Cycle Company was founded as a separate concern from the still successful musical instruments business.

From the outset Yamaha placed great store by competition – winning the Mt. Fuji hill climb with the YA1 in 1954; a year later the new 175cc YC1

also won. Both machines were distinctly European in appearance, but in 1958 Yamaha produced their first 'real' model, the 250cc YDS1 twin.

The twin was notable for two things – it was the first in a series of increasingly potent 250s; and in 1961 it also led to Yamaha's first venture into factory-built production racers, the TD1. Slow and hopelessly unreliable as it was, Yamaha soon learned, and from this duo sprang an empire which was to rule for over 20 years. On the road, it led to the YDS7, and ultimately the RD and RD/LC ranges; whilst on the track it culminated in the liquid-cooled TZ series which dominated almost every 250 and 350cc race of the 'seventies and early 'eighties.

With such a wealth of achievement to chose from, it's difficult to pick a pre-eminent model, but the first of the 'RD' series, the RD350 of 1973 will do as well as any other. This was the period when the 350 was one of the most popular machines in the biggest market of all, the USA.

The archetypal Japanese two-stroke twin. A close relative of contemporary TD Yamaha racers, the RD evolved into the acclaimed LC series of the 'eighties.

A development of the YR5, with which it shared a frame and the bulk of running gear and engine components, the first RD produced a sizzling 39bhp at 7500rpm. Under the heading 'Yamaha's 350 has come a long way . . .', *Motor Cycle Mechanics* suggested that 'As a 350, it makes a good 500'. This was the essence of a light, nimble and fast machine which, ridden hard, could hold its own in practically any company.

Part of the secret, new in '73, was reed-valve induction, in which a one-way valve of flexible 'petals' prevents blow-back through the carburettor, allowing a higher state of tune. Reed valves perform much the same function as the disc valves in Bridgestone's 350 GTR, but for far less cost and complexity. Even today, this remains the most common form of induction control on Grands Prix racers.

Yamaha called their reed system 'Torque Induction', and they had a point. The 350 boasted increased top-end punch without sacrificing mid-range power. This was a two-stroke which could be pottered with ease, yet offered that same manic rush of power when the engine came 'on the pipe'. Light (315lb), with a nimble chassis, good handling and a superb new front disc brake, the RD was both a peerless scratcher and moderately civilised. The cost? Just £455 in 1973.

SPECIFICATION: YAMAHA RD350	
ENGINE	347cc air-cooled reed valve two-stroke twin
HORSEPOWER	39bhp @ 7500rpm
TRANSMISSION	6-speed
FRAME	tubular twin cradle
BRAKES	disc/drum
TOP SPEED	105mph

From the RDs – the 250cc version was near-identical – developed the liquid-cooled 'LC' range of 1980, and then the YPVS 'Power Valve' models in 1983. Both became the favoured tools of a generation of street racers, creating an entire motorcycling sub-culture just as vertical twins had done 25 years earlier. Amazingly, the YPVS350 is still made, as the RD350R, in Brazil. Some legends, it seems, refuse to die.

'This was the essence of a light, nimble and fast machine which, ridden hard, could hold its own in practically any company.'

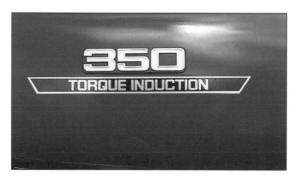

Norton Commando

....

'It literally tried to blow the cylinder head off the engine.'

Ingenious Isolastic engine mounting gave Bert Hopwood's original vertical twin a massive lease of new life. This was arguably the finest incarnation of the traditional British twin.

The Commando, in 750 and later 850cc form, was the final development of the archetypal British vertical twin. Essentially, it was yet another update of Bert Hopwood's 1948 design, in an attempt to rescue the famous Norton name from five years of financial disaster.

In 1962, partly due to the failure of the 250cc Jubilee and 350cc Navigator twins, Norton had subsided into partnership with the giant AMC group. Four years later, even worse was to follow, when AMC itself collapsed. The official receiver sold off part of the company to the Manganese Bronze Holdings group, and a new company, Norton Villiers, rose from the ashes.

Norton's new base was Andover in Hampshire, where in early 1967 a replacement for the 650 and 750cc twins was designed under a team led by Dr. Stefan Bauer. The result was the Commando,

which not only wore its cylinders inclined at a new, rakish angle, but – after the violent shakes of the 750 Atlas – featured a unique form of anti-vibration measure as well.

'Isolastic' was the name given to the system, in which the engine and transmission, including the swing-arm, were isolated from the rest of the machine by a sophisticated form of rubber mounting. Novel though this was, the Commando retained the clean, lean lines of its predecessors. It was light – around 400lbs. And it claimed 58bhp – fully 9bhp more than the Atlas. Less flatteringly, it retained dated non-unit construction, with the push-rod engine separate from the gearbox. Yet the British motorcycling public warmed to it, to the extent of voting it the *Motor Cycle News* 'Machine of the Year' for five consecutive years.

Norton's anti-vibration system, although

cynically dubbed 'Knickerlastic', actually worked. But the problem was that if handling was not to sutter – the rear wheel was effectively also rubber-mounted – the Isolastic bushes had to be in absolutely correct adjustment. Unfortunately this was quite a laborious operation using steel shims, and the penalty of incorrect shimming was either poor handling, the shakes, or both. Road test examples regularly had their 'Knickerlastics' shimmed solid, which helped handling at the expense of vibration. Not until 1975 did a more convenient vernier adjustment system appear, on the 850 Mk2A.

Even more troublesome was the Commando's other weakness, its crankshaft. Certain models, notably those with the highly-tuned 'Combat' engine, broke crankshafts and/or destroyed main bearings at an alarming rate. The high-compression Combat engine was also notorious for blowing head gaskets – it literally tried to blow the cylinder head off the engine. Although both problems were later solved, the Commando's reputation was tarnished.

Flawed as it was, in many ways the Commando was the best of the vertical twins, a handsome device with a strong, punchy power delivery which could humble theoretically more powerful machines. Although the 750 was a little vague at the front, the 850 was better, and handling was quite good providing the Isolastics were correctly shimmed. And a success it certainly was; 55,000 were made, 25,000 more than all Norton's previous post-war twins put together.

An 850 (actually 828cc) Commando appeared in 1973, and a more refined Mk2A 850 a year later. The last version featured a not very reliable electric start (an even less reliable version had almost reached production several years earlier), before manufacture ceased in mid-'77. Norton went on to develop and produce a range of rotary-engined models on a very small scale, limping from crisis to financial crisis in the process. Despite some heroic racing successes, it was a tragic end for one of the greatest names in motorcycling.

'Fastback' model – this one dates from 1972 – was the raciest of the Commando line.

Commando comfortably out-sold every other Norton model of the post-war years.

SPECIFICATION: NORTON COMMANDO	
ENGINE	air-cooled 745cc (828cc) OHV vertical twin
HORSEPOWER	58bhp @ 7000rpm (65bhp)
TRANSMISSION	four-speed
FRAME	tubular steel steel cradle, Isolastic engine mounts
BRAKES	drum/drum (later disc/disc)
TOP SPEED	110-120mph

Laverda 1000-3C

....

'It was bold, and it was brutal, and it said one thing loud and clear – power!'

If Laverda's 750SFC was a lot of a good thing, the 1000cc triple was almost too much. This was no mere superbike; this was a *musclebike*.

First launched in 1973, the Breganze factory's first production triple took over where the twin left off. The engine was a massive affair, its exquisite Italian castings deeply finned or just as deeply polished. It was bold, and it was brutal, and it said one thing loud and clear – power!

In the early 'seventies, even the best Grand Prix 500s developed no more than the 3C's 80bhp – yet this was a road bike. The engine responsible boasted twin overhead camshafts, three 32mm Dell'Orto 'pumper' carburettors (an extra squirt of petrol was fired into the cylinder when the twist-grip was cracked open), and the usual Laverda engineering overkill. Everything in Breganze, it seemed, was built big.

Typically, the engine had a deep, finned wet sump in crankcases which split horizontally. Less commonly, unlike the 120 degree crank layout of BSA/Triumph triples, the Laverda's two outer pistons rose together, with the middle one 180 degrees adrift. This gave the 1000 a characteristic off-beat exhaust note, as well as being credited with its thunderous response to the throttle from low rpm. Some years later Laverda adopted a 120 degree layout in pursuit of smoothness, but lost much of the engine's animal character.

As well as being vividly quick – geared for 138mph at 7500rpm in top gear – the 3C offered prodigious power right through the rev range. It seemed to matter little which of the five gears you happened to be in; twist the throttle, and she'd respond. Inevitably there was a price for such exhilaration. Enthusiastic riding could see fuel consumption plummet into the mid-thirties. Hard use was similarly punishing to tyres and chains; the big triple was never a cheap machine to run.

This ruggedness was echoed by everything else

Big, bold and brutal, the Breganze-built triple combined Z1-type power with much better handling.

about the 1000. It's a big machine, weighing over 530lb ready to roll (473lb, dry). At 31½ inches, the seat was particularly tall for its day. The controls, especially the clutch, are heavy, although a plus point was adjustable handlebars and footrests, which still haven't become the norm.

Although the big Laverda never handled as well as Italian sports contemporaries from Ducati and Guzzi, it was pretty good. At low speeds, the steering is distinctly odd, a feature accentuated by the standard fitment of a steering damper. The handling, not surprisingly, is heavy, although the 3C steers accurately and can chop line mid-corner. It is scarcely nimble, but a wheelbase of 58½ inches wasn't excessive. One of the penalties imposed by the wider engine was in ground clearance; the alternator cover could be made to ground on the right.

Early examples of the triple – 3CE in Britain – came with wire wheels and drum brakes similar to the 750SFC's. 1975 versions adopted twin front

Brembo discs, whilst the later 3CL sported cast wheels and disc brakes all round. Even with a fuelled-up weight of over 530lbs, disc-braked versions were sensational in their stopping power. Brembo simply had no equal at the time.

Our time frame doesn't quite permit us the ultimate triple, the 1000 'Jota' developed by British Laverda importer Roger Slater. The original Jota, sold from 1976, featured higher compression pistons, wild camshafts, bigger carbs (without air cleaners) and a tuned exhaust system. This added 10bhp to the 3C's 80bhp, and created a 140mph legend – the Fastest Production Roadster in the world. It was the ultimate man's machine; a superbike that needed Supermen to tame it.

Tuned 'Jota' version of the 3C was originally developed by the British Laverda importers and rapidly became a world-wide legend.

SPECIFICATION: LAVERDA 1000-3C

ENGINE	Air-cooled 981cc DOHC transverse triple
HORSEPOWER	80bhp @ 7250rpm
TRANSMISSION	5-speed
FRAME	tubular twin cradle
BRAKES	double disc/drum
TOP SPEED	132mph

The original muscle machine, Jotas were raced with as many as *three* steering dampers.

BMW R90S

Where the rest chased cams and cylinders, BMW's 'seventies Superbike stuck to its roots to produce arguably the best sports tourer of its time. 100mph cruising, with luggage, was effortless for rider and machine

The R90S first launched by BMW in the South of France in 1973 was arguably the first true superbike in a range of horizontally opposed shaft-drive twins dating back precisely 50 years. In fact, in their haughty and independent way, it wasn't until the 'seventies that the German factory seemed remotely concerned with what the rest of the motorcycle world might be doing. Yet when they did pay heed, the result was a memorable motorcycle.

The R90S was a stablemate of the 6 Series BMWs first sold in 1974, which were themselves a five-speed up-date of the 5-Series twins of 1969. The range comprised the 600cc R60/6, 750cc R75/6 and 900cc R90/6.

The mid-seventies, of course, was the time when the superbike race was gathering unprecedented momentum. In designing the 90S, Bee-eM deliberately set out to enter the fray. But inevitably their contestant would do things the Bavarian way. The engine was basically the same push-rod 898cc unit fitted to the R90/6. Bigger 39mm Dell'Orto carburettors and high compression pistons pushed power up to 67bhp.

By the time it appeared, the R90S was a non-starter – numerically, at least. Compared to the contemporary Kawasaki Z1, it had 15 less horsepower and a top speed perhaps 10mph slower. It had a 'mere' two cylinders, yet cost a great deal more. But, typically BMW, it had an extra something. It placed function higher than fashion, and so somehow amounted to more than the sum of its parts: the holistic motorcycle.

Perhaps the most crucial of these, a real novelty in 1973, was a handlebar-mounted 'bikini' fairing. It wasn't big, it probably wasn't particularly aerodynamic, but it did permit you to hold a high speed for far longer than on any Japanese four.

The seat, too, was comfortable – not very sexy, but welcomed by any rider with a long journey ahead of him. The suspension was more compliant than any other road machine of the time, and the ergonomics as a whole were unequalled. Add a fuel capacity well in excess of five gallons, a smooth engine (if not as smooth as smaller BMW twins), and a flexibility far greater than the Z1's, and the result was the mile-eater *par excellence*. The R90S was the Pullman carriage of 'seventies superbikes, a by-word for effortless long-distance capability.

The 90S also handled far better than large Japanese bikes of the period. With soft, long-travel suspension, it wasn't quite so taut as the best sports machines from Guzzi or Ducati. But it made the most of its relatively low overall weight (around 430lb) and the low centre of gravity inherent in the flat twin design. In the 'seventies you could have suppleness or you could have handling, but you

Although one of the most capable long-haul machines ever built, the R90S also tolerated scratching better than many subsequent BMWs. Its relatively light weight and a punchy, flexible engine came into their own on back roads.

couldn't have both – but the big Beemer came pretty close. And, thanks to twin Brembo front discs, it delivered class-leading stopping power.

Then there was the special factor that went some way to justifying a price tag of almost £2000, half as much again as the Z1. The finish, in classy silver/black or silver/orange 'smoke', was superb. Build quality was similarly in the Rolls Royce league. Yet the machine, with its wonderfully accessible engine layout, was simplicity itself to work on. And, most of all, it contributed to BMW's peerless reputation for mechanical reliability.

Of course the other defining quality of this 'ultimate' flat twin is that no-one else produced anything quite like it. BMWs are simply unique, which itself is reason enough to aspire to owning one. Ironically, during the 'eighties even BMW

themselves attempted to drop the range until thwarted by a world-wide clamour of indignation. They're still there, in original and four-valve form. For flat twins are as Bavarian as beer festivals and *lederhosen* – except that all 90S models were actually built at Spandau, Berlin. But this was still, for many, Bavaria's best-ever twin.

SPECIFICATION: BMW R90S	
ENGINE	Air-cooled OHV 898cc flat twin
HORSEPOWER	67bhp @ 7000rpm
TRANSMISSION	5-speed
FRAME	Tubular steel twin cradle
BRAKES	Double disc/drum
TOP SPEED	125mph

'BMWs are simply unique, which itself is reason enough to aspire to owning one.'

Moto Guzzi 750S

'Like all Guzzi vees, it had that special Mandello brand of remorseless, easy power.'

Prior to the 'sixties, Moto Guzzi were best known for two wildly different engine configurations. Ever since the first Guzzi & Parodi machine of 1920, they had promoted a succession of elegant single-cylinder designs with the cylinder horizontal-mounted. At the opposite extreme, their 500cc Vee-eight of 1956 was possibly the most complex and exciting Grand Prix racer ever produced. Along the way there were other layouts – parallel twins, triples, supercharged racing fours, fore-and-aft wide-angle Vee-twins – but the horizontal single and the V8 were quintessentially Guzzi.

But not any more. Mandello del Lario is now home to the most enduring range of Italian Vee-twins in motorcycling.

It is part of motorcycling mythology that the Vee-twin engine which has powered big Guzzis for almost 30 years began life as the powerplant for a bizarre military three-wheeler. Although only produced for four years from 1960, the 753cc six-speed '3x3' used tracked rear wheels and could almost literally climb the proverbial gable-end.

When three-wheeler production ceased, Guzzi sought another use for all that torque. The results were to become as sexy as the 3x3 had been grotesque.

In 1964, work began on the first two-wheeled prototype, under Guzzi's brilliant chief engineer, Ing. Guilio Carcano, the man responsible for *that* V8. A year later a prototype was hailed as the star of the Milan Show. The machine, now dubbed the V7, reached the shops in 1967.

To this one engine can be traced almost the whole of Guzzi's subsequent history for, more than any surviving manufacturer except Harley-Davidson, they have clung to their principles. In its original 703cc form, the twin produced some 40bhp at a leisurely 5800rpm. The engine, using many car-

SPECIFICATION: MOTO GUZZI 750S	
ENGINE	OHV 748cc V-twin
HORSEPOWER	53bhp @ 6300rpm
TRANSMISSION	5-speed, shaft
FRAME	Twin cradle, demountable lower rails
BRAKES	Twin discs/disc in Guzzi linked system
TOP SPEED	123mph

No motorcycle cobbled together in this way should be remotely this handsome — unless, perhaps, it was built in Italy. Tonti's 750S design stands out for looking good and going at least as well.

type engineering practices, was simple, remarkably solid and easy to work on. But the whole, although eye-catching with its metallic red tank with chrome knee recesses, was somewhat agricultural and heavy in appearance.

In 1967 Carcano retired. Lino Tonti, a veteran of Aermacchi, Bianchi and Gilera, took his place, and set about refining the V7. The first results were the V7 Special and Ambassador of 1969, both now with 757cc, bigger valves and 45bhp. Tonti was also later responsible for taking the engine up to 844cc for the GT850 and California of 1972.

Tonti's real breakthrough, however, came with the V7 Sport. His background was in lighter, leaner machines than the early Guzzi vees, and he set about remodelling the V7 in similar mould. By transferring the generator from the top to the front of the engine, he produced a machine which was both lower and sleeker than before, yet with more ground clearance. At the same time he added a fifth gear and reduced the capacity slightly to 748cc to permit the machine's use in increasingly popular 750cc racing.

The result, much refined and no less than 28kg lighter than the first V7, was the V7 Sport of 1972. A high-performance 'Le Mans' version, with half fairing and 'bum-stop' racing seat, was even more exhilarating (and brought the promise of the true Le Mans series which was to arrive in 1976). Like all Guzzi vees, it had that special Mandello brand of

By the 'seventies, handling was an Italian speciality. Firms such as Moto Guzzi showed the Japanese there was more to motorcycle design than simply putting a potent engine between two wheels.

remorseless, easy power. But now it was so much more *alive*.

Yet even here Tonti was not finished, for two years later he unleashed the 750S, now with two huge 300mm Brembo discs up front. Finished in all black with violent red, orange or green flashes across the tank and side panels, it was the most eye-catching machine of its era. In mid-'75 this became the 750 S3, with milder cam timing but the same 53bhp at 6300rpm. Now with a rear disc brake, the S3 adopted Guzzi's unique linked brake system. It was to be the last of Guzzi's sports 750s. And in more ways than one, it was the ultimate.

First developed for a bizarre military vehicle, much the same Guzzi powerplant survives today. But the 'seventies, when it was competitive for speed, was its hey-day.

Suzuki GT750

....

'At 90mph-plus, even the mildest motorway curve is likely to invoke a weave.'

Rod Morgan's GT750B, was the last of the breed when first registered back in '78. The B's most obvious distinguishing feature is the lack of stays on the chrome front mudguard.

In the days before anyone had even dreamt of emissions regulations, Suzuki's GT750, nicknamed variously the 'water kettle' and 'water buffalo', was the two-stroke answer to Honda's CB750. And to everyone's surprise it was the stroker which became a by-word for easy-going grunt, whilst the four-stroke Honda launched the tide of rev-happy multis which surrounds us still. Yet just five years earlier, Suzuki were working on a 50cc racing triple which revved to 19,000 and didn't have enough gears with 14.

For the time, the technical specification was mouth-watering; three liquid-cooled cylinders mounted transversely across the frame, mated to a five-speed in-unit gearbox by geared primary drive. The engine is piston-ported, and fed (in final versions) by three 40mm CV carburettors. With a chrome three-into-four exhaust, and very wide across the crankshaft, the engine was physically imposing. Less advanced by far, was the chassis.

Launched in 1971 as the GT750J, the Kettle enjoyed a much shorter model run than its Honda counterpart. The J was notable for its fade-prone drum front brake, lurid paintwork and four curious silencers whose black end-cones were adept at falling off, shortly followed by an ungodly racket as the baffles followed suit. The J was succeeded by the short model run of the 750K, substantially the same bike but with much-needed twin discs up front. The styling was somewhat in the manner of Wurlitzer.

1974 brought about the slightly less baroque GT750L. A year later the M appeared, with the 70bhp engine which was to last the Kettle until the end of its days. Compared to the previous 65bhp/112mph motor, the M was about eight mph faster and somewhat revvier, but still a big softy at heart. Perhaps it had become embarrassing to Suzuki to have a pussy-cat on the street, when its racing derivative (the machine crashed so

spectacularly at Daytona by Barry Sheene) was such a tyre-shredding missile on the tracks.

Instead, the GT majored on effortlessness and – unprecedented for a two-stroke – longevity. This was due to a modest rev ceiling of 7000rpm, and liquid cooling, which promoted durability by minimising temperature gradients and piston clearances. And everything was built big.

In this respect the Kettle was a complete success, regularly clocking mileages previously unheard of for two-strokes. Maintenance, too, was simple, with just occasional gearbox oil-changes and ignition points to look after. Ironically it was the electrics, rather than the engine, that usually proved the weak link when Kettles did break down.

But most of all the triple was appealing – and still is – for the way it went. Not only was it better braked and far more tractable than the Honda four, and easier to get away from the lights, it was smoother, too.

The handling, though, is distinctly mixed. Ridden with prudence, it's an attractive package. Although it feels much bigger and heavier than the CB750, the difference is actually only a few pounds. At town speeds it steers more neutrally, with far less

tendency to fall into turns and crisper low-down power.

At higher speeds, things get interesting. At 90mph-plus, even the mildest motorway curve is likely to invoke a weave. Ground clearance, although better on later versions, was slight. Even 'conveniences' like a digital gear indicator and vacuum-controlled fuel tap can't conceal the fact that getting anywhere quickly is a bit of a lottery.

The GT750 enjoys a unique place as not only the first, but the last of the big two-strokes, a demise jointly ensured by rising oil prices and increasing concern over emissions. When Suzuki announced what was to be the last of the Kettles in late '76, the writing on the wall, unveiled at much the same time, was the GS750, Suzuki's first big four-stroke multi. Apart from looking about a hundredweight lighter (it wasn't; only 25lb), the GS set the standards for the next generation by doing something the GT never could – it handled.

Huge and imposing, the 'Water Kettle' was the opposite of other road-going two-strokes: flexible, relaxed and reliable. But rising fuel prices sidelined large capacity strokers almost overnight.

SPECIFICATION: SUZUKI GT750	
ENGINE	liquid-cooled 3-cylinder 738cc 2-stroke
HORSEPOWER	70bhp @ 6500rpm
TRANSMISSION	5-speed
FRAME	tubular steel twin cradle
BRAKES	twin disc/drum
TOP SPEED	120mph

Kawasaki KR750 Racer

If the 'sixties was the decade of the screaming tiddlers, the 'seventies was the Animal Decade, the years of Formula 750, of brutal horsepower, skinny tyres and flexi-frames. From 1972 to 1978, Kawasaki's roadster-based triples, along with the even grosser Suzuki GT750s, were the quintessential racing superbikes. The example pictured, Mick Grant's 1976 KR750, was the ultimate development of the breed.

Surprisingly, Grant enjoyed riding his KR. 'At the time', he recalls, 'the press dubbed it an animal, but it was very rideable and extremely competitive, if not initially very reliable. The Suzuki's were definitely more of a handful, Yamaha's TZ750 was a jelly by comparison, and both were much heavier than the Kawasaki.' This particular machine, the only one ever made with magnesium crankcases, is the lightest KR ever built.

Grant's first outing on a KR was Daytona in 1975, when 'disastrous' gearbox problems prevented the machine ever completing more than five laps at a time. The KR's biggest handicap, however, was its over-stressed crankshaft. On early models, the fancy aircraft-type fuel quickfiller was of limited use, since the crankshaft lasted little longer than a tank of petrol. A crank life of 90 miles was a particular problem in the F750 world championship series, since most races were over 100 miles. Later examples, with improved crank design and peak revs reduced from 10,000 to 9500rpm, proved more robust.

Whatever its shortcomings, the KR had made immense strides since the introduction of its predecessor, the H2R, in 1972. The H2R was a heavily-tuned version of the 750cc H2 roadster (see page 70), retaining both the road bike's air-cooling and, more crucially, its blood-curdling handling.

Paul Smart, who rode in the Kawasaki America squad alongside Yvonne du Hamel and Art Bauman, remembers the H2R as 'absolutely atrocious . . . awful handling, totally unreliable'. Although it is Barry Sheene who will always be remembered for being spat down the road when his rear tyre cried enough, most riders had a similar experience. Despite this, and a process of 'constant de-tuning', Smart topped the US road race standings in 1972. Yet the HR2 was only really

tamed after Smart later had Colin Seeley build a frame for it, when it handled 'superbly'. Effective as it was, this 'defection' earned Smart no friends at Kawasaki.

In 'standard' tune, the KR's peak power was claimed as 120-plus bhp, with pulling power 'like a tractor'. A second-stage tune, involving different pipes, a 2mm shorter piston skirt and higher compression, gave perhaps 130bhp and was the practical limit of the KR's potential. Only once, at the ultra-fast Mettet circuit in Belgium, was Stage 3 attempted. Four mm off the piston skirt, lots of special porting and an even more radical exhaust produced an engine 'like a switch – either on or off. Completely unridable'.

Yet even in standard trim the KR750 was amazingly rapid. In 1975 Grant added no less than 7mph to the lap record for Ireland's NW200 circuit. At Macau in 1976, Grant lapped everyone except the runner-up. In winning the 1978 Isle of Man TT

'It was very rideable and extremely competitive, if not initially very reliable.'

on this very bike, he was speed-trapped at over 190mph. The figure has been questioned, even by Grant himself, yet KRs regularly clocked 180mph at Daytona, without the downhill advantage of the TT speed trap. Only in the last few years have *Grand Prix* 500s come to exceed those figures.

Despite this the big Kawasaki never quite achieved its potential. It's fragility prevented it ever mounting a convincing assault on the F750 title, although riders like Hansford, du Hamel, Ditchburn and Grant enjoyed the occasional success. When Yamaha put their full might behind their factory OW31, the KR's days were numbered.

SPECIFICATION: KAWASAKI KR750 RACER	
ENGINE	liquid-cooled 748cc two-stroke triple
HORSEPOWER	120bhp-plus @ 9500rpm
TRANSMISSION	5-speed
FRAME	tubular steel twin loop
BRAKES	double disc/disc
TOP SPEED	180mph-plus

Green only in colour, the 190mph Kawasaki triple (above) could shred tyres and lap records with equal vigour — just so long as the crankshaft held together.

Picture shows the final version of the green meanie, Mick Grant's magnesium crankcased KR750 of 1976. By then it had come a long way from the original modified H2 roadster.

MV Agusta 750S America

If any manufacturer of two-wheelers emulates the uniquely Italian flair of Ferrari cars, MV, surely, is the one. When Gilera pulled out of *grand prix* racing at the end of 1957, MV went on to claim manufacturers' titles at *every class* for the next three years. Even more astonishing, MV captured the 500cc crown every year from 1958 to 1974, through riders John Surtees, Gary Hocking, Mike Hailwood, Giacomo Agostini and Phil Read. The latter, with Read fighting off the growing (and now utterly dominant) two-stroke menace, must rank as one of the most dramatic and heroic 500cc series since the world championship began in 1949.

MV was founded as an aircraft manufacturer in 1923, and four years later was inherited by Count Domenico Agusta. After World War II, he established the Meccanica Verghera Agusta motorcycle factory at Gallarate, near Milan. The first MV racer, a 125cc two-stroke, was built in 1948 and won the national championship. But Count Agusta had his mind on higher prizes, recruiting Gilera's Pietro Remor to design a squad of MV four-strokes. Cecil Sandford gave the Count his first GP success in winning the 1952 125cc title, a class Carlo Ubbiali was to dominate for MV in the late 'fifties. In total MV claimed 16 500cc titles, nine at 350cc, five 250cc and seven 125cc.

The 750S America is not a race bike – not quite. But as a roadster it shares with Ducati's 750SS the mantle of the first 'race replica' superbikes; raw, uncompromising, exotic and expensive, street legal (but only just). Yet MV's first four-cylinder

Wickedly handsome, the vibrant red MV had the sort of glamour that even Kawasaki's much faster Z1 could not match. Almost every part of the dauntingly expensive Italian four was hand-crafted.

37 VOLTE CAMPIONE DEL MONDO

750S graphics (far left) trumpet MV's domination of the 500cc *grand prix* scene from 1958 to '74. But despite its racing pedigree, the shaft-drive roadster was heavy and didn't handle particularly well (left).

roadster, produced in 1967, could not have been more different. Of 600cc, it was a tourer – slow and, most unforgivable of all, ugly.

When the 750S arrived in 1971, it did much to restore MV's reputation. Good looking and fast, it was followed by the America in 1975. This, aimed at the US market, was styled to emulate the 500 on which Read had won MV's 37th (and, it turned out, last) world title the previous year. Red and silver paintwork gave the machine the look of the 'Gallarate fire engines', especially with the optional race-style full fairing.

The heart of this sensuous device, inevitably, was its 790cc four-cylinder engine – practically a scaled-up replica of the factory racers. With gear-driven double overhead camshafts, four Dell'Orto carbs (gulping unfiltered air) and four raucous straight-through megaphone exhausts, this was arguably the most exotic production motorcycle produced until Honda's NR750 came along 17 years later.

Exotic, yes, but imperfect. Despite high-quality suspension from Ceriani, the America was a disappointing handler, particularly at high speed. The fault seemed to lie with a frame design employing just a single backbone tube, and with the curious choice of shaft final drive. With a dry weight of well over 500lbs, it was also disappointingly heavy.

That engine, though, was memorable. Somewhat truculent at low speed, it found its soul through revs, emitting a piercing and unforgettable howl as the needle hurtled around the tachometer dial. Although true rear wheel horsepower was

somewhat less than the 75bhp MV claimed, it was substantially more than any other contemporary '750', rushing the red and silver MV up to 130mph and beyond. The America's successor, the 837cc, 85bhp Monza, was even more exhilarating.

The price, of course, was considerable. Even in their heyday MV roadsters were a very rare sight. Sales never met MV's expectations, and this intricate and hand-crafted machine was fearfully expensive to produce. By 1979, the company had ceased manufacturing motorcycles to concentrate on helicopter production.

'The 750S America is not a race bike – not quite.'

SPECIFICATION: MV AGUSTA 750S AMERICA	
ENGINE	air-cooled 790cc DOHC transverse four
HORSEPOWER	75bhp @ 8500rpm
TRANSMISSION	5-speed
FRAME	duplex steel cradle
BRAKES	double disc/drum
TOP SPEED	133mph

Benelli 750 SEI

....

Back in 1975, you'd go a long way to see one of these. Benelli's magnificent 750's place in superbike lore is assured: the first production motorcycle to boast six cylinders.

Although the transverse six is perhaps their best-remembered creation, the business founded by the Benelli brothers in 1911 had a long and illustrious racing history. A Benelli 250 won the last pre-war Lightweight TT, whilst another repeated the success in 1950. In the same year, Dario Ambrosini brought Benelli their first world title.

Then, in 1962, Benelli produced an astonishing 250cc four, which later grew into a 350 and then a 500. Thus equipped, the little Italian factory took on the mighty Hondas and MVs. Success didn't come until Honda pulled out of Grands Prix, allowing Kel Carruthers to take the quarter-litre title in 1969, but the battle was heroically fought.

Above all, it showed that Benelli undoubtedly knew how to make multis.

The 750 *Sei*, and its stablemates, the 350cc and 500cc fours, grew out of the extravagant ambition of Alessandro do Tomaso. Do Tomaso was an entrepreneur who attempted to rationalise and modernise mass production of motorcycles in his native Italy. He also owned Moto Guzzi.

Dubbed the 'Six pipe dream' in a test of the time, the most strident result of these aspirations was the 750-6. Suddenly all those 'too complicated' Japanese multis looked restrained. Finished in bright red, seemingly as wide as a bus but with acres more chrome, the *Sei* was a sensational eyeful.

Like other multis before it, the six wasn't actually that complex – it merely duplicated a lot of its bits. A single overhead camshaft topped off a 12-valve cylinder head fed by three Dell'Orto carbs.

As an exercise in corporate *machismo* – it was Latin, after all – the *Sei* was a magnificent success. The reality, however, was flawed.

These were quite small at 24mm (compared to four 28mm carbs on Honda's 750).

The wet sump crankcases split horizontally, revealing a crankshaft with no less than thirteen plain bearings. The single overhead camshaft is chain-driven. Primary drive is by a further chain from the centre of the crankshaft, an otherwise sound piece of engineering which unfortunately puts the five-speed gearbox in a very asymmetric position. As was to become widespread practice on later fours, the alternator was mounted above the gearbox to keep engine width to a minimum.

This was all very impressive, apart from two things: if, say, Honda had built the six, the detailing and finish would almost certainly have been better and it wouldn't have wept oil, as the Benelli sometimes did. And, most tellingly of all, the Benelli wasn't actually that quick. Road tests gave top speeds as high as 118mph, but 114mph was nearer the norm.

Visually impressive as it was, basically this wasn't a very powerful engine. Most engines develop less power than their manufacturers claim, but in the six's case the shortfall was considerable. Benelli claimed 71bhp, but the truth was nearer 60. Part of the problem, it seemed, was very high pumping losses, which also contributed to oil consumption as low as 300 miles per pint. At 37mpg, it was also greedy for petrol.

One-two-three-four-five-six! In 1975, no-one had seen a sight like this on the road. The Benelli excepted, they still haven't.

'The Benelli was magnificent, without doubt. But with hindsight it was probably also folly.'

What the *Sei* did deliver was unprecedented smoothness from a revvy engine which needed all of its five gears. Although wide and heavy at 485lb, it handled and steered fairly well, and stopped superbly with its twin Brembo discs. But, smoothness aside, all of this was offered in equal or greater measure by machines costing substantially less.

Kawasaki's Z1, for instance, cost some 30 per cent less than the *Sei*, despite 20mph more top speed and over 1 1/2 seconds advantage over the standing quarter mile. Even Honda's CB750, at little more than half the price, was faster. The Benelli was magnificent, without doubt. But with hindsight it was probably also folly.

As tiny in side-view as it is gross from the front, the six's performance was hampered by huge frictional and pumping losses and barn-door aerodynamics. (Left) Peak power was around 60bhp and performance disappointing.

SPECIFICATION: BENELLI 750 SEI	
ENGINE	air-cooled 748cc SOHC transverse six
HORSEPOWER	71bhp @ 8500rpm
TRANSMISSION	5-speed
FRAME	tubular twin cradle
BRAKES	Double disc/drum
TOP SPEED	114mph

Index